Into
Africa

**The thrilling story of William Burton
and Central African Missions**

Into Africa

The thrilling story of William Burton and Central African Missions

Edited by David Womersley and David Garrard

Includes the revised texts of:
'Congo Pioneer' by Harold Womersley (1973)
and
'Missionary Pioneering in Congo Forests'
compiled by Max Moorhead (1922)

NEW LIFE PUBLISHING

Published by Central African Missions

355 Blackpool Road, Preston, Lancashire, PR2 3AB, England

Tel: 01772 717830

Email: admin@camafrica.fsnet.co.uk

Includes the revised texts of:

'Congo Pioneer' first published in the UK in 1973

'Missionary Pioneering in Congo Forests' first published in the UK in 1922

This combined edition published in the UK in 2005

Copyright © Central African Missions

ISBN 0-9536100-6-3

Printed by Creative Print and Design, Middlesex, England

Produced by New Life Publishing Co.

Nottingham, England

Contents

Congo Pioneer

Missionary Pioneering in Congo Forests

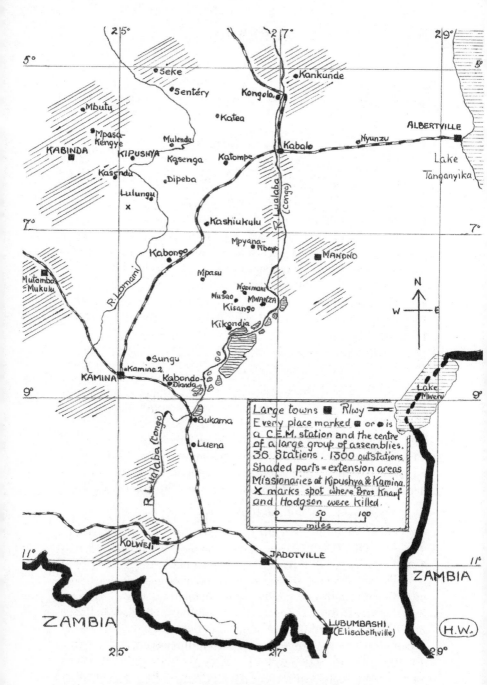

The Congo Evangelistic Mission field in 1964,
hand-drawn by Harold Womersley

Preface

When I first met William F. P. Burton I had no idea that I was in the company of a great man. He humbly made his way each day to a small office in central Johannesburg where, with meticulous calligraphy, he produced tracts to be sent far and wide. It was on his way home on the bus that I encountered him.

I vaguely recognised him as an old man from the church that I had recently started attending and where I had made a commitment to follow Christ. After several embarrassed waves we finally started talking and so began nearly a year of daily bus trips together.

I still did not realise that I was in the company of greatness. As time passed I realised that there was something profoundly different about this man from most others that I had met in my young life. There was a gentleness, a wisdom and sweetness of spirit that I had never encountered before. As many more years passed I began to realise what a privilege had been mine on those regular bus trips. I realised that I had enjoyed the company of an amazing apostle, a pioneer and a deeply spiritual man.

As I began my studies I would often look for the name W. F. P. Burton in the history books. To my amazement I never found it. As newer histories of mission were written I looked again and still his name was not there. Here was a man who had a massive impact on central Africa and had been instrumental in planting thousands of churches. Why was his name not in the books?

The problem was twofold. Firstly, Burton was British. The golden era of British mission had passed and the impact of both world wars had diminished the visibility of British missionaries. Few books were being written about British mission. The counter-colonial political correctness of the sixties and seventies was impacting severely on the true story of British missionaries being told. Even the impact of the Simba uprising and the slaughter of several British missionaries in the Congo did not make headline news! The second problem was that Burton was Pentecostal. The relatively small and slightly controversial group that he belonged to struggled to be accepted into mainline evangelicalism at the time. The Pentecostals had few resources, developed mainly in working class communities in the UK and thus were under-valued and their efforts were often ignored.

Hopefully these two restricting influences are passing and it is time for the true story of a great man to be told. My hope is that it will be read more widely than the circles of people who fondly remember Burton and his colleagues. This is an aspect of mission history that needs to find its rightful place in the wider record of the wonderful expansion of the church throughout the world.

Paul Alexander
Principal, Mattersey Hall
November 2004

Foreword

William F. P. Burton was a man ahead of his time. God brought together two giants with complementary gifts – William Burton, the dynamic, sometimes impetuous leader, anxious to get the job done and James Salter, cautious, concise, clear-minded, a good administrator and chairman. The African people, who have a great gift for analysing character, called one "The Rusher-Forth" and the other "Ina Banza" the chief's wise counsellor. My father, who worked closely in leadership with Mr Burton and knew him intimately, was ideally placed to write a biography of the great man. We are therefore happy to republish his gripping book: Congo Pioneer.

Burton and Salter were both gifted Bible expositors, ever in demand as speakers. Mr Burton had a unique way of expressing truth. Once in South Africa he took us to a church for their New Year meeting. Six leading men were invited to the front together to say something special, he being one of them. I have no idea what the others said but I shall never forget his two-minute exposition of a verse of Scripture delivered in his unique voice in that deliberate way he had.

Mr Burton was very human. His peanut tricks and sleight of hand would fascinate me, as a young lad home from boarding school. He loved children; he made everything so interesting for them. The children were not in awe of him as the adults often were. Some years later, he made me, a young raw missionary, feel wanted. I was not a builder, though like all missionaries in the early days I had to play my part. On one visit to Mwanza, he took me to see a new metal roof he was constructing. He embarrassed me by wanting my advice about a special ventilation system he was incorporating. True to form, Mr Burton was doing it with engineering precision! Another time, still in my first term, he actually sought me out, following me to my room, so as to tell me that he disapproved of a decision the senior missionaries had taken to exclude me from a committee because of lack of experience. He was the one who had nominated me! He was always encouraging the younger workers.

He was generous, ready to help fellow missionaries when it meant himself going without. When Bronwen and I were married, he gave us his old Chevrolet car, which came in so handy on our honeymoon. He was a perfectionist. His furniture was always exceptionally well made; much of it still remains today although the thatched house has been looted a number of times in recent troubles. The pelmets over the windows were hinged so as to facilitate putting up curtains. The sky window in the raised ceiling of his artist's room was beautifully constructed, flooding the place with natural light.

He was not always an easy man to work with. He expected the best from those who laboured alongside and this comes out in the second book we are including: Missionary Pioneering. He did not tolerate those who fell short of his expectations. He was single minded. Once we bumped into each other on a long lonely road; he was travelling west, I was going east. We had not seen each other for some months. Normally at such times we would stop and chat and ask how everyone was and enjoy some fellowship before continuing on our way. He came straight to the point "Ah, David," were his first words, "I was wanting to see you. What is happening about that matter I mentioned to you…?"

He was honest and straightforward in his dealing with people. In Missionary Pioneering he shows disgust, horror, anger, delight, at some of the letters he receives and some of the criticism levelled at him and the work. He was not afraid to express himself forcibly. Maybe that is the advantage of publishing letters that reveal his heart rather than writings and books that have been carefully scrutinised and at times toned down. This is also seen in his concern and tender care of sick and needy colleagues and even acquaintances so evident in his letters.

He was ahead of his times in many ways. Sometimes other colleagues held him back, not ready yet to accept his bold propositions. He was always prepared to accept a challenge. At one of our missionary conferences with some 55 people present, we were discussing the thorny problem of staffing for a new station we wanted to start at the extreme north-west of our work. The heads of stations did not want to release any of their workers; all were badly needed. No one volunteered. Suddenly, 72-year-old Burton jumped to his feet. "I'll go!" he cried to the abashed gathering, and he meant it.

Missionary Pioneering reveals how forward thinking he was. The book only covers the first five years of the work (1915-1920), yet already he was training evangelists and elders; he was treating the Congolese as leaders and fellow workers. This is one of his amazing captions that he wrote to go with one of the many of his photos that pepper the original book. "Two of our overseers. These men now take practically the same place and responsibility with regard to the young churches as the missionaries. Thus, if anything occurred necessitating the withdrawal of white workers, the local believers would still have steady godly men to whom to look for help and direction." Astounding!

The various letters and news items give a vibrant picture of those early days and show the forming of certain principles that have stood the work in good stead and contributed to its amazing growth. This makes the book very important.

The last time we were together was in Johannesburg. My wife Bronwen and I were returning from furlough, travelling north by road from Cape Town. Poor Bronwen got landed with typing a never-ending pile of letters and articles for him while he took me around the city showing me various fascinating places in which he had an interest for God's work. When it came time to leave, he peered into the packed van as we said our moving goodbyes. "Have you room for a little body with only a small suitcase?" he said wistfully. We then discussed the possibility of his visiting Kamina again and teaching in the Bible College for a few months. He wrote to us frequently. He was always "Mr Burton" to the missionaries but the last few years he began signing himself "Uncle Willie" to us.

His trip to Kamina never materialised. Just over a year after our goodbyes in Johannesburg, he had an abundant entrance into the presence of the Lord he loved and served so humbly. The "tramp preacher" was home.

David Womersley
Rushden
February 2005

Introduction

To a former generation of Pentecostals William F.P. Burton was a well known name. However, many of that era are no longer with us and the man and his exploits are for the majority today all but forgotten. Central African Missions, the successor to the Congo Evangelistic Mission, William F.P. Burton and James Salter's child and missionary organisation, celebrates its 90th birthday in 2005; it was decided to reprint two books concerning Burton and the Central African Church they launched under one title: *Into Africa*.

In a day when many question the validity of mission and the difficulties attached to outreach in a post-modern world, it is the hope of the publishers to inspire men and women of vision and faith to the same kind of commitment as was evident in this intrepid and godly Englishman and his colleagues. The mandate of the Great Commission still stands and although circumstances in our world have changed greatly opportunity for engagement in the spread of the Gospel to 'the ends of the earth', wherever those 'ends' may be, still holds fast. It is the purpose of this book to challenge believers and churches to greater involvement in the evangelisation of our world before the Second Coming of our Lord.

The first book: *Congo Pioneer*, written by Harold Womersley, himself a colleague of Burton's and also a man of considerable ability and calling, is a survey of the pioneer's life, ministry and influence from a Congo perspective. It deals not only with Burton the man, but with the work of the mission and the Church which grew out of obscure beginnings to be one of the most influential tools of evangelism in today's Central and Southern Congo.

The second: *Missionary Pioneering*, which was compiled mostly from Burton's early letters and reports, by Max W. Moorhead, covers the first five years of the Congo mission. Since that time the Congo Evangelistic Mission has gone on to plant a Church in Congo which has spread to many of the regions of the nation as well as to adjoining nations. Directly and indirectly it has been responsible for the establishment of more than 5,000 local churches, some of which number among the largest local churches in the nation.

The Congo Evangelistic Mission or Burton's Mission, as many knew it in the early years, has gone through a number of name changes resulting from the country being called Zaire in 1972 and then back to Congo in 1997. The Trustees of the mission decided that it was only right to give the Mission a name which would indicate its wider sphere of interest: Central African Missions. CAM is presently in addition to its involvement in Congo also active in Zambia and works in partnership with a national body of believers in church planting in Ethiopia. It is also open to the leading of the Lord as and where opportunities become available in other areas of the African continent. Pioneering was at the heart of William F.P. Burton and were he alive today he most certainly would be the first to "lengthen the cords and strengthen the tent stakes" (Isa 54:2). This aspect of Burton's vision continues in CAM.

It is only right that a man who himself wrote over 20 books, and countless articles covering a variety of subjects from children's stories to missionary exploits, scientific examination of Luba religious beliefs and practices and the collection of over 1,000 proverbs in the Luba language, should have a book or two written about him and the way in which he was used of God to establish this body of believers in the Congo. In all of this it is acknowledged that all the glory must go to God alone.

Editorial notes:
The integrity of the original works has been maintained throughout although outdated terms and those which have a pejorative connotation today have been changed or modified. Archaic language has been updated although where this includes the adjusting of the Authorised Version the changes do not reflect any particular translation other than where this is indicated. Corrections to the spelling of African, and Kiluba names have been made where applicable and foreign terms which are no longer known have been adapted so as to facilitate understanding to a wider readership. William Burton's personal testimony regarding his healing from cancer has been added and some sections which do not appear to be relevant have been excluded. The photographs which have been included have been chosen for historical value and not for artistic excellency. It needs to be remembered that some are nearly 90 years old.

David J. Garrard
Mattersey
February 2005

Congo Pioneer

1
Kapamu is dead

It was icy cold at London Airport and the V.C. 10 was three-and-a-half hours late in taking off owing to a 'go-slow' strike. A funeral was being held up for me in Johannesburg and I was getting anxious.

It was Tuesday January 26th 1971. On Sunday morning a phone call to our Preston Office from South Africa announced that William F. P. Burton, founder and pioneer of the Congo Evangelistic Mission (now CAM), had been called home some hours before.

Only a series of miracles had enabled me to accept the invitation to take part in what proved to be a most impressive and unforgettable ceremony. A rush to Preston from farther north, prayer and discussion with our Trustees and ceaseless phone calls followed. The missionary secretary of Assemblies of God and ex-CEM missionary Walter Hawkins achieved the impossible in obtaining a seat on the plane and in getting me to the Airport on time. Through the barrier, my dear wife's goodbye ringing in my ears, then – this annoying delay.

So 'Kapamu', that energetic, tireless preacher, Bible teacher and missionary had gone to be with the Lord he had loved and served with passionate abandon. 'Kapamu' was the name given to him by the Congolese tribesmen and means 'The Rusher-Forth'. He was always ready at a moment's notice, day or night, to rush forth to pray with some needy soul or to see to some urgent Mission business hundreds of miles away through forest and swamp. In the years before we had motor roads he had a handful of picked carriers who, at the call of the drum, would gladly rush off with him, taking light loads of camp kit but doing double journeys at Kapamu's pace to any part of the CEM field.

His co-founder and pioneer James Salter used to say, 'Willie Burton is always a step ahead of everybody else.' He needed little sleep and spent hours every morning with his Bible and his Lord in prayer and intense study and was still out and about before everybody else, well prepared for preaching, Bible teaching, building, writing and indeed any job. He was here, there and everywhere, ahead of everybody in speed, skill and accomplishment yet never ruffled, never excited, never impatient. For 65 years he had served God ceaselessly, 57 of them, from 1914, in Africa...

Suddenly we were off and soared quickly to 33,000 feet, trying to make up for lost time. Five hundred and fifty miles an hour was far too slow for me; impatient with the stop at Zurich, I cheered up a little as dawn broke over snow-capped Mount Kenya. A brief stop for refuelling at Nairobi and now, in brilliant sunshine, we rose to still greater height and finally came down to the familiar burning heat of Jan Smuts Airport where CEM missionaries Harold Berry and Horace Butler awaited me with brotherly warmth and, it seemed, relief. Romans 8:28 had been fulfilled again. All things had worked together for good to them that love God, to them who are the called according to His purpose.

Five hundred people poured into Fairview Church, Johannesburg, for the funeral service; nephews, nieces and families filled the first four rows. But for the obstacles of time and distance, hundreds more would have been there from all over South Africa, Rhodesia (Zimbabwe today), Zambia and Zaire (then still called Congo and now back to Congo), for William F. P. Burton was loved and respected in a unique way throughout that vast sub-continent.

The service began at 9.30 a.m. and, together with the gathering at the graveside, went on for nearly four hours! Many people came to the cemetery who could not get to the church. It was more like a convention than a funeral and, though emotion ran deep, the note of victory sounded loud and strong. Senior missionary Jim Fowler led us into the presence of God in moving and fervent prayer. The singing was triumphant, the praying resonant with praise and the many tributes paid were grateful testimonies to the rich ministry, self-sacrifice and warm friendship of Willie Burton.

I had worked very closely with our leader for a lifetime, but even I was amazed at the breadth of denominational and independent representation, and that not in a general or mere respectful acknowledgement of an outstanding teacher, writer, artist and missionary, but in an intimate, loving and long-standing recognition of a humble yet gifted man of God, a true Apostle of the New Testament order. During the following days I read correspondence from Pentecostals of all shades: Brethren, Methodists, Anglicans, Presbyterians and many others from Britain, Europe, America, Australia, New Zealand, the Far East and all over India and Africa. Many were thanks for precious ministry by pen or preaching and many were seeking further light on personal salvation in Christ, the work of the Holy Spirit, service for God and missionary problems. There were piles of letters and papers but our 'Tramp Preacher' had only a couple of suitcases of this world's goods.

The minister of Fairview Assembly of God, Louis B. Potgieter, spoke most eloquently on Zechariah 11:2, 'Weep, O Fir for the Cedar has fallen'. Cedar he was, prince among preachers, giant among men. Seeing that our Congo Church leaders could not be present, Pastor Potgieter invited the executive members of the large Bantu, Indian and Coloured sections of the Assemblies of God of South Africa – all friends of William Burton – to represent them. They sang movingly in Zulu and read the Scriptures in English.

Closing a pithy testimony to Willie Burton's intensely zealous ministry, one of the Congo missionaries, Elvyn G. Lee, cried out, 'He did not burn out for God, he went out burning!' Yes, still blazing for God at almost 85!

It was a tremendous privilege to give the funeral address and to speak of his unrivalled qualities of leadership, his unremitting service to God and for the Congo whether on or off the Field, his unusual gifts dedicated to God, his versatility as a preacher, writer, artist, poet and naturalist; also as a practical builder, map-maker and lover of men, black, white, young and old. He was truly a Prince with God and an Apostle to men. Surely he merited the 'abundant entrance' that Peter speaks of in 2 Peter 1:11; the qualities mentioned in verses 5 to 8 were certainly evident in him. As Paul says, he was 'always abounding in the work of the Lord'. He abounded in the gifts and graces of the Holy Spirit and was a daily seeker of souls – he won 13 people to the Lord in the last ten days of his life – and was a daily builder-up of the saints. Up to the last, his usual request when arranging to take meetings was, 'Please, brethren, let us have a meeting every night and three on Sundays.'

Willie Burton did nothing by halves, but wholly, abundantly, with all the energy and spiritual enthusiasm of a totally sanctified and dedicated man of God. He poured out his life, strength and exceptional talents in white-hot boundless service. No wonder the Congolese, with their apt gift of naming every European, called him Kapamu, 'the Rusher-Forth', the one who bounded out to answer any call, day or night. All who are born of God may enter the kingdom, but all will not have that abundant, triumphant, glorious entrance. Some will slip in almost shamefacedly, but Kapamu will surely bound through in triumph.

We later learned that on the very day that he was called home two other pioneers and great friends of his were also called, A. Howard Carter, Pentecostal Pioneer of Great Britain and world-renowned

Bible Teacher, and Ralph M. Riggs, Assistant Superintendent of the Assemblies of God of USA, author, and one-time pioneer missionary in South Africa. In fact Mr Riggs was very closely connected with our Congo work in the very early days. What a picture! All old pioneers, all friends, all believers in the abundant life of the Holy Spirit in experience and service, entering together into eternal life in abounding glory and triumph.

Another aged pioneer, J. R. Gschwend, Swiss missionary to the Basuto and founder of the All Nations Publishing Company led in prayer, but before he did so he prophesied under the power of the Holy Spirit saying, 'The work of My servant is not finished but is beginning anew... The battle is not yours but Mine... Victory is assured.'

Pastor Potgieter had arranged for the African pastors to be the pall-bearers into the church, while Congo missionaries bore the coffin out of the church and six of Willie Burton's nephews were pall-bearers at the cemetery. With the triumphal singing of 'Forever with the Lord' our brother's remains were laid to rest. David Newington of Emmanuel Press spoke about the 'Shock of Corn' ascending in full age in Job 5:26, and Harold Berry of World Outreach read the committal with deep feeling, remarking that it was peculiarly fitting that he should have the honour of committing our brother's remains seeing that William Burton had held him in his arms as a baby, committing him to God's care and service 57 years before.

Surely we are overrating this man? Willie Burton hated flattery, artificiality and false praise. No! We are simply trying to show in this book what God can do with a totally dedicated man. We could say much more; it may indeed be an understatement of what he was to God and man. But if, by it, one humble young man could see the vision and begin to ask how could he withhold himself when such a man as William Burton could deny himself and all earthly ambitions, laying his exceptional gifts at the feet of Jesus, then it will be a fitting memorial to such a man of God.

2
Born and born again

Some months before he died, William Burton stood with us in the garden of my sister's house in Redhill, Surrey, and pointed out the landmarks familiar to him from childhood: the ridge along which Chaucer's travellers rode the Pilgrim's Way from Winchester to Canterbury, the woods where he used to collect birds' eggs as a boy, and the valley close by our house – one of the few places in Britain where fuller's earth is obtained – where he used to dig for fossils. Collections of his specimens of birds' eggs and fossils can still be seen in Reigate museum.

Just below, in the bottom of the valley, is a beautiful old white house which stands out clearly, a house of character and charm, now squeezed and jostled by intruding blocks of modern flats yet still retaining part of its large, old-world garden. This was the old Burton home, lying between the twin towns of Reigate and Redhill and just within the borders of the latter.

It was here that he grew from babyhood to young manhood (though he was actually born in Liverpool on March 24th 1886, while his father's ship was in dock; his mother had to be rushed to a nearby hospital for the event: Willie was in a hurry, as he was for the rest of his life!) It was here, too, that his godly parents systematically taught their growing family the principles of salvation and to know and to love the Word of God. Parents and grandparents on both sides were keen believers and witnesses for Christ, as were many uncles and aunts. One uncle was greatly used in establishing Brethren assemblies in Switzerland, while an aunt was for twenty years a missionary with the China Inland Mission and barely escaped with her life during the Boxer Riots of 1900.

Grandfather, Colonel Burton, after an active life in the Indian Army, spent several years preaching to the Negro slaves in America and later was one of the leading figures in establishing the 'Open Brethren' assembly at Shrewsbury Hall, just near the white house.

It was at Shrewsbury Hall that Willie's father, George, met his future wife, a certain Miss Padwick, who was of aristocratic stock and connected with a branch of the Marlborough family, owners of the manor in Canvey Island and whose family crest was a greyhound – a most fitting emblem for the future 'Kapamu'! A young woman of great gifts, strong personality and at the same time deeply spiritual, she imbued young Willie with much of her nature. It may be trite, though nevertheless true, to say that most great men owe much to their mothers; certainly Willie Burton did to his. During the long absences of her husband who became commodore of the Cunard fleet, she made it her life work to train her young family in the Scriptures, in the art of living, in the study of nature and in practical things. She made arrangements for her sons to go to a carpenter's shop during holidays to learn the use of tools. Often she would say to Willie, 'You may be living in the far off wilds some day and have to make your own furniture.'

From earliest childhood, Willie's mind was turned to Africa and his parents encouraged this. He did not know till many years afterwards that, before he was born, they dedicated him to God's work in Africa. He was about three or four years old when a lady showed him a missionary picture book of Bishop Hannington's work in Uganda and the great African king Mtesa; from then on he always said, when asked what he was going to be when he was grown up, 'I'm going to be a missionary!' When he was about six years old a freed slave, Evangelist Thomas L. Johnson from USA, visited his grandmother who lived nearby at Shaw's Corner, and placed his hands on the little chap's head, asking God to send him to his people in Africa.

Like any normal boy, however, Willie Burton was no stranger to trouble. Once during the school holidays he was experimenting in the attic and found he needed a small mammal. No time to search the woods, so he caught a cat in the garden and, with some difficulty, killed and skinned it and was intently boiling the bones when his mother returned from paying a call. The cook met her at the door.

'There's a terrible smell coming from the attic, ma'am, I hope Master Willie is all right!'

Young Willie was soon found out and made to bury the debris at the bottom of the garden, strip, bathe and bury his suit too, Norfolk jacket and all. The stench hung around for days and the poor gardener complained bitterly; Willie ran to his usual safe retreat at Grandma's round the corner.

'Willie, how would you like to go with me next voyage?' The lad could scarcely believe his father was serious – what a perfect adventure for a 14-year-old.

'Do you really mean it, Father?'

'Yes, I do. I could drop you in New Zealand and you could stay with your uncle for a few months, then I could pick you up again on my return.' He frowned. 'The only snag is, I can't take you as a passenger and at the same time have you with me in my cabin. Ah! I know what we can do – I'll sign you on in the ship's company as cabin boy!'

During Christ's life on earth, the devil often tried to take His life in order to bring to nought the purpose of the Cross; he sometimes does the same to God's called ones in order to ruin God's purpose for them. At least four times this was true of Willie Burton, and the first was during that trip.

In a fearful gale in the South Pacific, when the ship was heading for Port Chalmers, heavy seas swept the decks. The lad was turning in for the night after walking with the officer on watch. He fought his way down from the bridge and groped across the slippery deck, when suddenly a burly sailor shouted against the wind, 'Look out, Captain's kid!' and seizing him round the waist, swung him into the scuppers and held him tight. And only just in time, for a moment later a mighty wave came thundering down upon the deck and would have washed the lad straight overboard into the boiling ocean. The sailor landed young Willie, drenched, but safe, in his father's cabin. The captain, white as he thought of his son's near escape from death, thanked not only the brave sailor but an overruling God. I've stood there at Port Chalmers and ruminated on Scott's ill-fated Antarctic expedition, and on others who have sailed from that port, and also of God's pioneer whose life was nearly lost, but the One who calls will never allow His plans to be thwarted: His purposes must be fulfilled.

During his stay in New Zealand, Willie and his Doctor uncle one day visited a farmer patient. After the visit the farmer walked with them to the gate, then laid his hand on the boy's head and prayed, 'Lord, save this lad's soul and send him out to preach Thy Gospel.' Then after a pause he added: 'And I have a strong presentiment that it will be in Africa.' At any point during his childhood Willie Burton later recalled, he could easily have yielded to Christ, for he was often under deep conviction but, as he said, 'I knew the way of salvation but did not accept it, simply because I lacked decision and put it off. At school and later at St. Laurence College, Ramsgate, I lived a reckless, carefree life. Then, at 17, I went to work as an electrical engineer and soon got into sin and sadness. However, conviction deepened and I knew my need of a Saviour, but again there was that lack of decision. I knew well the truth of the Lord's Second Coming and of the eternal doom in hell awaiting the impenitent, and would sometimes awake in terror at night and, hearing all things so still, would fear that the rest of the family had been caught up and that I would be left to a Christless eternity.'

3
God calls, but we must answer

After leaving St. Laurence College, Willie Burton took a course at Redhill Technical College and another at Liverpool University, the latter while training with Dick, Kerr and Co. (now General Electric) in Preston, Lancashire. At 19 he was sent to Batley, Yorkshire, on new tramway construction work between Batley, Dewsbury and Wakefield and was at first somewhat bewildered with the local dialect. When he and his mother arrived at Wakefield railway station and enquired the way to an address they had been given, the first man said, 'Aye, Missus, it's ower t'brig 'n oop t'broo.' Thinking he must be a foreigner they thanked him and tried someone else. Again, it was, 'Ower t'brig 'n oop t'broo.' After a number of enquiries, all with the same perplexing reply, it dawned on them that this was the South Yorkshire dialect. Eventually they found a kind interpreter who said smilingly, 'Over the bridge and up the hill.' (Actually 'broo' is pure Anglo-Saxon 'brû'.)

William Burton's conversion, after many years of conviction, growing concern and indecision, was brought to a head by a visit to London. A friend invited him to one of the Evangelistic Services being held in 1905 by the famous Evangelists R. A. Torrey and Charles A. Alexander, who were conducting great campaigns in England. There he came under such deep conviction under the anointed ministry of Dr Torrey that he could not rest nor sleep, and so it was that, a few days later at Batley, Yorkshire, he knelt by his own bedside and accepted Christ as his Saviour and Lord.

He writes in *Missionary Pioneering in Congo Forests*: 'On August 3rd 1905 I knelt by my bedside in Batley, Yorkshire, and claimed the promises in John 1:12, Romans 10:13 and John 6:37. Well do I remember the prayer which I prayed: "I am only a lost undeserving sinner, O God, but I take the Lord Jesus to be my Saviour, and please take me to be Thy servant. I ask this in Jesus' Name."'

He adds: 'If I had died as I knelt down by my bed I should have dropped straight into hell, but I rose from my knees saved, rejoicing and on my way to glory.'

Now it was neck or nothing. All for Christ, Christ for all. All his boundless energies were turned to Christ, his people and his service. First he must find other like-minded out-and-out children of God who would help him in fellowship and witness. He himself records: 'On rising from my knees I cried, "Now, Lord, You must direct me to godly companions with whom I may have fellowship." Then, looking out of my bedroom window, I saw men erecting a tent under the direction of a man who looked like a preacher.' In true 'Kapamu' spirit he shot out of the house and across the road, made himself known and found he was talking to Evangelist James Gilchrist who was about to start an evangelistic campaign. Mr Gilchrist used to take the 19-year-old young man to his home in Bradford where the whole family helped him in studying the Scriptures and encouraged him in preaching.

Willie attended every meeting, testified whenever he had a chance, and began at once his lifelong ministry of witnessing for his newly found Saviour and winning souls to Christ. Though able to discourse in highly technical language on very many subjects, he always preached the Gospel in simple uninvolved speech, just as Jesus did. No wonder he was to be so successful in winning souls among every possible age group in every land he visited. Children would flock to 'Uncle Burton'; the old loved him, young men and girls would listen to him with awe, and countless thousands would attribute their conversion to his direct, vivid, logical, assured presentation of the 'glorious gospel of our Lord and Saviour Jesus Christ'.

Burton grew to love Yorkshire, learnt the brogue and later could even tell tales in the broad dialect. He loved Yorkshire chiefly because it was the scene of his conversion and saw him become a child of God. One of the many who helped him during his first years as a Christian was Mrs Japp, a lame lady who lived in Leeds. She would invite him to play tennis with her son; Willie Burton at that time loved tennis and cricket, and being both quick and left-handed could be a formidable opponent. He always wrote and painted with his right hand but, having broken his arm badly near the elbow while at college, preferred to use his left arm in games. Then in the evenings Mrs Japp would say, 'Willie, come and sit beside me and let me show you these Scriptures that I have been looking up for you.' He learnt much from her of such subjects as victory over sin, justification by faith, guidance by the Word, imparted and imputed righteousness and Christian fellowship.

Some months later he saw from the Scriptures that those who trusted in the Lord Jesus were baptised on confession of their faith in

Him – Acts 8:12, 37 and 38. He saw that it was by a burial, an immersion (Romans 6:24). He wanted to obey and be baptised on the spot, and indeed was immersed as soon as it could be arranged, though it brought upon him some hard criticism at the time as he had been both 'christened' and 'confirmed' in an evangelical Church of England in Redhill where his mother usually worshipped.

Impetuous as Moses, he now wanted to rush off to the farthest corners of the earth – anywhere, but preferably Central Africa. He felt strongly within his soul a call to preach the Gospel to heathen lands. However, God is not often in a hurry, and the potential pioneer and founder of what would become one of the largest Churches in Congo needed training and character development: it was to be over eight long years before he could finally sail for the African Continent.

4
Just warming up

During the few years that followed his conversion Burton applied repeatedly to various evangelical missions working in Central Africa but was rejected because of inexperience. He spent much time on his knees, pleading for the heathen and felt desperate because he could not go to take the Gospel to them. Once in his impulsiveness he nearly joined a ship going to Brazil and at another time almost left for China. He read avidly all the missionary books on which he could lay his hands. His parents were perfectly willing that he should be a missionary, and of course always had been.

Two reasons for the long delay soon became clear. The first was that Willie Burton had a sister still unmarried, his mother was fast becoming an invalid and his father's health and sight were failing. All these might become dependent upon him and he read in 1 Timothy 5:8, 'If anyone does not provide for his own, and especially for those of his own house, he is worse than an infidel, and has denied the Christian faith.' This Scripture shook him somewhat. The second was that God had an experience for him of which he then knew nothing. Jesus had told the apostles to tarry in Jerusalem until they were endued with power from on high. He was becoming hungry for more power in service and witness and sought earnestly at Holiness meetings and conventions without complete satisfaction, till God in His mercy and grace endued him with the glorious baptism of the Holy Spirit. 'You shall receive power after the Holy Spirit has come upon you and you shall be my witnesses,' said Jesus in Acts 1:8.

Meanwhile he had been transferred back to Preston and had forged ahead in his profession. He had invented an anti-submarine device which, it is said, would have been of great use in the war which followed, had he not come to the conclusion that a Christian should use his talents to save life rather than to destroy it, and so thrown his invention into the River Ribble.

He became more and more active in witness, had a large and thriving Sunday School class of young men and did much open air work both in the villages around Preston and in the town itself. He visited the ships on Preston dockside, playing his banjo, singing the Gospel and winning sailors to Christ. A Christian barber was a great help to him and together they went about preaching in mission halls, in tramps' lodging houses and in market places. He began then to look upon himself as 'just a tramp preacher' – a title which stuck for the rest of his life.

About this time, Willie Burton found, and joined up with, a group of believers then meeting twice a week for Bible study under the guidance of Mr Thomas Myerscough; here he received a solid grounding in the fundamentals of God's Word. He wrote: 'This was an immeasurable blessing to me. He taught us how to ferret out for ourselves the precious truths of the Scriptures. From then on I formed a habit of being up early for at least two hours' Bible study and communion with God at the opening of the day.

'In 1910 we came into that wonderful blessing, the gift of the Holy Spirit and enduement of power. I sought and received this gift, praising God in new languages which I had never learned. Also we discovered that Jesus heals bodies as well as souls, so that we began to lay hands upon the sick, anointing them with oil in Jesus' Name. We saw many wonderful healings in answer to prayer.

In the nominal Christian churches and the Keswick Movement there was much violent opposition to all this. Many hungry souls came to our meetings and went away filled with the Spirit, but they were mistrusted and shunned in their own churches, so they came to us and there gradually came into being a new non-denominational church.'

During the previous five years or so, the power of the Holy Spirit had fallen as on the Day of Pentecost, in 'waves of liquid glory' and attested to by speaking in other tongues, in many places throughout the British Isles; in Croydon, Kilsyth, Southsea, Belfast, Halifax and in South Wales the flames descended, but notably in All Souls Church of England, Roker, where the vicar, Rev A. A. Boddy, started the Sunderland Conventions, the magnetic centre for the growing number of groups of believers filled with the Holy Spirit. In Sunderland there is a plaque which still records that this was 'where the fire fell and burnt up the debt'. (These groups of Pentecostal believers came into being because they were ostracised by their denominational churches. Thank God, today that spirit of mistrust, suspicion and persecution has almost disappeared. It is said that there are now as many Spirit-filled believers, exercising the gifts of the Spirit, in the historic churches as in the organised Pentecostal churches.)

William Burton was now white-hot and his burning, unconventional ministry flowed in all directions like streams of molten gold. He became a real 'tramp preacher', walking all over Lancashire and the Yorkshire Pennines to hold meetings in cottages and on village greens in his holidays. Many assemblies of believers today owe their beginnings to those meetings.

Some leaders were nervous of his unorthodox style and forceful personality but not so Thomas Myerscough. This great Bible teacher started the first Pentecostal Bible School in Great Britain and our 'fire-eater' plunged into the studies with typical enthusiasm. His habit of intense concentration on the Word and prayer during the early and late hours of each day enabled him to master the subjects with rapidity and to contribute much himself. This period settled his doctrines in more or less permanent channels; all but one or two remaining basically unchanged throughout his long ministry. I have by me notes of some of those early, detailed studies, written in his neat and beautiful though microscopic script. Later, while pastoring a church, he taught regularly in that same school which helped to train George Jeffreys, later founder of the Elim movement and E. J. Phillips, its General Secretary, James McNeill of Kilsyth, James Salter his co-pioneer, F. Dean Johnstone another Congo pioneer, Frances Jameson of South America, Edmund Hodgson the Congo martyr and many other missionaries and leaders.

And it was Thomas Myerscough, Overseer who signed the ministerial certificate from the Preston Christian Assembly which read: 'I hereby certify that William F. Padwick Burton was, with the general consent of this Assembly, ordained as a minister of the Church of God on 18th June, 1911 and was commended to the Lord with prayer and the laying on of hands for the propagation of the Gospel in Africa.'

A remarkable sign came to him at this time. He had had trouble with his teeth, so decided to trust God alone for healing. A perfectly new and strong set of teeth grew, most of them remaining till his death; this sign was attested at the time and, since then, has been recorded in articles and on radio programmes.

Delays continued. He later wrote: 'I learned many lessons during that time of waiting. I learned that God is not in a hurry and impatience is sin (Proverbs 19:2, Isaiah 28:16). I learned also valuable lessons in church guidance and discipline. God showed me that His delays are not denials. Among many precious promises were "I will make all my mountains a way" (Isa. 49:11), and "As you go step by step, I will open up the way before you" (Prov. 4:12). 'Mother was called home to Glory in March 1911 so I resigned my job hoping to leave soon for Africa but it was three years before I sailed.'

Meanwhile he gave himself to full-time ministry, first at Bracknell in Berkshire and then at Lytham in Lancashire. He and his co-workers, he wrote, 'commenced in private houses and as the Lord added to the church we built halls'. From 1912 to 1914 he lived with Mr and Mrs Beech at Warton. Here there was forged another important link in God's leadings. Mrs Beech's brother, Mr Charles Heatley, a jeweller in Johannesburg, had recently visited his old home and family and brought the news that he had received a Pentecostal baptism in the Holy Spirit in South Africa, through the ministry of Evangelist John G. Lake of America. This aroused great interest; Willie Burton was welcomed into the Beech home and, when he finally left for Africa in 1914, carried a letter of introduction to the Heatleys.

'Mr Burton,' writes Mr Tom Finch, 'used to come by train for a mid-week service held in different farmhouses in the Parbold area. He would walk from Rufford Station to Parbold, a matter of 3 ½ miles, and preach to the farmers on the way, and on at least one occasion he followed Philip's procedure with the Ethiopian Eunuch and baptised a farm labourer in a pond.' Others recount similar unorthodox ministry. Pastor J. Nelson Parr tells of another occasion when Burton went to minister in Manchester, won a soul on the way and upon confession of faith in Jesus promptly baptised him in a pond by the roadside.

His independence caused him to be eyed askance by some Pentecostal leaders; they considered him a reckless young man, as indeed he was. He cared for no man, only his Lord. On the other hand, he couldn't see eye to eye with Pastor Boddy because he still sprinkled infants in his church and called it baptism. Burton strongly maintained that baptism was by immersion and for believers only. Donald Gee, referring to the same period in *The Pentecostal Movement*, comments that 'The matter of infant sprinkling became a very vexed question'. Burton also joined issue with the renowned and wealthy Cecil Polhill, one of the Cambridge Seven of the China Inland Mission, founder of the Pentecostal Missionary Union and sponsor of some early Pentecostal missionaries. He felt he could walk the life of faith better without sponsor or committee: an Apostle to be led of God and not ordered by men. Even his mentor and father in God, Thomas Myerscough, finally felt he could no longer support this young firebrand against these leaders and his hitherto warm and sympathetic friend Pastor John Nelson Parr also lost interest in the rebel, even though he himself has often been considered a rebel in a similar way.

Now completely on his own, he again tried various channels of missionary service to see if God would open any specific door. William Burton's call at first was to 'the black man', then more generally to

Africa and finally more particularly to Central Africa and Congo. When praying for the heathen he often saw in a vision an African man with a large white growth over one eye: he later recognised this man in an open-air meeting in a mountain village in Basutoland (today's Lesotho).

On one occasion he rushed off to Liverpool to offer himself to Dr Karl Kumm, the founder of the Sudan Interior Mission. He considered West Africa and began to study Hausa. Then he tried Charles E. Hurlburt of the African Inland Mission. Both these doors failed to open. Then C. T. Studd became interested in him as he, too, was planning to go to Congo to a spot in the dead centre of the African Continent. 'Come with me,' said he, 'tongues and all!' But Burton had no inner witness that this was God's plan for him. He began to realise that he must wait for God's time, when He would provide the right man and lead them to pioneer some other equally needy Field where Christ was not named.

A short time before, Willie Burton had stopped on a street in Preston to have a chat with one of the Bible students, James Salter, who was just going out into full-time service:

'Jimmy, did you ever think of God's command to go into all the world and preach the Gospel to every creature? And did you ever consider Africa's need of the Gospel message?'

'Jimmy' certainly had, and as Burton failed to go first with one, then another possible partner – and there were many, James Salter knew in his heart that God had planned for him to be Burton's partner in that great venture for God in darkest Congo. A lifetime later he was to write to Willie Burton, then a vigorous eighty-year-old, still travelling all over South Africa and Rhodesia (Zimbabwe) and rarely preaching for less than an hour: 'My dear Willie – As I sit alone by the fireside you are much in my mind. I wonder how you are and wish I were at your side as in the early Congo days.... The bringing of us together was surely of God. I think back and see you getting ready to go to the Mission Field with so many folks, John Young of West Africa, Alma Doering, Jim McNeill, Fred Johnstone, C. T. Studd and others, and finally us two linking up, yes, it was God. I would do it all over again....'

The coming together of these two men, totally divergent in character, training and background, was very moving to those who knew them. One was from a wealthy home with every advantage in life; the other was a poor orphan who worked in a mill from an early age. One was brought up in comfort, with a public school education; the other in hardship and largely self-educated.

James Salter has often told us how, when he left school at twelve, he and his older girl cousin used to walk each morning from the centre of Preston to the mill where they worked at Walton-le-Dale three miles distant, where they had to start work at 6 o'clock. They finished at 5:30 in the evening and walked the same distance back. On cold, biting winter mornings the young twelve-year-old, wearing a cloth cap on his head and clogs on his feet but no overcoat on his back, chilled to the bone, had to snuggle under his cousin's shawl to keep out the cold wind.

Yet both men became known as intelligent, educated, outstanding preachers, gripping writers and well-known Bible expositors. As missionary pioneers they fitted together like a key to a lock. In temperament one balanced the other, Willie was headstrong and bold; Jimmy was cautious but brave. They were brothers and pals and, in their single days, wore each other's clothes with complete disregard as to whose they happened to be! God moulded them and shaped them to fit together in order to work together for Him. Workers together with God. How fitting that the ever-observant Congolese named the one 'Kapamu', the rusher-forth to help, and the other 'Inabanza', the wise counsellor. In 1965 the Congo Evangelistic Mission held a great, and packed, meeting in Spurgeon's (Metropolitan) Tabernacle, London. It was for a twofold purpose: to celebrate the Jubilee of our pioneers' entry into the Congo Field, and to bid goodbye to the Womersleys and the Brinkmans, returning to the Field, and Burton, travelling to South Africa. The whole congregation was deeply moved at one point in the service when the two old pioneers put their arms round each other, and, their voices breaking, testified to their lifelong service for God together.

Three months after that talk in Preston, Burton and Salter met in a public park in Shrewsbury and made a solemn and prayerful pact to work together in evangelising the part of Central Africa that God would lead them to. That pact was never broken. The devil would make many attempts right down through the years to prise them apart, but they always gained the victory.

5

Introducing Africa

At last, in May 1914, God showed Willie Burton that the time had come, and even gave him the very day on which he must embark for Africa. He had been selling some of his black-and-white drawings to meet the cost of the fare to South Africa and, at the last moment, a lady gave him a sum which just made up the amount to £14, the cost of a 3rd class passage to Durban. On June 5th, God removed the last remaining barrier and he set sail in SS *Galeka*, happy in the thought that his dear 'bishop' Thomas Myerscough, and friend John Parr were now behind him in prayer, along with Preston and other assemblies of loving and praying saints.

The voyage was good but the water rough; on one occasion, prayer was made for a very seasick believer, who was immediately healed. The two of them preached the Gospel on 20 of the 21 days of the voyage; several souls were saved, and each Sunday the believers on the ship broke bread together in memory of Christ's death. Then there was the train to Johannesburg, where Mr and Mrs Charlie Heatley met him and took him to their home. Mrs Heatley was quite worried because Willie Burton insisted on pitching his tent in their large garden, although it was mid-winter! But Burton wanted to get used to roughing it right away. After some days, however, they prevailed on him to stay indoors for a while; time enough, they thought, for him to sleep rough when he got to Central Africa.

The months that followed were filled with hard work and fruitful ministry. The Pentecostal revival which had burst over South Africa through the preaching of John G. Lake from Dr Dowie's church in Zion City, USA, Mr Bryant and others was still flowing in full spate along the Rand (Gauteng) and other areas. The Apostolic Faith Mission, the Full Gospel Church and other Pentecostal groups were forming and increasing rapidly. The famous church in Rochester, New York, had sent out George Bowie to found the Pentecostal Mission of South Africa and many of their missionaries were actively engaged in evangelising among the various Bantu tribes 'with signs following'.

Willie Burton was a tremendous help in stabilising many newly-formed assemblies that were full of zeal for their new-found Saviour and rejoicing in their Pentecostal experience, but as yet largely untaught in the Word of God. He often gave three or four Bible readings a day on doctrine and church order, as well as preaching the Gospel in all its fullness, and had remarkable results in conversions and healings among white, black and coloured peoples. Usually the first Bible reading of the day was held at 8 a.m. at Jeppe in Johannesburg for about 30 preachers and workers, though for some days he gave a series of studies on the Levitical Offerings at 6 a.m. 'and', he said, 'we had delightful times'.

During his stay in Johannesburg the devil twice tried to stop the work that God had for Willie Burton. Some years ago he showed me a spot a mere stone's throw from the present Fairview Assembly of God Church where, crossing a piece of wasteland on the way to a new chapel recently opened by Charlie Heatley, he was beaten up by a mob. He was able to testify to them, however, and later two were soundly saved and one baptised in the Spirit; after the brethren arrived in Congo, the 'mob' sent an offering of £5 for the work! The second occasion was when he was invited to visit a very deep gold mine with a party at Benoni, and was discussing geology with a doctor. (Remarkably enough he found that the doctor's wife came from Broughton near Preston and had heard him preach on Preston Market and could recall his message.) He was examining the face of the rock with a naked acetylene flame when suddenly a black workman shouted and dragged him back. The lamp flame was only two inches away from the end of a fuse attached to a heavy charge of dynamite in the rock, which had failed to explode on the previous shift. He recorded at the time, 'Another two inches and in a matter of seconds we should all have been mangled corpses.'

The opportunity soon came of spending three months in the mountains of Basutoland (Lesotho) to gain missionary experience with Mr and Mrs Edward Saunders on their Mission Station. Soon after he arrived, the missionaries' eldest boy, Owen, then about nine years old, was saved (Later, as a young man, he was to serve with the Congo Evangelistic Mission on the Congo Field). Edward Saunders had a great vision for missionary work among the African people; once he clearly saw in prayer a large map of Africa and felt that the South African believers should step out to evangelise all the unreached parts of East and Central Africa. To the end of his life he backed up with all his power first the efforts of the Pentecostal Mission of South Africa then those of the Congo Evangelistic Mission. His family paid for the beautiful building that housed the Saunders Memorial Press at our Katompe Station and for some of the printing machinery.

Willie Burton gained invaluable lessons in missionary work while in South Africa and unlearned many preconceived notions. He also learned a good smattering of Sesuto and a little Zulu which was a big help in understanding the Congo Kiluba, as all languages of the 'bantu' group of Central and South Africa follow the same grammatical structure. He also picked up and used a limited amount of Afrikaans, or South African Dutch, which was much appreciated by the Dutch-speaking believers.

Then the devil tried again. On August 4th 1914, Burton walked the 16 miles from their camp in Basutoland (Lesotho) to the border town of Ficksburg, South Africa, for their mail and stayed late to listen to the news of the declaration of war on Germany. On the return journey, he lost his way among the rocky hills and dark gullies, got entangled among the thorny aloes and at last in despair prepared to spend the night with his back resting against a rock. Just then dogs began to bark and voices called down the mountain side, 'Who is there?' He called back, 'I'm a white man and I have lost my way!' 'Don't move, we're coming down!' Soon the kind Basuto came with lanterns and conducted him to the safety of their village and gave him food and shelter. In the morning, before putting him on the right path, they showed him where they had found him – on the very edge of a deep ravine. Two more steps and he would have been dashed to pieces. Again God saved him for his life-work, and by the Africans to whom he was called.

It was at about this time that Willie Burton was struck by the healthy climate of this mountainous land with its peaks towering to 11,000 feet, and wrote to Mr Myerscough that for any intending missionaries not strong enough for the enervating tropics, Basutoland (Lesotho) would be ideal, and the need was great. Vast areas knew nothing of Christ. Just then, David Fisher from England was looking for just such a place. David, weakened from several years in Congo, burned to return to Africa. Two elderly ladies, Miss Billing and Mrs Watson, were led to go with the Fisher family who were looking to South Africa for a suitable field. Burton met the party and strongly advised them to go to Basutoland (Lesotho). They saw God's hand in this and went.

In 1920 David Fisher fell sick of typhoid and died; a man was needed to care for the growing work. With others, our assembly in Halifax prayed much for this little band. J. G. Gschwend of Switzerland had recently entered the London Pentecostal Missionary Union Bible College to train for service with W. F. P. Burton in the pioneer Congo Evangelistic Mission. Smith Wigglesworth, the 'Apostle of Faith', told the students that a Moses had died and a Joshua was needed. A series of miracles took Mr Gschwend to Basutoland (Lesotho), where he married Miss Eveline Mahon, a missionary daughter of the family whose story W. F. P. Burton told in: *When God makes a Missionary*. And so the Mount Tabor Mission passed to the Swiss Pentecostal Churches, whose Family Kast are still working there at the time of writing (1973). And so links in the chain of God's work are formed; we are workers together with God. Meanwhile Willie Burton returned to Johannesburg where, in the home of Mr and Mrs Heatley, he met Mrs Saunders' younger sister, Miss Hettie Trollip.

During this time, Congo was beginning to open up rapidly. The Berlin Conference of 1908 had turned it from a privately owned Congo Free State into the Belgian Congo, administered by the Belgian Government instead of by King Leopold II. This intelligent and progressive monarch played his part in stopping the flow of myriads of human lives into the slave-trade of the West; he employed Henry M. Stanley and many others of all nationalities to bring civilisation and education, and even rail and river transport to the almost impenetrable jungles of the Congo basin, but he nevertheless stained his reputation with blood. The land was too vast for one man to rule, travel too slow and conditions too primitive for adequate supervision, and his agents, often conscience-less adventurers, cruelly forced their primitive workmen to bring in more and more of what Sir John Harris and other reformers dubbed 'red rubber', bringing shame on the name of an otherwise well-intentioned ruler.

Most of these efforts, good and bad, were concentrated on Lower Congo, apart from at least three rubber-collecting stations in what became known as 'Katanga' – Fundabyabo, Kinda and Kisengwa. For the most part, the eastern side of Congo was being dominated more and more by encroaching Arabs who, for many years, had been carrying away hordes of men and women to the slave-markets of Zanzibar, while half-caste Angolans were draining the population of the South for the slave-markets of Bié.

Copper, together with other minerals, drew Europeans to Katanga, and the rail pushed its way up from South Africa, a link in the dream of a Cape to Cairo route. White men trickled in from all directions, mostly seeking a fortune.

It is a thrilling thought that the first white man, apart from the handful of Portuguese who lived in the Lower Congo in the 16th century, was the missionary, David Livingstone, who walked the forest trails of Congo in 1871.

By 1878, brave missionaries of the English Baptists and the Livingstone Inland Mission penetrated the fever-stricken mouth of the Congo River and as far inland as Stanley Pool, followed by many others, all on the western side. The price was heavy. When Dr Samuel Chadwick of Cliff College laid his hands on me, he said, 'Remember, 50 old Cliff men in the days of Dr Grattan Guiness laid down their lives in the Congo.' By 1913 the Africa Inland Mission and the Heart of Africa Mission (Worldwide Evangelisation Crusade) had entered Congo from the north east via Sudan.

In the South, F. S. Arnot, who had played with Livingstone's children, had made an exploratory journey into South Katanga as far back as 1886 and from 1890 to 1906 several pioneers of the Christian Brethren, including Dan Crawford, followed. In 1910 the provincial capital Elisabethville, now Lubumbashi, came into being and the American Methodists, led by Dr John M. Springer, occupied Kambove in 1913 and Lubumbashi in 1917.

So from three sides undaunted missionary bands slowly percolated through forest, swamp and savannah on foot, by canoe and occasionally by bicycle. They suffered fevers, dysentery and hunger gladly for Jesus' sake to win the lost to Him, but the land was so vast, 910,000 square miles in extent and nearly half of it dense forest, that the task was gigantic. Happily, most missionary societies worked together in spreading out as widely as possible.

In spite of the rapid advance and in spite of the fact that at least two new workers stepped into the gap left by every missionary who died or who was invalided home, people in enormous areas of the country still had not heard the Name of Jesus.

Cartographers in Africa's maps
With savage pictures filled the gaps,
And o'er the inhospitable downs
Placed elephants for want of towns.

Willie Burton studied all the maps available and, though they had greatly improved since the time when Dean Swift wrote those lines, names of places were still very few indeed, rivers ran in the wrong direction and mountain ranges were completely misplaced. There was little guidance as to population or settlement of people. However, the old rubber-trading camps were marked and, as far as he could see, Fundabyabo in South Katanga seemed a suitable place to begin and was far from any other missionary.

A few years earlier a Belgian expedition under Baron Dhanis had conquered and driven out the Arab slave-raiders, and the population of Kivu and Katanga had welcomed the white people as saviours. From then on the doors to the great undeveloped central region were open wide for Europeans.

In 1914 a party of four men, three Americans and one South African, all of the Pentecostal Mission, had left South Africa, seeking for unevangelised people with whom to commence mission work. They went by boat to what was then German East Africa, but there met many difficulties: one member turned back and a second died; war was declared but the men escaped capture, crossed into the Kivu mountains, eventually walked hundreds of miles to a point on the Congo River and took a boat southwards, back to South Africa. One, a Mr Ulyate, was very weak with fever, so the captain of the little river-boat put them off at Mulongo where a missionary of German extraction, F. Zentler, welcomed the two, George Bowie and Ulyate, and nursed the sick man. In conversation he told them of the teeming population across the river and the enormous country without a missionary. He himself had more than he could tackle on the Eastern side of the river and gladly took George Bowie to visit Mwanza where Kajingu, chief of the large Budye section of the Baluba tribe, welcomed them and said he would give them land if they would settle there.

There appeared to be endless chieftainships beyond; they heard names like Ngoimani, Mpyana Mbayo, Munza, the great chief Kikondja of the riverine people, Kasongwa Nyembo and the greatest of them all, Kabongo. Hundreds of miles of populous country stretched North, South and West. Surely God had brought Zentler and Bowie together to choose Mwanza – which actually means 'The Place of Beginning' – as the starting point for a tremendous venture for God?

This was surely a miracle; God's timing was perfect, for a few weeks later F. Zentler, to all intents and purposes English, but, owing to his parents having neglected to take out naturalisation papers, technically German, was taken to Stanleyville (Kisangani today) and interned as an alien. After three weeks Ulyate was strong enough to travel and the two men managed to reach Johannesburg, though Bowie was now very weak and for some time lay between life and death with a temperature of 104°F. Ulyate fell ill again and passed away some months later.

One of the problems facing Willie Burton at this time was the matter of quinine; he was thrown back on God as his soul agonised over this then vexed question. As believers in divine healing, the Pentecostal Mission, though experiencing extraordinary physical miracles in the course of their ministry, lost most of their missionaries labouring in the malaria belt, nine almost at one time, because they refused to take prophylactic doses of quinine. He wrote to James Salter about his concern: 'For myself I would gladly go into any fever-stricken hole in the Name of Jesus, because "greater is He that is in you than he that is in the world". Brother, if the power of God was not upon me, I would acknowledge it and humbly seek the cause of failure, but people are being continually both saved and healed. The Lord has been kind enough to use these poor unworthy hands for the healing of numbers during the Convention. If I were allowing anything between myself and God, this would not be. But now these malaria victims are dying and of course some of the Spirit-filled missionaries are taking quinine and they don't die, and they ask me which gives God most glory? To take this stuff and live, or refuse it and die? I would rather die than disgrace His cause, but then there are millions of dark heathen who don't know Christ, and I must live to carry the Gospel to them. I am certainly up against facts, and want God's glory only.'

In early June 1915 James Salter arrived in South Africa. Owing to the war, he could not get a passport, so he sailed without one; people said he would never be allowed to land. He was convinced, however, that it was God's will that he should go and, when the situation was explained to the South African authorities, they stretched a point and let him land, provided he rectified the matter in Pretoria, which he did.

He joined Willie Burton and together they were used to impart outstanding blessing among the people. Souls were saved in every Gospel meeting they held. At one open-air meeting near a railway station many of the people were so gripped by the Word of God that they missed their trains! Healings were common, and the Name of Jesus was honoured in every case. Prayer was asked for a boy in agony because of a painful swelling of the eye, ear and throat. They prayed at once; then Burton hurried to the house to find that the lad had been perfectly healed exactly when they had asked Jesus to do it. A woman with terrible rheumatism was unable to move her head or lower her limbs; she was immediately healed after laying on of hands and very soon got up and dressed and, in the exuberance of new-found strength, went to lay hands on a dying man next door who leaped up, healed and was heard singing:

> 'Arise my soul, arise, shake off thy guilty fears,
> The bleeding sacrifice, on thy behalf appears.'

Just before they left for Congo, a woman brought a little boy whose foot was twisted from birth and who had to wear a special boot. When the brethren prayed for him the little lad began to cry because the foot was hurting. They took off the boot and before their eyes, the foot straightened out and soon was perfect.

They discussed whether or not they would take quinine after reaching the malarial zone. James Salter said he would not take it but would trust God. Burton decided to take it so as not to be a burden on others who might have to waste their time nursing him. Both had many serious attacks of malaria. Both survived. One could apply Romans 14:3-5, 'Let every man be fully persuaded in his own mind'.

Meanwhile an advance party of two of the Pentecostal Mission had been chosen to leave for Congo and distant Mwanza. Burton and Salter, understanding that independent missionaries would not be permitted to enter the country, applied to travel with them and enter nominally under the Pentecostal Mission, work with them through the long wet season and, on receiving permission from the government, establish their own work and proceed to Fundabyabo.

The two men were Joseph Blakeney, an American, and George Armstrong, a retired builder and contractor who was going to see to the building in order to release the younger men for preaching. Blakeney and Burton went ahead on June 30th, a band of about 150 friends seeing them off at Johannesburg station with prayer, tears and song. Willie Burton was asked to go ahead with Joseph Blakeney because he could speak French, having had a French governess as a child, and this was, and still is, the official language of the country. They were able to get their goods through customs with little difficulty, and had interviews with helpful high government officials who granted permission for the Pentecostal Mission to be established at Mwanza. The Vice-Governor gave them a special shooting licence to help provide meat and offered much useful information about the interior.

By the time all the formalities and interviews were through, 'Daddy' Armstrong, as the three younger men called him, and Jimmy Salter had arrived and they turned their faces joyfully and prayerfully towards the unevangelised North.

But it was to be seven and a half long weeks before they completed the 450 miles of difficult and almost disastrous journey to the place to which God was calling them.

6
Heading northwards

Having failed to get him killed, the enemy of souls was subtle and flattering in his efforts to keep Willie Burton from full-time service – and full-time was little time enough – among the Bantu peoples.

While in Basutoland (Lesotho), his friends in Johannesburg wrote with tempting offers of a job as electrical engineer on various mines; he could work among the black folks there, evangelise in his spare time to his heart's content and, moreover, be able to finance his own work.

Willie Burton won the victory. An engineer's salary was a temptation but, on consideration, totally inadequate to meet the needs of such a work as he envisaged. Being a spare-time preacher was not his idea of evangelising the lost. Time and again in his correspondence he refers to the Mission that he felt God was calling him to found and to lead: only God's provision could make possible such a work as that. He stood on Philippians 4:19, 'My God shall supply all your need according to His riches in glory by Christ Jesus.'

And now, after twelve months of practical missionary experience, he was actually on Congo soil, heading north as fast as the construction train would take him and his three companions. Already God had worked miracles of provision for them, a guarantee of what He could do in the future. They had little in the way of equipment to take with them into the unknown, but, in the nick of time, a substantial gift arrived from Preston for Willie Burton, enabling him to buy many essential items at a sale, such as buckets, a tin bath and cooking utensils, as well as a canvas wash basin, folding table and chair. He also bought a bicycle and a good camera, besides food supplies.

Elisabethville (Lubumbashi today) proved expensive for four of them and they found that they would have to travel further by river boat than they had thought, since at one point (actually between Kabondo-Dianda and Kapamai where today we have a string of thriving, healthy churches) two groups were at war, and the road was therefore dangerous. This extra river travel would cost them more than they had planned, and they found they had insufficient funds to get them to their destination.

The night before they were due to leave, Burton went for a walk in the moonlight after the others had gone to bed, to think over and pray about this problem. Turning a corner, he almost collided with another European. Mutual apologies turned into a friendly chat, a witness concerning the Lord Jesus Christ and salvation, and finally, in response to the questions of this interested stranger, their missionary journey northwards. 'When does your party plan to leave?' he asked. 'Tomorrow, sir,' replied Willie Burton. 'What have you in the way of baggage?' Details were given. 'Well then, I think I can help you. I am the manager of the construction company that has laid the new railway line between here and Kambove, 130 kilometres (80 miles) north. The work is finished and should have been handed over to the Government last week. However, matters are temporarily held up so I am still in charge. I have a goods train going up tomorrow and you may use one truck free as I am strongly in favour of foreign missions.' Again God had undertaken. If the Government had already taken over, it would have cost £15 or more for them and their goods.

At Kambove they stayed with the American Methodist missionaries, Mr and Mrs Guptill, at the first station the latter had opened. Finding themselves obliged to stay there a month, waiting for the next section of line to be completed, they jumped at the chance of gaining more missionary experience and spent some days with Brethren workers at Mount Koni and also met others from Dr Fisher's distant station at Kaleni Hill, later reckoned in Northern Rhodesia (Zambia now), and close to Sakeji, where our missionaries' children still go for their English primary education. All these folk were extremely friendly and helpful and one of them, Mr Anton, taught the new arrivals much concerning the construction of Bantu languages.

Then they were away again on the very first passenger train to run to Tshilongo, which was to remain the railhead for some years. Next came ten days' tramp over the highlands and wide savannahs of the Kibara plateau and down, down the little winding path to the steaming valley of the Lualaba or Congo River, shining in the distance. For this trip, a friendly Portuguese trader was able to supply them with porters, the only means of transporting goods where there was no railway.

At Bukama, the highest point of navigation, they met their first major difficulty: there was no boat and food was fast running short. Though the river was 200 yards wide the water was unusually low, being the end of the dry season, and they were told that the little steamer was stuck on a sandbank 46 miles downstream. James Salter records that Daddy Armstrong caught a good supply of fish but he also caught a good dose of fever, as all along the riverbanks and swamps malarial mosquitoes rose in clouds and bit them severely. Willie Burton hunted antelope on the plains and the meat was sufficient to barter for a certain amount of food – maize, peanuts and sweet potatoes – from the village people.

The missionaries prayed hard and fervently and on the 14th evening they were told, 'Tomorrow morning two empty barges will be at your disposal going downstream to the steamer.' So they were up early to pack their gear on board. Let William Burton tell the story: 'It took two days to reach the steamer but they passed like two hours for we were fascinated by the strange birds, the crocodiles and the hippos, the great herds of antelope on the plains on each bank, the broad marshes alternating with dense patches of oil-palms festooned with creepers.

Waterfowl in their thousands rose like black clouds from the sandbanks. Solemn fish eagles perched in the palms, then swooped down to the clear water to rise with great silvery fish in their talons. Beautiful butterflies flitted to and fro. Nests hung from the reeds along the banks. Brilliant little kingfishers did a thriving business in tiny fishes and all nature seemed most charming and attractive.'

The steamer, the 'Louis Cousin', was reached – a burning oven of heat and sweat. Twelve long blistering days and eleven long sultry nights passed before the steamer floated clear of the sandbank. Nature lost its charms, birds and butterflies enchanted no longer, antelope ceased to fascinate. Daddy Armstrong was becoming weaker, Jimmy Salter succumbed and lay prostrate beside him in the stuffy cabin. Joseph Blakeney went down too with malaria, but managed to stagger ashore to attend the funeral of poor Daddy Armstrong who died of blackwater fever and was buried under a solitary palm on the bank of the river forty miles from human habitation. None to mourn but the voice of the African bush – the trumpeting of elephant, the roar and cough of lion, the mournful howl of hyena and the eerie blowing of hippo.

On that little river steamer was a party of naval men, an Englishman in charge, a younger Belgian officer and some naval ratings; they were taking a small boat, in sections, to Lake Tanganyika for the East Africa Campaign. It was called the 'Mwanza' – not after the Mwanza of the missionaries' destination, but the one in German East Africa (today's Tanzania). Nine years later, Teddy Hodgson and I crossed the lake in that very boat, now a trading vessel, and at Albertville (today's Kalemie) on the Belgian side we saw, recently salvaged, the large German ship the sinking of which by the little Mwanza contributed considerably to the ending of the campaign.

The night that Daddy Armstrong died, the English officer, an old and experienced campaigner, took Willie Burton on one side and said, 'I have had long experience with these African fevers, let me give you my advice. The old fellow is dead. The young one may be dead tomorrow. Ahead the tribes are at war. Food is extremely scarce. Blakeney and you may be saved yet, if you turn back at once to civilisation. Otherwise you will all die. The barges leave for Bukama again tomorrow. My advice is, go back, young man, go back!'

Burton felt this to be the greatest crisis of his life. If his three companions all died, he would certainly be blamed. Needing solitude to think and pray this through, he walked out into the moonlight and wandered along the riverbank. A hyena yelped and laughed in the distance. Hippos were snorting and wallowing in the reeds close by as the young missionary paced up and down, trying to weigh the situation correctly. 'Was I mistaken in this call of God?' he mused, 'if so, far better to turn back at once and find some other field of labour in South Africa. Was I right in risking my life and the lives of others on this forlorn hope?' The future of the Congo Mission, still unborn, hung upon a thread. He was wet with perspiration, not with fever this time, nor with tropical heat, for the night had grown cooler as the dawn approached, but with the sense of responsibility which weighed heavily upon him.

As he fought this fearful battle the hyena's shriek mocked again and the hippos snorted in derision. He prayed again and groaned before the Lord, but as he prayed God's call welled up anew within him, stronger than before! God's call must be obeyed, whatever the cost. Were not his old school friends gladly giving their life's blood in Flanders at that very moment for an earthly king? Could he not face death for the King of kings? If this was God's will, and he was more convinced every minute that it was, would not God see the matter through? It was surely God's responsibility, not Willie Burton's. His but to obey, and obey he would. Forward with God! He squared his shoulders and, as the first rays of a smiling sun gleamed over the horizon, he marched back on to the boat to nurse his sick companions, tossing and moaning in their fever.

Jimmy Salter was too weak to attend the funeral; indeed, the grave was left open a few more hours as the captain fully expected him to die too. Joe Blakeney's fever was worse; he had almost to be carried back to the 'Louis Cousin' with a raging fever of 105°F.

The turning point of a battle is not the end of the struggle; Willie Burton had gained a mighty victory, but the fight went on. Jimmy was still delirious. Joe hardly knew whether he was on his head or his heels.

Willie himself kept going with the greatest difficulty, though he still managed to hunt antelope during the day to help feed the passengers and crew, helping to ward off a threatened mutiny because food was agonisingly short. And he still nursed the other two during the long nights, snatching an hour or two's sleep here and there.

In spite of all, they maintained their testimony. Everybody had admired fine old Daddy Armstrong: even in his last moments of feverish suffering, he praised his Lord and Saviour and his voice was heard throughout the ship. And the fortitude of Jimmy and Joe in extreme suffering impressed those naval men and the two or three Greek traders on board, as well as the African crew. Pain and patience need no interpreter. At the graveside, too, Willie seized the opportunity to preach the Gospel. Many were impressed by his simple illustration of the South African level-crossing signboards, 'Stop! Look! Listen!' At least one man heeded the warning.

Then came the welcome morning when the little steamer slid sweetly off the sandbank into deep water; the engines chugged again and once more they headed northwards, downstream, along the constantly winding, twisting river towards their goal. Little fishing villages slipped by; the huts, built almost entirely of papyrus stalks and grass, blending in colour with the dry thick growth of the plains, quickly melted into the landscape. Clumps of waving palms and cream of tartar trees beckoned them from bend to bend. Once more the fish-eagles, the kingfishers, the diving birds, the antelope held them fascinated.

Yet that nagging fever still persisted; their heads throbbed with pain; their temperatures fell only to soar again. Jimmy and Joe, still lying in their stuffy, tiny cabin, with no room to have a proper bath, tossed and turned till their blankets had to be wrung out, dripping with perspiration. The noise, too, on that small vessel was shattering. The yells of the crew, the clatter and bang of the heavy mahogany logs of firewood as they were pitched across the iron deck to feed the boilers, the spasmodic clang of the stokers' spanners on the side of the boilers to check the water level, the ceaseless chug of the engines, not to mention the laughing and arguing of the passengers and the squalling of the babies, turned the journey to three days and nights of increasing nightmare. Now and again a clatter, a bang, a thud, sudden and louder than usual, would seem to crack their skulls wide open.

It was with relief and thankfulness to God and a feeble 'Hallelujah' on their dry lips that they crawled out of their bunks and staggered to the shore at Mulongo, where they were to meet Mr Zentler and have fellowship with him at his station two miles away. He would give them useful information about that magic-sounding name 'Mwanza' and tell them how to get there. With some difficulty, they pitched their tent and had a good wash down before meeting a couple of Greek traders, from whom they bought eggs and tinned fruit; it tasted like nectar from heaven. The local Chief most kindly sent a young goat to make broth and even fresh vegetables. They had tasted nothing like it since leaving Kambove over six weeks before: bliss indeed! Salter and Blakeney were refreshed and renewed in strength. But where was Mr Zentler?

At that moment, a smart young man came up and greeted them in English. 'Good morning sirs, I am Peter Tyungu, a Christian worker. Brother Zentler has gone and left me here to take his place. He left you this letter. Anxiously, Willie Burton opened it. 'Dear Brethren,' it read, 'I welcome you in Jesus' Name but regret I cannot greet you in person as, being of German nationality, I have been interned but I fulfilled first my promise to Brother Bowie and arranged with the Mwanza Chief to put up a mud-and-wattle house for you on Kayembe Hill. Sorry I have nothing with which to welcome you but this sack of rice which I have cultivated here. May the Lord bless you exceedingly.'

Peter Tyungu handed over the rice, adding fresh vegetables of his own and with pride showed them his fine band of young converts. It was eighteen months before Mr Zentler was allowed to leave the country and Willie Burton could express his thanks and enjoy fellowship with him.

The next day they were ferried over the wide Congo River to the Western bank and faced the last lap of their journey, 22 miles of mostly uphill march to Mwanza. Porters were engaged to carry their scanty possessions and the sack of rice. Jimmy Salter was still too weak to walk, and was carried in a canvas hammock. Joe Blakeney was now strong enough to ride slowly on Willie Burton's bicycle, while Burton himself walked behind the caravan of men along the winding trail across the plain, then up and up through the forest-clad hills into the unknown.

As he plodded slowly along, mile after painful mile, reaction set in after the strain of all those weary weeks of responsibility, the loss of Daddy Armstrong, the nursing, the hunting, the wrestling in prayer. Utter exhaustion gripped his tired body and his breaking nerves. His frame shook, his legs ceased to function, he sank on to an anthill then completely collapsed.

Was this, then, the end? Had he failed after all? He felt to be sinking... sinking... sinking.

Suddenly the unconscious Willie Burton felt a warm glow. He later described it as a delightful, comforting sensation, something like that of warm water being poured over his body and trickling down from head and shoulders to limbs. His head stopped throbbing, his eyes cleared, and energy returned. He stood up, stretched himself and began to walk, and, as strength increased, he found himself running, singing, laughing in sheer exuberance of spirits. He caught up with the others and finished the 22-mile journey, in spite of the climb, more fit and fresh than when he set out.

This was surely a miracle. Exhaustion to exhilaration! What had happened? He did not know till he returned to England on furlough in 1921, six years later. After a meeting in North London at Mrs Cantell's, the rendezvous of all Pentecostal missionaries – and many other evangelicals of the day, a lady approached him and, diary in hand, asked him what he was doing at 8 a.m. on September 1st 1915.

Somewhat startled, Willie Burton thought hard; suddenly he remembered. 'Of course,' he thought, 'that was the day we arrived at Mwanza. And it was about 10.30 in the morning when I sank into a helpless coma of utter exhaustion and oh, so suddenly recovered and jumped up with a miraculous inflow of new strength. I simply could not forget that! But this lady says '8 a.m.!' Suddenly he smiled as he remembered that Mwanza is about two and a half hours ahead of Greenwich time!

'Why?' he asked the lady. She told him how at that moment she had a strong prompting to 'Go and pray for Mr Burton'. She was busy and put the thought from her. Again the impulse came, so she left her work, as she prayed, the burden seemed intolerable. She wrestled on until the burden lifted, then praised the Lord and returned to her work; she was so impressed that she entered the matter in her diary. How they praised God together! All through the years that followed, prayer warriors in different parts of the world, prompted by this heavenly telegraph, have brought sudden deliverance to God's servants when no earthly post could have brought news of the need in time. 'Workers together with God,' indeed! How many other tragedies might have been averted if all His children had been at their heavenly listening-post?

7

Mwanza: the place
of beginnings

A tremendous and boisterous welcome greeted the party at Chief Mwanza Kajingu's enclosure. Thousands yelled and shouted, happy that the white men had kept their word and sent their 'brothers' to live among them. Hundreds crowded round and conducted them to the top of Kayembe Hill to the house they had built among the rocks and trees.

The house?

Before them stood a structure built of poles from the forest laced with split bamboos, with clay pressed into the framework of the walls, and the whole roofed over with poles and grass thatch. It was bigger than anything the local folks had ever attempted before but in the intervening months, termites had done their destructive work and the walls bulged dangerously, the thatch and the walls gaped widely and the whole structure seemed likely to collapse at any moment.

The three young men were so delighted to be there however, that their spirits rose to God in glad Hallelujahs, praising Him for His obvious leading and miraculous deliverances on the way. God was good. After all these years of waiting, eight or nine in Willie Burton's case, they had arrived where God had sent them to win souls and found a church to His glory. Mwanza or Fundabyabo, it was all the same tribe and this was clearly His starting point; who knows where they might finish? Complete greenhorns in Congo ways and means of building, nevertheless they enthusiastically 'set to' and propped up the sagging walls with a few forest poles left over from building, pitched their tents inside, stored their goods, and made plans for a more permanent house.

During the next few days, crowds of men, women and children thronged Kayembe Hill to gaze at the curious white men, watching with wonder their every move and gesture. They were only too glad to sit around and listen to what the strangers tried to tell them in a glorious hotchpotch of English, Zulu, Swahili and the few odd – very odd – words of Kiluba they tried to pick up day by day. One thing was clear: they were always talking about God, using the Swahili name for Him, 'Mungu', and pointing to the sky.

Willie Burton soon discovered the word for 'blood' when a young fellow, who was helping them, cut his finger and another shouted, 'Mashi!' It was a beginning; but how could one say, 'The Blood of Jesus Christ cleanses us from all sin', or 'We have redemption through His Blood'? It seemed hopeless. Here was a field ready for the seed of the Word of God and one that would surely produce a bounteous harvest. Chief Mwanza Kajingu had a densely populated district. In every direction the forest was broken by village after village, revealed by clumps of oil-palms, banana groves and fields of manioc and maize. Other large chieftainships – all of the great Baluba people group – stretched out beyond to the north, west and south.

They had been told that a quarter of a million souls lived within a 37-mile radius, and beyond that, many times that number who had not yet heard of Jesus. The nearest missionary at that time was Dan Crawford of Luanza, 15 days tramp to the east; that is, some 180 miles over the great Kibara plateau. Northwards and westwards one could travel for weeks among people who had never heard of Jesus. Dr Piper of Kapanga and Dr Fisher of Kalene were nearly 300 miles to the south west while Mr Whitehead at Waika was fully 350 miles to the north, and Dr Morrison at Luebo was 400 miles to the west. That was a vast area of Baluba and Bekalebwe people.

They must get down to serious language study at once. They had Dan Crawford's Sanga New Testament and J. A. Clarke's excellent duplicated Sanga grammar, and a Hemba vocabulary. But although these related dialects were a tremendous help, they soon found that Kiluba is a language in its own right and further removed from these than French is from Italian.

Each day as the sun went down Burton and Salter used to sit on the large rock on the projecting shoulder of Kayembe Hill and gaze across the wooded country that lay below them, rolling away mile after mile southwards to the River Lovoi and away beyond to the Kikondja Hills and Lake Kisale 40 miles away. As they saw the smoke curling up from the evening fires, revealing scores of villages around, they would pray for each one in turn that God would save those precious souls sitting in darkness outside Christ. The children used to gather to watch, and they tried to chat with them and ask the names of the villages they prayed for.

One day, Willie Burton had an inspiration. Searching in his pockets he drew out three small objects: a key, a penknife and a button. He held up the key first and said slowly, 'Key! Key!' Soon the fascinated youngsters realised they were having a lesson in white man's language. 'Key! Key!' they choroused gleefully. Then the second object, 'Knife. Knife.' A pause. That was more difficult. They giggled but had a go. 'Nah-eefi. Nah-eefi!' Not too bad. They waited expectantly as the button was held up, but this time there was complete silence. After a moment of bewilderment they were soon shouting one after another, 'I ki ka? I ki ka?'

Notebook and pencil at the ready, Willie Burton quickly scribbled down 'I ki ka' – 'What is that?' He'd got his first phrase, and a veritable key to the language. He pointed to one thing after another, 'I ki ka?' The lads soon caught on and cried, 'Tree!' 'Rock!' 'Boy!' 'Head!' 'Arm!' and so on, in their language. In his element, the zealous missionary noted down pages of words before the youngsters tired. This was just a beginning which was to lead to bigger things and a stock of words and phrases, not always accurate, but which led them speedily into a working knowledge of the language.

It was Jimmy Salter, however, who made the first attempt to preach. 'He shows a remarkable gift for languages,' wrote Willie Burton, 'and I think he catches the thoughts of the people more quickly than I and is most diligent in putting down words and phrases'. Just a month after their arrival he announced, 'I am going to preach in Kiluba.' It was Sunday morning and a big crowd had gathered outside the Chief's enclosure in the village just below the hill. 'What are you going to preach about, Jimmy?' 'Pilate and the Crucifixion,' was the surprising reply.

Such an advanced subject soon found the novice out of his depth but he bravely kept on repeating one particular phrase – like a gramophone with the needle stuck in a groove! The more he said it, the darker became the frown on the Chief's furious countenance. 'The ruler was a bad man,' was what Jimmy Salter imagined he was saying. He was not really very far out, but his vocabulary was limited; 'mulopwe' certainly does mean 'ruler' – or 'chief'. 'Mulopwe udi muntu mubi. Mulopwe udi muntu mubi', (The Chief is a bad man. The Chief is a bad man), he persisted, with complete disregard for his tenses. The crowd was silent. The chief ground his teeth in rage. Men began to reach for their spears.

'Come on, Jimmy,' said Willie, 'let's get back to the hill.' They quickly said polite goodbyes, extricated themselves and made for home. 'The village', he records, 'was like a swarm of disturbed bees behind us'. Once home, they flung themselves down before the Lord and prayed for the people and their feeble efforts to make them understand the Gospel message, and also for food to be supplied, for their cupboard was literally bare.

An hour or two later the two men heard the noise of an approaching crowd. They waited anxiously. 'Hope this isn't mischief,' muttered Burton. Far from it! Over the brow of the hill came the men, one dragging a goat, another with half a dozen chickens, yet another with a wooden bowl of eggs. Then came women with baskets on their heads with sweet potatoes, manioc flour, cucumbers, groundnuts and all kinds of food. A large crowd brought up the rear. The man in charge said, 'This is a present from the big Chief. He isn't really bad, we didn't know you were hungry!'

Later they would often laugh with the Chief over this misunderstanding which brought blessing of another kind and met a dire need. Today, every one of those villages round Kayembe Hill and far beyond has its place of worship; morning and evening the drum sounds and songs of praise reverberate among the hills and valleys. A large percentage of the population has believed on the Lord Jesus Christ as personal Saviour and gathers round His table every Sunday morning to remember and to worship Him.

It was about this time, however, that a bombshell exploded in the missionary camp. For some time Joe Blakeney seemed to have been ill at ease and referred often to his wife, left behind in America. Then he told them, 'An abscess, which I thought was healed, has broken out again in my side. The fever has left me a wreck. I shall only die if I stay here. I'm going back to civilisation.'

Funds were low, and the other two gave him every penny they had left to help him get to South Africa. Years later Blakeney, when quite an elderly man, wrote to the Field to say he realised he had made a mistake in leaving the others in the lurch; could he be forgiven and come back and he would try to make up in service? Circumstances made it impossible for him to return, but a sweet correspondence of fellowship continued until he died shortly after in Switzerland.

Now they were reduced to two. Apart from the food they were given that Sunday morning, they had no stores except for a box of blue mottled soap. The rainy season was upon them; they had no money – just a leaky shed over their heads which might collapse at any moment – and the promises of God.

The next morning, things looked still worse, for a soldier arrived with a letter from the Government official who lived at Kikondja, forty miles away.

'I am coming in two days' time to see the piece of land you have applied for. It must be surveyed and a demand sent in to Elisabethville (now Lubumbashi) for official approval.'

Willie Burton wrote: 'This was a real dilemma. The land was one mass of tangled forest and creepers. The Government required us to cut a clear path right round the boundary of our 100 hectare (over 200 acre) plot. This meant cutting down many big trees, hoeing away grass and undergrowth through which it was difficult to force one's way, so a gang of 30 or 40 men would be required. How could we pay them?'

They prayed about it at once. As they rose from their knees a young man came to the door. 'Will you sell me a piece of soap?' 'No,' they said, 'but if you and your pals will bring your axes tomorrow at sun-up and help us to chop a path round our land, you shall all have a big bar each!'

Early next morning over forty lusty men, each with his axe on his shoulder, turned up for work and by the time the official arrived to measure and map the land, the boundary was neatly cleared, everybody was happy and they still had plenty of soap left.

And God had yet another miracle of provision to work. A well-known Jewish trader, Joe Dubin by name, sometimes called and had a meal with them. The Colonel in charge in Tanganyika sent urgent orders to him to recruit four thousand carriers for the expedition against the Germans. Dubin's assistant, always a hard man, abused his powers and with a company of police, raided the Mwanza villages forcing men to go, beating them with the hippo-hide whip and firing his revolver at those who attempted to run. The Chief appealed to the missionaries to stop this cruelty. They replied that they had no authority but would pray.

Then one night an urgent call came from a dying white man at Kabumbulu 18 miles away. Burton set out, storm lantern in hand; he waded through a swamp, was drenched with dew from the long grass and scratched with thorns, but reached the dying man by dawn. It was Dubin's assistant, ill with blackwater fever. Next day Dubin himself arrived, sick with malaria.

For a week Willie Burton lovingly nursed the two sick men and, when they were convalescent, he read the Word to them, witnessed and prayed with them. The result was that the assistant called the Mwanza man who had accompanied the missionary and said, 'Tell the people I am ashamed of what I've done, I'll never force another man against his will.' When the Mwanza folk heard this they said, 'God has answered prayer. Only He could change the heart of such a man!'

Dubin wanted to pay the missionary. 'No, I've done it for Jesus' sake,' was Willie Burton's reply. It was near Christmas, and soon two sturdy carriers arrived at the Mission, each with a huge box marked, 'A Christmas box from Joe Dubin.' They contained everything they could have wished for – tea, sugar, cheese, jam, tins of meat, fruit, flour, cakes, biscuits – the lot!

With the sudden departure of Joseph Blakeney just a month after arrival, not only was the pioneer party reduced by 50% but every responsibility was now thrust upon the two younger men. Not that they were totally unprepared, for their plan had been to work in association with Blakeney and Armstrong for a year or so until the Mwanza Mission was established, then to move out and found their own work in some other needy area. William Burton felt strongly led of God to establish a new work that would develop into worthwhile proportions. He was a man of vision, energy and practical ability; he saw big, he thought big, he built big. He was a glutton for work and, throughout his life, seemed to do as much as two or three ordinary men. James Salter was one with him in heart and mind. He never had any other thought than to back up his friend in everything that conformed to what they considered to be the will of God.

Of necessity, Fundabyabo receded into the background but not entirely; on occasion, Willie talked to me about it. But for many years his mind and energies were fully occupied in trying to keep pace with this fast-growing work: the increasing responsibilities, the multiplicity of open doors within that huge area of 200 miles by 400, and the development of an indigenous church. However, a thriving assembly was established there during the 1963 revival.

The Government rightly required someone to replace Mr Blakeney immediately as 'Legal Representative' or 'go-between' for Mission matters. As the only one of the four with a knowledge of the French language, Willie Burton had already conducted what correspondence had passed between them, so he began to do at once what was needed: namely, to make as thorough a survey of the district as was possible, and over as large an area as possible, and to make a scale drawing to submit to the Government. Thus he gained an intimate knowledge of every hill, stream, path, village, forest, plain and swamp. Having already some knowledge of surveying and possessing a prismatic compass and aneroid barometer to measure altitudes, he was able to make such a thorough job of it that it became the substance of later and more official maps.

All this hard work and constant travelling served a double purpose, for he preached the Gospel in every village he visited, in every group of huts and to every individual that he could. For instance, the ferryman who paddled him across a river, the young fellow who carried his cycle through a swamp, the old woman who cooked him a few mealie cobs and the child he nursed upon his knee – all received the Gospel in a pleasant, personal and telling manner. In this way, too, he was able to obtain a remarkable grasp of the Kiluba language and, never wasting a moment, seated at ease round the evening log fire, after the evening Gospel meeting, he gained an unrivalled knowledge of Luba proverb, history, custom and lore.

Though preferring to enjoy each other's company, he and James Salter were often obliged to take turns in travelling, while the other worked on the station. James Salter was never happier than when tramping from village to village preaching Christ, and insisted on doing so even when racked with fever. They both suffered a great deal from attacks of malaria and, during the next two years, both were often on the verge of collapse and considered going south for a break. But both were urged on by the impelling force of their call to seek out and win the lost for Jesus.

'Here I am down with another dose of fever and a temperature of 102°F,' Willie Burton wrote at this time. 'However I think the worst of it is over and I want to write if only a few lines in acknowledgement and thanksgiving for your gift. How I praise God for all His care. I'm rather shaky and my head is all on the swim so that I feel you will not mind if I make the one letter do for both of you. I have just returned from a four days' trip and we had some blessed meetings at some large villages. They heard the message for the first time and asked me to visit several big villages up among the hills.'

And Jimmy Salter: 'After leaving Kikondja I had to go bare-legged for two days, the paths being flooded. The evil-smelling mud, oftentimes up to one's middle, was a sore trial... my legs are scorched with the sun and my feet have inflamed sores all over them.'

'I had a time of mighty blessing among the wild, lawless folk of Ngoimani and Lubinda,' Willie reported, 'Chief Lubinda's withered arm was restored whole like the other instantaneously in answer to prayer, at his own request. He pleaded with us to return to tell them more. As I was too weak with fever, Jimmy went and spent two weeks in follow-up work in the Ngoimani Valley, which eventually led to the opening of our second Mission Station.'

'Then I heard Jimmy was lying sick in the temporary house that I had put up so I sent one of our Christians to help him. Two weeks later Jimmy came staggering back, pale, haggard, a living skeleton. Some of the Christians wept when they saw him. He had been five days semi-conscious at Ngoimani with blackwater fever. The faithful Christian brother, only recently baptised, Katamina by name, prayed through night and day for victory, neither eating nor sleeping till healing came. Brother Salter rose, but instead of resting to recuperate, set out, scarcely knowing what he was doing, preaching among the wild villages beyond.'

Katamina followed, fed and cared for him by day and watched him by night, and finally guided him safely back to Mwanza. There was always a special bond, right to old age, between the missionary and this Congolese brother who during that time saved his life at least twice.

In many places the people were eager to hear the Gospel. 'They gulp it down without stopping to chew,' wrote Burton, 'and then come for more... You see it is all new to them, never a whisper has reached them before. Mark 16:15-18 is being fulfilled again. The "signs" Jesus promised are our "credentials". Not only are people saved by believing on the Name of Jesus but as we lay hands on the sick they are healed in His Name when their own fetishes and witch-doctors have failed. We have eaten palm nuts which it was thought a witchdoctor had deliberately poisoned, but with no ill results. We are still in the same age and on the same business as when Jesus sent out his disciples, so His promises and His commands are the same too.'

The welcome was not always so enthusiastic, however. In some areas the people were wild, ignorant of the missionaries' real intentions, and even hostile. Witchdoctors and leaders of secret society cults were afraid their own influence would diminish in favour of these foreign whites, and instigated bitter persecution. Those who suffered most from this were the first converts from heathenism, and particularly those who went out to evangelise distant parts.

The very first convert was a half-brother of Katamina, Nyuki – or Honey Bee – by name, who, as a sturdy lad of 15, believed on the Lord Jesus Christ three months after the missionaries' arrival at Mwanza. Their new house, just being completed, was struck by lightning and completely destroyed. The missionaries used this as an illustration of the brevity of life, and the lad later testified that this was when the Lord struck his heart. A few days later they were thatching their kitchen to use as temporary quarters and Nyuki was throwing up the bundles of thatch grass to them; during a break while tired arms rested, the message was driven home and late that evening the lad came to make open confession of his belief in Christ. He became a firebrand, helped in the opening of Ngoimani and later in moving farther afield to the south. Once he was poisoned for the Gospel's sake, because he was winning souls from idolatry; a long battle with the powers of darkness followed, but the victory was won and he still lives to serve Christ even though now, as I write, he is an old man (1973).

With calls on every hand to bring the Gospel message, growing groups of believers to care for, correspondence, building, language study and travelling, the two men, often weakened by fevers, simply could not cope; it was only by the energising power of the Holy Spirit that they could accomplish their Herculean tasks. But even then, they could only use one tongue, two hands and two feet each; more workers were an urgent necessity. But where could they be found?

In a prayer meeting the day they left Johannesburg, a sister had prayed, 'Lord, find the brothers some faithful African believers to help them there in Congo.' Burton thought, as he afterwards recorded, 'My good woman, we are going where Christ has not been named. There cannot be any Christian helpers!' Nevertheless, God knew better. A few months after their arrival at Mwanza, Burton and Salter were preaching to a big crowd seated around them on the end of the Mission Hill when they heard, coming across the valley below, a crowd of people singing a Sankey tune, one they had certainly not taught the people.

Up the hill they came, and over the brow – about 30 travel-stained men, women and children with tears of joy running down their faces. They had walked 740 miles from Angola and brought letters of recommendation from missionaries there. Thirty years before, they had been carried away to slavery and now had been released. Just about the time that dear lady was praying in Johannesburg, God had moved them to try to return to their childhood home in Lubaland. These believers were a great help in the early days and most of the new stations that were opened had one or more of these families or others that followed them, to help the missionaries. God's plans are wonderful and His timing perfect.

Missionaries as well as national evangelists were sorely needed. Originally, Mr and Mrs Richardson and Mr and Mrs Blakeney were to have pioneered the work. The former had worked for some years in East Africa, but Mr Richardson had died while travelling with the Bowie party. Now his widow returned from America to South Africa, and, together with another lady, she was sent to help. They gave yeoman service for over a year, chiefly in opening the Kabondo-Dianda station to the south; but repeated fevers eventually caused them to leave. The station was left by Mrs Richardson to Mr Salter, who incorporated it with the Congo Evangelistic Mission (today's Central African Missions).

In March 1918, Burton decided to go to South Africa to recruit more missionaries. He had been in regular correspondence with Miss Hettie Trollip ever since their meeting in 1914 at the Heatleys' home in Johannesburg, and had worked with her relatives, the Saunders, in Basutoland and stayed with her younger sister and family, the Raines, in Bloemfontein. He felt freer in mind to go because another young man, Victor Gatzke, whom Burton had baptised in Pretoria swimming baths in 1914, had joined them to put in some work on the buildings and in the villages, so Mr Salter was not left entirely alone.

On May 23rd 1918 William F. P. Burton and Hettie H. Trollip were married near Craddock in the Cape. It was a simple but most blessed ceremony of supreme dedication to united service for Jesus in Central Africa. Sister Burton became a veritable 'Mother in Israel', so gentle in manner but so strong in character and so utterly dedicated to the Congo work. Brought up at Beaconsfield, a large, typical South African farm on the Karoo, she was extremely practical in all household and farm matters as well as being a schoolteacher. In later years she was to be a tremendous help to young lady missionaries, to whom she taught many things useful in those primitive days, such as the making of soap, starch, cornflower and peanut oil. She worked particularly among the women and girls and ran a rescue centre, and later a training home, most of her missionary life. 'Mrs Burton's girls' are well known and bear the stamp of her spiritual and practical influence, most of them being wives of pastors and other workers.

After their wedding, Burton wrote: 'Your kind gifts have been a real Godsend. On the day of our marriage I only had just enough to pay for the rings and certificate. A camera had served as an engagement ring – it was more useful! Next day a longstanding debt due to me of £2 came which enabled me to bring my wife to Johannesburg, then money came in for our outfit – and so we've gone on.'

They brought back to the Field with them a printer, Mr C. Bakker, as they hoped to set up a printing press. Also Miss Anna Toerein, a fine, experienced and educated worker of good Dutch family, and a lively, energetic lady from America, Miss Anna Rickhow, just out of Bible School. It was planned that others should follow.

With these new workers, the number of missionaries rose to seven. Their spirits rose in proportion, now the work would forge ahead, many needs would be met and much ground covered. They looked into the future with faith and joyous anticipation of a growing, widening and deepening work of God.

And most of all they longed and looked for an outpouring of God's Holy Spirit – A Luban Pentecost.

8
The power of God's Spirit

For a long time, in fact, the missionaries had been looking, waiting, trusting for the power of God's Spirit to fall upon the growing, maturing church. The Word had been taught carefully, prayer meetings had been held regularly, much blessing had been received, but the fullness of the baptism of the Holy Spirit had not been experienced.

Further setbacks in the work had occurred and the missionaries' ranks had been thinned again. Sisters Richardson, Hodges, Meester, Aaronson and Henderson had left, three through long ill health and constant fevers and two because of marriage. Miss Brookes had died on the way out, travelling with Miss Henderson, and had been buried at Kaleka not far from Daddy Armstrong's grave. Victor Gatzke, after over two years of hard work, had returned to South Africa and Mr Bakker had left after a few months because of his inability to learn the language. This was a heavy blow, as a printing press had been promised as soon as our printer could prepare the way. The co-founder, James Salter, had gone to England for a badly needed furlough and to recruit new workers

This thinning of the ranks seemed to be experienced by all pioneer missionary movements, almost always because of rough conditions of living, lack of balanced diet, lack of knowledge of how to adjust to country, climate and people and most of all through fevers and dysentery. In later years the Mission had a magnificent record of long years of service, 20, 30 and 40 years being common and many second generation missionaries following their parents in the same glorious service.

Another problem had worried them for some time, concerning that fine band of men and women who had been such a tremendous help to them, and still were, in preaching the Gospel around Mwanza. Regarding this, Donald Gee, in his book *The Pentecostal Movement*, writes, 'A rather strange hindrance had occurred owing to the new church at Mwanza being joined by a company of freed slaves returning home to Lubaland from Angola. While away these folk had blessedly received the Gospel of Christ, but the denominational prejudices which they had imbibed from their missionaries, were against the truths embodied in the Pentecostal testimony. This was sufficient to set them against it themselves, and to cause them to hinder the others.'

This hindrance, worsened firstly by the fact that these brethren were quite illiterate and so could not discuss things from the Scriptures, and secondly when a few of them tried to stir up the younger converts against the teaching of the baptism of the Holy Spirit and of Divine healing, blessings of which they had never heard, produced bickerings, jealousies and the like. Some of the more intelligent men, however, learnt to read and, having seen what the Word of God said, for their part caused no further difficulties.

There were not only jealousies between the Angolans and the local Baluba Christians, but also between two sections of these returned slaves, for half had come from one denomination and half from another. And not only that, a group of men of the Bekalebwe tribe had returned with Mr and Mrs Burton after their long trip to Bwana Tshofwe, or Kipushya – 15 days' journey north west. These, too, had their sharp differences with the local Baluba as well as with the returned slaves, as their hero who had brought them the Gospel with Willie Burton was Shalumbo, who had also returned from Angola with the first party.

However, the Lord showed that He could work in spite of all hindrances; in fact, these hindrances merely served to throw them more on God. He alone could, and surely would, deal with the backbitings, the squabblings, the discord, the misunderstandings, the dissensions and even the hidden sin which was now rearing its ugly head. There were only three missionaries then on the Field: the Burtons and Miss Toerien. They were convinced that the Holy Spirit would sweep all these things away and bring blessing, unity and joyous service.

It had been the custom to gather together every few months for a time of prayer, study and mutual exhortation; invitations were sent out to the farther outstations to come in and join the local Mwanza believers in a week of special study of the Word and waiting on God early in January. Much prayer was made beforehand. The missionaries felt that the whole future well-being of their testimony would depend on what happened. They had come out to declare 'the whole counsel of God'.

The Word of God burned within their souls. 'Jesus... commanded them that they should not depart from Jerusalem, but wait for the promise of the Father, of which Jesus said, you have already heard Me tell you. For in reality John baptised with water but you shall be baptised with the Holy Spirit not many days from now... But you shall receive power, after the Holy Spirit has come upon you and you shall be My witnesses both in Jerusalem, as well as in all Judea and in Samaria and in the furthest extremities of the earth'. 'Then Peter said unto them, everyone one of you needs to repent and believe the Gospel, and be baptised in the Name of Jesus Christ for the remission of sins, and you shall receive the gift of the Holy Spirit. For the promise is for you, and to your children, and to all that are afar off, even as many as the Lord our God shall call.'

'So with earnest crying to God,' wrote Burton, 'and with hearts brimful of love to all parties, we raised a definite note from the commencement of the convention, upon the supreme necessity of God's children being endued with power from on high... For the first three days of our meetings we ceaselessly hammered upon the one dominant note of submission to God's Word.'

Worship started around six o'clock in the morning and meetings were held till evening, some for the teaching of new hymns, some specially for men, women or children separately, but the main meetings were the Bible studies morning and afternoon.

On the fourth day of the gathering, Thursday, January 8th 1920, there were about 160 or more present. Burton felt led to minister on God's purpose in enduing His people with power from on high. He showed how God did not necessarily select the learned and wise, but that He bore testimony to those who were His witnesses 'with signs and wonders, and with many miracles, and gifts of the Holy Spirit, according to His own will' (Hebrews 2:4).

They then read together Mark 16:17-18. 'And these signs shall follow those who believe: In My name they shall cast out demons; they shall speak with new languages; they shall take up serpents; and if they drink any deadly thing it shall not hurt them; they shall lay hands on the sick, and they shall recover.'

There followed a most solemn and heart-searching time. The Holy Spirit's convicting power rested upon the people and many who had previously resisted the Word of God confessed that these signs did not accompany their testimony. Men and women came crowding out to the front, tears streaming down their cheeks. 'The whole of the front of the chapel was a tightly-wedged mass of earnest men and women with their heads down and their shiny backs heaving with the emotion of their prayer.'

And then it happened. In a matter of minutes the power from on high was falling and rapturous praises were ascending to God, first in their own language of Kiluba and then in tongues which they had never learned, praising and adoring the Lamb who was slain for their sin. This was God's moment. Many under deep conviction and a sense of their own insufficiency groaned in spirit and wrestled their way through to joyous victory and liberty. The noise of this visitation was heard in a village a mile and a half away! The spirit of prayer was so intense upon them that for three hours the whole place was swayed by God's Spirit. They prayed and prayed, glorifying the Name of Jesus.

Then, after a time of quiet before the Lord, confessions began, together with promises of restitution, which were later carried out. Mountains of pride were broken down, valleys of mistrust were filled up, and the crooked places of schisms, suspicions and party spirit were made straight. They laughed and hugged one another, with cries of 'Hallelujah! Isn't this wonderful?' What peace and joy reigned among them!

That wonderful meeting went on till 3 pm. It had started at 10 am! Five hours before the Lord! Distrust had turned to delight, jealousy to joy, resentment to rapture. They couldn't count all who had been baptised in the Holy Spirit in that meeting, but later they reckoned from testimonies given that at least 120 men, women and young people had received the power from on high.

The whole work was transformed. Quarrels were settled, debts paid off and stolen property restored. At the end of the week, no one wanted to go home. Questions were asked and answered, advice was sought and given from God's Word and men volunteered to preach Jesus anywhere – even among the waiting villages of the Kisale swamps with their clouds of mosquitoes. Anywhere with Jesus! Anything for Jesus! Willie Burton asked for youngsters to volunteer to clean out the pool used for baptism, which had silted up with slime. An old man stepped forward. 'I'll do it!' he said. Up till then, he had always tried to impress the rest of the church with his superiority and spirituality, always too dignified for dirty work. But now – any job for Jesus!

Several of the Bekalebwe, too, received the power from on High that day. They were gloriously filled with the Holy Spirit, and were now friends with everybody, Baluba, Angolans and all. A few months later, they joyfully led the Johnstones, new workers from Britain, to their distant home and became the backbone of the evangelistic staff at Kipushya Mission.

As for the two factions of Angolans, the two old men who led them now took sides in the new dispute. One accepted the truth; the other naturally led the opposition. The missionaries' prayer and friendly advice seemed fruitless. Then one night God awoke the one and told him to go and pray for his rival. He went, prayed for his startled enemy and laid hands on him in Jesus' Name to receive the blessing. Bickering now turned to blessing as the Lord filled the other mightily with the Holy Spirit. The noise brought others running to see the fight – but the two old antagonists were hugging each other and praising God in new tongues!

Now, other believers who had been unable to attend the Conference wanted the blessing at any cost. Every village evangelist, every pastor, the day-school teachers, the carpenters and other workmen – all were filled with the Holy Spirit. The meetings swelled in numbers and grew in fervour. Bands of men and women went out to witness in the villages around. Souls were won on every hand. Miracles of healing were recorded. Signs and wonders followed the preaching of the Word in Jesus' Name, according to the promise.

The following week, a party of men set out for the Kikondja chieftainship and the villages around Lake Kisale. The teeming thousands of fisherfolk welcomed the message, given in simplicity and power. An evangelist's house was built and, after much prayer, a fine man of God, tall and impressive, intelligent and now filled with the Holy Spirit, felt led to go. His wife felt the call too, quite separately. The elders and the missionary had the witness that Ngoloma was God's man. And so it turned out to be. John Nelson Parr reading his friend William Burton's letter in Manchester, took Ngoloma and his wife specially upon his heart, took a personal interest in him, and became his prayer-partner until Ngoloma was promoted to glory. Four years later, missionaries built a station there, constructed a boat, and evangelised along the rivers and lakes; today there is a string of 150 assemblies along those waterways.

Here was the secret of expansion. From now on the blessing spread; it was like a forest fire of wind and flame, engulfing the countryside. Prayer and the teaching of the Word brought down the Latter Rain of God's blessing and the land was soon covered with the lush growth of a healthy church. It is still spreading, farther and wider than the missionaries' wildest dreams. Over the years that followed, station after station was opened, chieftainship after chieftainship conquered for Christ. By 1960 there were 65 missionaries on the Field, with many others on furlough and many training in Belgium; there were 14 stations and nearly a thousand churches.

Today (1973) this now completely indigenous movement has few missionaries, but over 2,100 assemblies, many large, and 125,000 believers gathering in God's house to break bread Sunday by Sunday. Primary, Secondary, Bible Training and Nurses' Schools, maternities and dispensaries have all grown and play their important part. In all this we see, on the one hand, the energising power of the Holy Spirit and, on the other, the wise leadership, vision and skill of William Burton.

9

A vision with a task

Samuel Chadwick's definition of a missionary has always intrigued me: 'A vision without a task makes a visionary. A task without a vision makes for drudgery. *A vision with a task* makes a missionary.' If this is true, then W. Burton was an ideal missionary: no hazy visionary, for he had both a vivid picture before him and a mighty task on his heart. The old Hebrew prophets called their visions 'burdens' – a task was involved. The burden lifted when the vision was fulfilled.

A vision is essential, for 'where there is no vision', said Solomon, 'the people perish'. Paul said, 'I was not disobedient to the heavenly vision.' His vision showed him not only the people's need, but how to set about the task to which he was being called. 'I will make you a *minister* and a *witness*,' said the Lord: a workman and a witness, a servant and a preacher. 'And I'll deliver you from the people to whom I now send you,' added the Lord Jesus, making it clear that suffering was involved. Then the programme was outlined before him – to open their eyes, to turn them from darkness to light, and from the power of Satan to God, so that they may receive forgiveness of sins and a place of inheritance among those who are sanctified by faith that is in me.'

What a vision! What a programme! It's all there: the needy people, the power of God, the light of salvation and forgiveness of sins, complete deliverance from all the oppression of Satan, faith, and sanctification. It includes the inheritance of the baptism of the Holy Spirit as typified by entering Canaan, and also by the coming kingdom of our Lord and Saviour Jesus Christ. So much for Acts 26! There is still more supplied in the other accounts in Acts 9 and 22: persecution, water baptism, Jews and Gentiles, prisons and palaces, and further visions yet to come.

William Burton certainly had a vision, and the vision revealed the task. And he went at it with all the strength, intelligence, dedication, spiritual perception and power that God supplied constantly, according to his need. He was to a great degree inspired by the example of Hudson Taylor and the scriptural pattern of the China Inland Mission, though he did not rigidly copy others, realising that every country, every people and every age would require modification of methods in preparing a people and building a church that would please the Lord.

He bought a copy of Roland Allen's: *Missionary Methods: St. Paul's or Ours?* and read it with fascination and approval. It seemed so similar to his own ideas, yet he saw clearly that many things which applied to China and its peoples did not necessarily apply to Central Africa and the Bantu, particularly in Christian Education, as no one in Mwanza knew anything of books, or even of writing and reading. Not only that, but missionary practice was controlled to a large degree by governmental laws. James Salter was completely one with him in his vision, often referring to it in early letters and articles.

First, William Burton's vision was of an *indigenous Church*. This was a revolutionary idea in those days. Missionaries to those who were perceived as primitive peoples, whom the tentacles of European civilisation were scarcely yet reaching, considered that a strong, if benevolent, parental control was essential. They usually imposed a copy of their own particular denomination in doctrine, worship and organisation upon their converts. William Burton and James Salter endeavoured from the start to form a church that was reliant on God and that looked to Him and His Word rather than to the rigid rules of man, and one that would begin to share the burden of responsibility right from the start. Even before they could read or write, the converts were encouraged to witness. However, reading was essential to those who went out into full-time service and eventually to all except those who were too old – and it was pathetic to see even some of the dear old folks, in spite of white hair and failing eyesight, struggle to master the magic signs that revealed the Word of God.

It was a long and uphill task, but well worth the struggle, and whatever success our missionaries have had through the years in developing indigenous principles, it is almost entirely due to the insistence and encouragement of Willie Burton. At first, the aim was not to establish Mission Stations, but to camp in a village and preach till a nucleus of believers could be formed into an assembly, then pass on to another and so on until we had covered the Field.

However, we soon found that we should never get round the thousands of villages, often miles apart, in this way. We had to establish a base from which to work and from which to replenish our stocks. We were obliged to have a centre where we could systematically teach believers to read, write and do simple arithmetic so that they could read the Word of God, enter up their records and reckon up church offerings. We needed a place where we could train national workers, by whom our labours could be multiplied indefinitely, and the country covered with the Gospel as quickly as possible. The key to the indigenous church was the indigenous worker, and such had to be trained. There were also complications of mail and delivery of goods that would greatly hamper a totally itinerant preacher in a land of long distances, remote forests, no motor roads (at that time) and few means of communication.

Secondly, his vision was of a *simple Church*. Many societies had complained that their older stations had developed into small 'towns' and that many of their missionaries were so involved in the central organisation that they knew little of the way of life in the bush areas, and less of the mental processes of the Congolese. From the start, William Burton determined to have small decentralised stations.

Not only simplicity of organisation but simplicity in worship was his aim. The Breaking of Bread, as he conducted it, lacked any suggestion of ritual: he encouraged the people in their assemblies to use a lump of their stiff manioc mush or pudding for the bread. It was just as much their daily bread as a wheaten loaf to the European, or the unleavened cake of the Jews. He also found that the sticky red pods or buds of the 'mwilembwe' plant, a variety of 'rosella', mixed with water, was a practical and easily-obtained substitute for wine. The plant was grown behind most of the people's huts for the sake of the edible leaves. Better still he gave them slips of hedge-mulberry because these cuttings grew very quickly, bore profusely and made a still more acceptable wine. The mulberry was far more suitable than the wild grapes, 'mañanza', which certainly grew in the deeper forest regions, but were rare and difficult to find in any quantity. He felt that the memorial remembrance of Christ's body and blood was more important than the material emblems, and that if he insisted on the use of European bread and imported wine there would never be a Communion service held in the bush assemblies. After all, Jesus commanded his disciples to 'do this in remembrance of Me' and used as emblems what was to hand.

All the meetings Burton held were simplicity itself: no frills, no formulae, no special uniform, no titles other than 'elder' or 'deacon'. Even funerals, dedication of believers' children, water baptisms and weddings were completely informal. He never went a step further than the examples given in the New Testament. But although he reduced formalities to the absolute minimum, it had to be the Scriptural minimum, and nothing less than what the Word declared or the apostles' taught. For instance, I have known him interrupt a brother when he has given thanks for the bread and the wine together, or just mentioned one of the elements. He would quote from the Bible to the effect that both Jesus and Paul emphasised that both elements were meditated upon separately and separate thanks were to be given for each.

Thirdly, his vision was of an *instructed staff*. New workers were invariably allotted to older ones, he and Mrs Burton taking a good share. When younger missionaries from other stations visited Mwanza, he missed no opportunity of instructing them by all sorts of interesting means in missionary life, the country, the people and their customs, the language, what to do and what not to do in dealing with the Congolese themselves, with white traders and with Government officials. Mr Burton was full of fascinating items of information about birds, beasts and butterflies! He was so well informed that the younger missionaries, somewhat overawed, thought he knew everything – and he certainly seemed to. He loved to teach and had such a charming manner that we all, young and old, never tired of his tales, his folklore, his fables and his proverbs.

He certainly helped us to understand the people of the country and their fascinating language and background. He saved us from many pitfalls and rid us of wrong ideas about the land in which we had come to work.

He was particularly helpful in regard to the language. By 1923 he had prepared very detailed notes in duplicated form of its structure and vocabulary, and by 1928 a rule was applied in the Mission which continued until the big evacuation during the war of independence in 1960-61. This rule said:

1. That no new worker shall use English in any contact with the Congolese or preach through an interpreter after the first welcome meeting, where such was held. (There was no such fuss made at Mwanza itself!)

2. That every new missionary must study the language and pass successfully two written examinations, one after six months and the other after twelve months.

3. That every missionary must make an attempt to preach in public in the local language no later than six months after arriving on the Field. Failing this he or she would be sent home.

All this put people on their metal. They realised the necessity of speaking the language of the country and the seriousness of their calling. 'No man worth his salt will waste God's money by fooling around,'

Willie Burton would say, 'and remember that the saints of God have sacrificed to send you out. Be your best for Jesus!' Down went noses to the grindstone! Out came paper and pencils to jot down every new word and phrase! Every opportunity was seized to try to talk with the Bantu and understand them. Some managed to splutter out a testimony or a sermonette in three months, others just scraped in with something more polished within the six months, but not one missionary failed the stiff examination, though it may have been pretty close!

Though dealing with this matter so firmly, he could be delightfully humorous. 'I know this language is difficult,' he said to us one day, 'because Mr X (an Englishman we knew, the caterer on the biggest of the river boats) said to me' – and here he imitated the man's rich cockney speech- '"Lengwidgis?" he said, "Lengwidgis? Why, I kin speak sebn lengwidgis, I kin speak this 'ere Swahili like a blinkin' naitive, but es for this bally Baluba lingo, I jes' cawn' t stamick it!"'

It was necessary to practise even the tones of the language, as so often a high or low tone of one single vowel, or a long vowel, instead of a short one, can change the meaning of a word. Some never could quite get the difference between 'mani' which means 'oil', and 'mani' which means 'leaves', and confusion often resulted. Another poser was 'bangi' = 'different' and 'bangi' = 'many'. Yet another puzzle was 'makonde' = 'fishing nets' and 'makonde' = 'bananas'. About a hundred or so of these pairs of words exist, differing merely in a tone.

Burton told us of the surprising richness of the language. In 1915 he had collected 1,500 words which had been increased to 15,000 by 1920, all of which were in regular use. This latter figure, he said, was double the usual vocabulary of many Bantu tribes and compares more than favourably with the average Englishman's vocabulary. His collections of fables and of 1,800 proverbs are unrivalled and were published by the Judicial Revue of Katanga (*La Revue Juridique du Katanga*) as was his: *L'Ame Luba* (The Luban Mind), a treatise used today as a textbook in universities.

The vision being so clear and the task so heavy, it was necessary to plan carefully and prayerfully, looking to the Holy Spirit to guide every step. This Willie Burton proceeded to do – a glance at the mission map will show the pattern.

It will be remembered that an area 600 miles by 350 miles now lay before our two pioneers. There were three main stages of development in evangelising this enormous area.

First, having established the work at Mwanza, where God had most miraculously directed them, they occupied a strategic place 150 miles south of them (10 days' trek), and soon afterwards another one 240 miles north west (15 days' trek). Thus lifelines were flung out to two big chieftainships, Kabondo-Dianda and Kipushya.

The second stage was to open up places in between, mainly along those lifelines; they were the most populous and strategic areas. From Mwanza, they moved to the well-peopled valley of Ngoimani, then on to Kisanga where a large district was being organised into the new and powerful chieftainship of Ilunga Mwila; then, continuing in a direct line to the north west and more than halfway to Kipushya, a station was opened at Kasongwa-Mule which was the centre of a group of big chieftainships.

Meanwhile the area around Kipushya was opened up and the chieftainships of the Bekalebwe opened to the Gospel. It was found wise to open an entirely new station among the Basongye peoples around Katenta, so that other related sub-tribes could receive the Gospel.

Southwards, Bunda and Nkulu chieftainships had received the Word of Life. Then Kikondja with its dense lakeside population, along the road to Kabondo-Dianda, had a station built at the invitation of Chief Kikondja, the greatest Chief the missionaries had so far seen. Beyond Kabondo-Dianda, to the north west of it, Busangu station was opened, covering much of the ancient territory of Kasongwa-Nyembo.

Gradually at times, and with revival speed at others, the 'filling-in' process continued. The biggest step was perhaps the taking over of the American Methodist Station at Kabongo, the centre of the 400 to 500 year old Luban (Baluba) Empire. The previous year, two other important centres were opened and stations built: at Katompe (Katombe) among the Bene Mpai, and at Mutengu, which joined up with Kipushya and Kabongo in spreading the Word among sub-tribes in-between. Later, the Kasongwa-Mule station, after a period with no missionaries, was reopened as a new station at Kashiukulu.

To the extreme south east, the testimony spread till a new station could be opened at Kisamba in the Bupemba swamps and lakes beyond the Congo (Lualaba) River. This was later moved to Luena on the railway south of Bukama. On the Kikondja side of the river, the work had spread southwards to Bukama and beyond and, finally completing the southern arc, to the new town of Kamina on the railway between Kabondo-Dianda and the north east. Kamina was really the reopening of the old Busangu and Nsungu stations. From there, in later years, the work spread still farther up the line north-west to Mutombo Mukulu (Kanyama).

Meanwhile, further strides had been taken in the extreme north. Katenta station had been moved to the more convenient new motor road at Katea, and Kongolo, a very large town on the railway, motor road and river, was opened as a mission station. For some years a small station had been operated at Nseke, and this work was now incorporated in the new district.

Following the improved administrative system after the war of 1939-45 motor roads were built, and the growing of commercial crops of cotton and peanuts was introduced; most of the stations were in line with these routes, and eventually all of the then thirteen main stations of the CEM were linked up with this road system. It was wonderful to be able to travel, for instance, from Luena in the south to Kabondo-Dianda, then to branch northwards to Kikondja, Mwanza, Ngoimani and Kisanga, right on to Kashiukulu and out into the main northern road. This latter continued from Kabondo-Dianda to Kamina (for many years the main shopping centre as well as the site of the District Administrative Offices and the central office of the CEM). From there one could travel either north west to Kanyama and the Kasai, or directly north to Kabongo. Just after this the first-mentioned road joined, and it was possible to go straight forward to Katompe, Katea and Kongolo, or one could branch off beyond Kabongo and take another road to Lulungu, to which place the Mutengu work had been transferred.

All these are a somewhat bewildering mass of names, perhaps, to those not familiar with Congo, but to those of us who have walked those trails for weeks on end, cycled on forest paths, canoed its waterways or waded deep through its stinking swamps, it comes as a thrilling realisation of that vision, seen so long ago. As we poked our white faces – sometimes the first ever seen – between the trees to behold some savage tribal dance, to hear the hopeless heathen cries of death, to see the silent poisoned arrow fly 'thupp!' into the body of man or beast, never did we dream that motor horns would bleep or railway trains clank and roar through those lonely forest glades, though we did envisage points of light shining in every village, assemblies of God's people witnessing to those still in darkness.

The third stage was one which most of us had not even envisaged, but to which we were carried by the momentum of Willie Burton and James Salter. There had always been a clear understanding between the evangelical missions concerning areas and boundaries: the Gospel must 'be preached in all the world for a witness... and then shall the end (of the age) come (Matt. 24:14). The only way to establish a Christian witness in every part of the country to which God had called us was for each society to have its own recognised region, thus avoiding overcrowding in some centres and the neglect of vast inland areas. Every society had plenty of work without encroaching on another; but there was one exception, where there had been an inrush of people from the bush to mines or capital centres and the local missionaries simply could not cope.

Thus the tin mines of Manono, the vast copper regions of Lubumbashi (formerly Elisabethville), Likasi and Kolwezi and the commercial diamond mines of the Kasai received an enormous influx of CEM believers who formed their own assemblies. No missionary opened these or lived permanently among them; it was purely a movement of Congolese believers. They went quietly ahead with their normal witness to the unsaved and praying with the sick, and have over the years built many places of worship. In these assemblies, the believers are mostly Baluba and Bekalebwe people, the rest being converts won from round about and from other tribal people working on the mines. They use their own Kiluba language in the meetings, though Swahili and French are also to be found.

Since the Church founded by the CEM has been completely independent, the work has doubled; to think that early newsletters of Burton and Salter reported 'Our evangelists are now *six* in number' (July 1918), and in 1972 there are over 2,100 assemblies and 2,500 workers, and numbers are still growing. If Willie Burton could see the picture today – and maybe the Lord will let him do so – he would see that the vision was real and the accomplishment of the task far greater than he could have imagined.

But often it was accomplished in the face of terrible setbacks. After the First World War there was the fearful Spanish flu which swept people away in thousands. There was for many years the heavy drain of recruiting men and their families for the mines. The assemblies shrunk sadly, but foundations were laid for future mining-area churches. Several unusually heavy rainy seasons in the days of footslogging made the country one vast swamp and hindered the spread of the Gospel. Fevers and dysentery struck time and time again. Seven missionaries died of blackwater fever, one of malaria with pneumonia, others of paralytic seizure and of other conditions of climate and overwork – 14 altogether. Seven little graves mark the sacrifice that parents have made, far from help and civilisation.

Often church buildings have been struck by lightning and totally destroyed, and at least four times missionaries' dwelling houses, scarcely finished, have become a blackened ruin in a matter of minutes. During the rebellions of 1960 to 1963 missionaries' houses, schools and even churches have been destroyed by every type of rebel – and there were many – and their goods looted. The first two missionary martyrs of that period were Edmund Hodgson and Elton Knauf, murdered on November 23rd 1960. Numbers of Congolese preachers and believers were killed for Jesus' sake.

In the early years the Roman Catholics persecuted us with vigour, provoking fights between Catholic and Protestant believers, trumping up false charges against evangelists and pastors, ridiculing the work by stirring their people to sing ditties composed by priests against Protestantism, and trying to prevent lands being granted for new mission stations. Years of prayer and faith brought about a miracle of change, so that today that type of persecution is no more.

During those turbulent years the enemy of souls almost got the CEM turned out of the country. Complaints were made about the outpourings of the Holy Spirit at two of our stations and a certain government official wove a plot from this to get rid of the foreign Protestants.

At our Field Executive meeting in January 1929 William Burton read out an urgent letter from the Governor of Katanga Province summoning him to Elisabethville (Lubumbashi) at once. The British Consul also requested his presence. The meeting decided that he should leave as soon as possible and that I should accompany him. I had been soaked to the skin twice by heavy rain on the 130 mile cycle ride through the forests and over the rivers from Busangu, and had slept twice in local huts, so didn't look forward to a 400 mile journey by cycle, boat and train without a decent suit for the interview. We sent a man on foot to tell my wife I should be away for an extra two weeks. It would take him a week to get there.

The day after we arrived, Burton applied for the interview. The Governor's secretary let us see that we were in for serious trouble and arranged the meeting for the following morning. We then saw the Consul who gave us to understand that we were as good as out of the country. We discussed with him the possibility of moving to Tanganyika Territory (Tanzania), and wrote a letter to Dar-es-Salaam to ask if there was room for a Mission our size. We then went back to the hotel room and gave ourselves to prayer. In the evening we called on Judge Guebels, well-known poet and author and friend of William Burton. The Judge, being a Roman Catholic and knowing that there was trouble brewing, was cool and formal in the extreme. It was clear there would be no help from that quarter. Back to more prayer. Vain was the help of man; we were thrown back on God. As we prayed our faith rose. God had called us. He would help.

The next morning, making ourselves as presentable as possible, we were early at the Governor's palace. The great man sent his attaché to deal with us. This huge, rather frightening, military-looking man held a sheaf of papers in his hand and looked gravely at us. After assuring himself of our identity he handed Willie Burton the papers. There were several foolscap pages of charges against us, mostly false, and some minor technicalities. For example, we had allowed the grass on one station to grow more than 20 centimetres high (8 inches), thus encouraging mosquitoes! (Through the window we could see grass five feet high!) Others were more serious, but nothing criminal. A mass of all sorts of possible unproved charges were brought on the assumption that there would be sufficient to bring us under suspicion of being an undesirable element.

William Burton thought I turned white. I thought he did. He bowed to thank the stiff official and prepared to leave to think things over. As he raised his head the official stared at him and suddenly gasped, 'Who did you say you were? Burton? Burton? Not... not... surely not the one who buried his friend under the palm tree out there on the bank of the Congo in 1915?' 'Yes,' said William Burton, 'I am that man.' The attaché's whole manner changed. 'You remember that young naval officer to whom you spoke about his soul, and gave him a New Testament?' 'Yes.' 'I was that young officer – and I accepted Christ, and now read my Testament every day. Now, let's have another look at those papers!'

We never saw them again. We went home happy. The Lord had done it! No charges were brought against us, and it all resulted from a faithful word of witness and a faithful God.

10
Down to earth

An assortment of red, brown and white slabs of wood, 15 by 9 centimetres and 1 centimetre thick with a hole neatly drilled through each one, hung on a cord behind the office door.

William Burton was busy writing at his desk, books and papers heaped up all around him.

'What are these bits of wood for?' I asked, eyeing them carefully as I closed the door. 'Oh, they're samples for the CSK' (Le Comité Spécial du Katanga), he replied, scarcely looking up. 'I'm just writing to them,' he added, 'before we go in to breakfast.'

It was 7 a.m. I hadn't been up very long, tired out after yesterday's gruelling cycle ride through the bush. He had already been up some time, had had his usual couple of hours of prayer and reading the Word, and was now clearing his correspondence before starting the main work of the day. He turned to his typewriter, a somewhat battered old office model which he had acquired during his previous furlough, and clattered and banged out his letter to the CSK.

Ever since he and James Salter had settled at Mwanza he had been intrigued by the many kinds of timber in the Congo forests. So different from the 'Mopani' forests of Southern Africa, where one sees miles and miles of the same kind of tree or the endless monotony of wearisome thorn-scrub, here was a surprising variety of trees of all kinds, breathtaking in their beauty, with every shade of green to red reflecting from their leaves in the sunlight, and every kind of bark from the smooth grey skin of the great wild fig to the dark rugged ridges of the 'blood walnut'. There was everything – from the tall and stately 'muvula', often nicknamed 'African Oak' because of its similar grain, rising 50 to 100 feet before beginning to throw out its mighty arms, to the useful little 'muswaswa', meaning 'the tree that everyone likes'; from the truly magnificent 'mpafu' or wild olive with its mighty trunk and myriads of edible fruit, to the common 'kilubanshimbi', showing off with its huge scarlet tulip-like flowers splashing colour over the green of the forest.

He had soon found that the Baluba had a name for every tree and plant. Though they had little interest in flowers and blossoms, so fascinating to the white strangers, they knew the use, if any, of every tree and forest creeper. They knew that the 'kipapa' (mahogany) made the longest-lasting canoes, so they made them for the fisher-folk, and the 'mutondo-mashi' (type of walnut) was the best for making signal-drums. They knew that the 'mulalapulumba' was strong, straight and resistant to borers so was fine for beams, and that the 'mushelele' was good for hoe and axe handles. The women knew all the trees that were good for firewood, those which smoked too much, or left too much ash, and others which burned bright and warm, even on a windy night – and so on.

The 'CSK' was similar to the old British Chartered Companies of India and Africa. They leased from the Government all the rights of 'above, below and on the ground', so they had the monopoly of game rights, land tenure, forestry and mining rights. Permission now had to be obtained from them for our Mission land concessions, building permits, shooting licences and even the right to cut down timber for planks, buildings and furniture – and in some places – Kongolo for example – where wood was scarce, even the right to chop firewood.

Word soon spread that this missionary Burton had an encyclopaedic knowledge of trees, plants, rivers, hills and the Congo countryside in general. They tapped his knowledge and he generously supplied information that saved the CSK much time and money. He took a lot of trouble in making those beautiful wood samples, and before posting them he addressed labels with all relevant information – Luba name, other name where known, hard, medium or soft wood. He indicated whether or not it was subject to destruction by termites, boring beetles or damp and pointed out the location and type of country where it was grown and its possible uses etc.

All this information duly appeared in the subsequent CSK timber catalogue, and he had their thanks – but nothing else. William Burton always considered it part of the job to help everyone in any way they needed. It was not a waste of time, for his vast and practical knowledge helped other missionaries starting new stations and saved them from spending time on making experiments that he had already done so thoroughly. He was well placed for such experiments, for the Mwanza forests are a veritable paradise of good timber; on the other hand, no-one else would have been so thorough and complete in his experiments as he! They wouldn't have had enough time. Neither had he, but he did it.

Maps, too. We have already seen our practical Burton rushing forth, trekking from end to end of the work, preaching, answering calls, attending to Mission matters, measuring lands for new stations. Wherever he went he took with him a prismatic compass, aneroid barometer and the simplest mapping materials necessary. In every new area, villages were plotted and mapped, streams, hills and the direction of paths added in. Little by little, over the years, a sufficiently accurate map of the whole Field was built up only to draw the envious attention of government officials and territorial administrators, most of whom had not much training in survey work, and whose compasses were not of the prismatic kind.

Some such were actually jealous. When Edmund Hodgson and I were engaged in similar work, a Belgian recruiter of the 'Bourse de travail du Katanga' (Katanga Labour Exchange), known locally as 'Bwana Nyoka' or 'Snake Boss', threatened to have us and our leader William Burton charged as British spies.

'For what purpose,' he enquired, 'do you live among the people, learn their language, map every village, hill and stream? Missionary work? Bah! You're nothing more than the paid spies of the British Government!'

Others were sympathetic and friendly and, of course, borrowed the maps to copy! The 'high-ups' heard, and once more William Burton's hard and skilful work was incorporated in their own – not that he was the one to receive the kudos! However our missionaries found the maps invaluable, and lovers of the work and prayer-partners bought them for a shilling each and saw with their own eyes the marvellous development of the work in answer to their prayers.

You will remember that, when he was a child, his mother arranged for her boys to learn carpentry and the use of tools.

'You may be living in the far off wilds some day and have to make your own furniture,' she had often said to Willie.

He was now glad of the experience. His early efforts were not always eminently successful. There was an enormous, heavy old ironing table at Mwanza and Willie Burton laughingly told us how it had originally been a bed! It looked massive enough to have accommodated Henry VIII and all his six wives at once!

'It was so high and hard that it hurt my elbows when I prayed by my bedside so I turned it into a table and tried again!' he explained.

The later pieces of furniture he made are still there at Mwanza as I write, as solid and beautiful as ever. He always tended to make things on the massive side and all were of solid mahogany! Mahogany was so common there that it was used on the river steamers for firewood.

Not everything was clumsy or heavy however, for when baby David was expected, the father-to-be made the most exquisite cot, with fine, slender slats and tall, chamfered uprights to take the mosquito net. There was a sliding side, neat and smooth-working, so that mother could slip the little one under the net quickly and safely out of danger from the anopheline or malaria-bearing mosquito then so common.

Alas, it was not to be. That precious, perfect little baby suddenly and unexpectedly died, apparently bitten by some creature of the tropics: a centipede it was thought. No creature was found, but a tiny puncture was there on the baby's body. Eight years later my own son David occupied that cot for some time, while my wife and Mrs Burton wept together and prayed.

William Burton was practical in every way. He was by training an engineer and, when he built a house, school or church, engineering principles were carefully followed. Every building he has put up looks as though it will be there till the millennium. The church which stands on the end of the Mission Hill, just by the rock where he and James Salter prayed for the people each evening at the very beginning, is very plain outside, but inside, the tall pillars, made of very large, rough burnt brick, looking more like stone, together with the extremely neat roof structure, are a picture of precision.

Canework furniture is lighter to move about and cooler in the tropics than the wooden kind. While staying with Mr and Mrs William Finch in Lancashire in 1914, Mr Burton was struck by a cottage industry and small assembling factory at nearby Mawdesley. People would prepare withies and peeling-cane in their houses, then assemble chairs and tables, weaving them round with split cane, as well as making trays and baskets. 'Just the thing for Congo!' he thought.

Back on the Field, he enquired where the 'nkodi' cane could be found which the men used for their bow strings and women to strengthen the rims of their baskets. To his surprise he was directed to seemingly endless quantities of great lengths of half-inch thick supple cane along and under the water in local streams, ideal to split, peel, scrape and roll ready for weaving. He found that the 'mushelele' tree that the men used for hoe handles was plentiful and made suitable chair legs, which could be wrapped around neatly with strips of black and white cane. The black was produced by steeping the cane for two or three days in a special kind of sticky mud. Burton arduously compiled lists of dyes and inks made from mud, roots and berries, as well as many kinds of poisons in regular use, African medicines from roots and barks, remarkable if not always helpful, edible fruits, and varieties of trees and hedge plants with their various uses.

In time an industry developed on Kayembe Hill which provided spare-time work for scholars, Bible School students and girls in the rescue home as well as full-time work for the jobless. The increasing white population of officials, traders, mineworkers and others, created a market even in distant towns. Everybody wanted the strong, handsome cane furniture from the Mission. The Governor kindly accepted, and admired, a pair of beautiful chairs of the Burton design. It was at a time when funds were low and expansion great; all profits went into the work. Other missionaries were helped and encouraged to do the same on their stations, and some did, particularly Kabondo Dianda. Other stations concentrated on good wooden furniture, notably Ngoimani, Kisanga and Kashiukulu. Eventually the cane furniture industry was turned over completely to the Congolese as their own 'cottage industry' which continued to flourish in the Mwanza area for years.

A casual examination of a rush-bottomed chair gave Burton another idea: rush mats and carpets as well as chair bottoms. The only suitable rush he could discover was the Bible 'bulrush' or papyrus. This, he found, could be cut, peeled, dried in the sun, twisted then plaited into flat strips and sewn up with home-made sisal string. Young lads jumped at the chance of making string and Mrs Burton's girls sewed the mats and carpets. Again other stations were encouraged to try this new venture. Different places had usable quantities of one thing or another, timber, cane or papyrus. Katompe and Kabongo stations found papyrus suitable and developed their own designs and styles, using raffia string instead of sisal. Kabongo in fact made it a major industry, sending carpets up to four metres square to towns hundreds of miles away, the income paying for several new school buildings. They added brush and basket-making.

While in South Africa, particularly at his wife's home, he picked up useful information about the breeding of animals and in 1918 obtained a very good billy goat to improve the strain of the undersized goats of the Baluba. Consequently the Mission herd improved tremendously, and many of the local herds too. Those of us who later opened up new stations received help and instruction in goat breeding; it surprised the black folks to see that the whites wanted goats for milk as much as for meat. 'Fancy feeding a human baby on animal milk!' they said. But when such goat's milk saved the lives of many of their orphans they understood, and even began to clamour for it. The same thing applied to fowls; many of his improved strains spread to other stations and the village evangelists and many others were greatly helped.

Then, of course, there were the vegetable seeds and tropical fruit trees of many varieties. Many a time, missionary visitors to Mwanza would leave for home with a few young guava, orange, lemon or other trees and hedge-cuttings in their luggage; every station got the 'Mwanza touch'.

At the same time he kept abreast of modern knowledge and discoveries. He was quite thrilled on one occasion to read of the discovery of the 'carbon test' used in the estimation of the age of trees and timber. He had been anxious to discover at what period of history a certain Congolese ruler had lived; this he did by taking out a boring from what had once been the chief's fence-poles, but were now giant trees, and counting the annular rings. Only the year before his death, experts confessed that he astonished them by his knowledge.

Two things stand out concerning this practical side to his nature. One was his anxiety to pass on all he discovered to others, black or white. The other was his willingness to learn from others. It sometimes seemed that his knowledge was so wide that there couldn't be much that he could glean from others; yet he was learning every day. He was extremely observant and, wherever he moved, knowledge and information would stick to him like pollen to a bee. And, like the bee, he was equally willing to deposit it with others to benefit them.

Yet all this was quite incidental to his main task. He still travelled, preached, taught the Word and won souls in a degree as great, if not greater, than any other man.

11
Artist and poet

'What is that in your hand?'

Willie Burton's mother had gathered her five children around her by the fireside to tell them tales from the Old Book, as she did every evening, and to teach them special verses of Scripture; usually there was a selected one for each child.

That evening, the story was of 'God's personal Talk with Moses' in Exodus 4, and young Willie's special bit was verse two 'And the Lord said to him, 'What is that in your hand?' And he said, 'A rod.'' The children were enthralled by their mother's vivid description of the great and mighty God taking a personal interest in Moses. He had a special job for him to do, using what Moses already had in his hand; his shepherd's rod, used every day with his sheep, could be used with God's power to lead Israel.

Turning to Willie she said, 'What is that in your hand?' He looked down – he was always scribbling and drawing on every bit of paper he could lay his hands on. He looked up again – 'A pencil, Mummy'. 'Willie, use that for God. He has put it there. Use it in His service.'

He often told us of this. He never forgot the lesson and, after he was converted, he dedicated this remarkable talent wholly to God. His mother taught him all she could; she was no mean artist herself and had studied under Thomas Linnell. Young Willie became exceedingly adept with both pencil and brush, his delicate flowers and finely drawn trees being specially remarkable. He was always a rapid worker, though amazingly painstaking. It would take him but half an hour to draw an exquisite sketch with Indian ink, with extremely fine lining, delicate palm fronds – almost waving, it seemed – rippling water, birds poised for flight, grasses and sedges along the bank and a canoe nosing its way through the reeds guided by a Congolese, paddle in hand.

Scores of people all over the world have shown me their autograph albums, proudly turning to Willie Burton's page: a picture in black and white or colour, well worth framing. He was thorough, quick, skilful, and always the best he could be for God and man. Hundreds of homes where Willie Burton has enjoyed loving hospitality have on their walls beautiful Congo scenes, usually a river scene, always containing palm trees and thatched huts, always with life in them: children swimming, a hunter with bow and arrow, a woman with a waterpot on her head, river birds diving for fish, antelope feeding on a grassy plain. He was prodigious in his output and generous to a fault in giving. 'Freely you have received, freely give,' was his motto. He always liked to give that little bit extra, believing that 'the fat of the offering is the Lord's'.

As in everything he undertook, he poured all his energy and intelligence into it. The best for God! And it was only for God that he did it. Countless people have said, 'Every morning when I come downstairs and look at that picture I lift up my heart and utter a sincere prayer for Brother Burton and the CEM.' He made no personal profit; he not only gave much of his work away, but he also sold as much as he could, but only that he might give more. People who did not know that it was a ministry to help others have often criticised him for painting so much. They did not realise that he worked at least as many hours per day as any other worker and usually did his painting in the quiet of the early morning before others were astir, or immediately after lunch when most folk were taking their siesta during the hottest hour of the day.

Once, after an unusually heavy dose of criticism from well-meaning friends, he confided that he had decided to paint no more and had just thrown his box of paints and brushes away. If this were God's will, then He would give him grace to deny himself the joy of putting God's handiwork on paper. Knowing something of how the Lord had led him to this unique service, and the great help it had so often been to the Mission and to individuals, it seemed strange that it should be God's will to give it all up. We had a long talk and prayed about the matter.

By the next mail a parcel arrived from a dear friend in Lancashire who had much appreciated his work. The accompanying letter said how much the Lord had blessed him through this ministry and trusted that others would be similarly blessed, and would he accept the enclosed gift to help him to carry on the good work? With trembling hands Burton opened the rather heavy packet to find a wonderful box of paints, far better than the ones he had thrown away! With tears in his eyes he acknowledged that the Lord had not taken away what was 'in his hand' but wanted him still to use it in His service.

William Burton assiduously tried out every possible form of expression of that type of art, usually with great success. Some of his finest work was in pen and Indian ink. He tried linocuts, which were excellent for some subjects, then copperplate and even dry-point. Most of his paintings were done in watercolours, some in gouache and much in oils; with these he could have made a fortune. Monsieur Pierre Ryckmans, when Governor General of the then Belgian Congo, accepted with grateful pleasure a beautiful night scene of a Congo River ferry, the log fire glowing within the ferryman's hut door, and the canoe gliding across in the moonlight for the benighted old couple on the other bank. William Burton became widely known as one of the very best artists in the Congo, his pictures being so true to life in the tropics. He gave a set of pictures to the Congo Protestant Council for use on greetings cards.

The South African Academy in Johannesburg accepted four pictures in 1938, and the Orange Free State Society of Arts and Crafts sent him a very warm letter of appreciation for a number of pictures exhibited there, remarking on their high quality and indicating that they had sold a number of them to admirers.

Twice he decided to take extra courses to improve certain aspects of his art that he felt were not quite up to his high standard. In reply to the submission of one lesson, the 'John Hassall Art Schools' commented on 'the remarkably high standard' of the work; the book illustrations were of 'a very high standard indeed' and the lettering 'above the standard of the lesson'; one drawing was 'remarkably clever' and 'could be used in every way successfully and professionally'.

When travelling he would often stop the car, jump out and pull out his tiny paintbox, do a lightning sketch, jot down a few remarks on the scene and get back in the car panting 'I just caught that sunset before the light changed', or 'that morning glow edging the forest in pink', as the case might be. From his tiny art pad, with its 'shorthand pictures', as he called them, he would later build up most exquisite impressions in delightful colour – his photographic memory and vivid imagination supplying the rest of the material.

Fred Ramsbottom tells of one particular journey: the sun was pitiless, the car broke down, the parts had to be tied up with wire. With great difficulty, much sweat and loud clatter the old vehicle was urged on to reach the Lomami ferry before sundown. Suddenly Burton cried 'Stop!' Out he jumped, climbed the bank and out came the tiny paint box.

'But we'll never get across before dark!' called Fred.

'Come up here, just look at the blue, the purple, the gold in this setting sun!' came back the reply.

An exasperated Fred could see no colour but red! A few days later

– 'A little surprise for you, Fred.' There on the table was a breath-taking picture of that sunset with all the blue, purple and gold that in his anxiety he had failed to see. Burton added, 'You were so worried you couldn't see the beauty the Lord had put there to encourage you!' Fred says he gulped a 'Thank you' and 'Praise God', and learned the lesson.

Lying on the desk before me as I write is William Burton's sample book. Somewhat tattered, its pages carry a fascinating selection of many of his favourite subjects. Hundreds of people have turned its pages: friends invited to choose something for a present, prospective customers leafing through for a subject they would like to buy, enthralled by the variety, finding it difficult to select. Eventually one would be chosen and, from the rough sample, an individual work of art would emerge.

Among his paintings there is the village under the shady oil-palms, the calm river scene, the gorgeous purple hills of Kisanga, the roan antelope on the Lulungu plains, the borassus fan-palms near Kongolo, the fishing islands of the Lualaba, the moonlight shining over the water, the striking Soswe Peak, the lovely Ngoimani village, animals drinking at sunrise, the eerie forest, the Lomami Ferry going to Kipushya, and the tower-like anthills of the south.

Burton kept a large envelope of rough pencil drawings for further reference – jotted down in all circumstances on all kinds of scrap paper, quickly sketched in odd moments, just as things happened. Black boys fishing with rod and line, an old man telling tales in the firelight, a solemn line of elephants marching through the forest, dogs dozing by the dying embers of a village fire – one alert, head raised, all living, moving. Or again, a flight of pelicans on the marshes and the golden-crested cranes by the river, vultures gathered to swoop, crocodiles, buck, buffalo, tortoises, mothers feeding babies or pounding flour with pestle and mortar, fowls chased and squawking, goats feeding, a chief with exotic head-dress, a man carrying a heavy load of building poles. They're all there. Preliminary studies in hand for the illustration of an article or book, a blind old man, a baby being washed – endless in variety, moments captured for ever.

Always fascinated by the bird life of forest and swamp, William Burton began to make models carved from soft white wood and painted in natural vivid colours. At first they were for ornaments, colourful presents for Christmas. Then he found that Baluba youngsters could imitate them and showed considerable originality so he encouraged them. Today the brightest of them, a Mwanza Christian, shows his own private exhibition of original art in towns and centres all over Congo.

All for God. Assemblies, churches, Mission homes, individual Congolese and missionaries have been helped, often privately, always in the hour of greatest need, just by a few spots of paint put in the right places by the skilful, dedicated, generous hand of Willie Burton, utterly sanctified to the Master's use. But painting expressed only some things; preaching expressed others, and prose others again. But when all of these failed to voice the dramatic upsurge of his soul, William Burton found yet another outlet in poetry.

During his first furlough in England in 1921 his words set to the music of 'Swanee River' seized the imagination of young people throughout the assemblies and was sung in missionary meetings everywhere.

The following unfinished poem was found among his papers. The last line, added in pencil, is probably the beginning of the last stanza. William Burton's thoughts, right until the last, were centred in the cross:

Crucify! Crucify! Let the Galilean die!
　Priests and mob the sentence give.
　'Tis not fit that He should live!
Nail His hands, to the tree.
　Made a curse for you and me.
　God has laid our sins on Christ.
　See the Lamb is sacrificed!

Burdened down. Burdened down.
　Rugged cross and thorny crown –
　Till a sturdy black man came,
　helped Him drag the cross of shame.
All alone. All alone! Christ the great Creator dies!
　Friends, disciples stand afar.
　Jibes and insults drown His cries.

Dripping red! Dripping red!
　From His feet, His hands, His head!
　Gaping wide. Gaping wide.
　Livid spear thrust in His side.
Bitter cry! Bitter cry! Why must I forsaken die?
　Earthquakes shake the hills and rocks.
　Darkness overcasts the sky.

This God's boundless love to us. This God's estimate of sin...

William Burton's nephew, Owen Saunders, produced the follow-ing poem, apparently written not long before his uncle's death, which was read at the funeral in Johannesburg. Many were moved by this cry from the heart of one who remained a missionary to the very end.

The yearning cry of a pensioned-off missionary

I long to tramp those little, twisty footpaths once again
        Shut in by tangled walls of grass and mighty forest trees,
Blistered and scorched by tropic sun or soaked by tropic rain
        The pain of weary limbs and aching body would be sweet.

I long to see the dainty spoor of tiny antelope
        Or mighty tread of herds of buffalo and elephant,
But more than this I yearn to wander through your leafy glades
        Accompanied by crowds of laughing, bumbling boys and girls.

Oh, shall I ever stand again mid throngs of eager folk
        All listening as we tell how Jesus died to bear our sin,
Then rose alive to vanquish Satan and to set men free.
        The joy when they raise hands to show us that they trust in Him!

No earthly thrill like that when stepping forward with a shout
        They cast their idols, charms and fetishes into the flames.
We stand around and wave our Bibles in triumphant song
        'All hail the pow'r of Jesus' name, and crown Him Lord of all.'

The moon rides high among the stars. Folk slip away to sleep.
        And as we tuck ourselves beneath mosquito nets at night
We praise God who has given us th'inestimable joy
        To preach His Word and see the dark folk reconciled to Him!

12

Author and raconteur

Willie Burton had always had a gift for telling stories, especially to children. Their eyes would grow rounder and rounder as he told his version of the folk tales of Central Africa that he had heard so often round the camp fires in the villages of the Baluba.

After the day's trek, and the last big Gospel meeting at night, the carriers and many local folk would draw closer to the roaring log fire, push up the remaining logs till they crackled and blazed, and tell their stories.

To encourage the Congolese to give their very best, Willie Burton would put a franc piece on the arm of his folding chair and promise it to the teller of the story judged the best. Young chaps would volunteer eagerly, hoping to win the prize; old men would quietly wait, pretending not to be interested in money, but casting a sly glance now and then to see that the franc piece was still there. Then, out the stories would come: perhaps the one of how the hare made the leopard stir the porridge with his tail, or how big brother hyena carried the story-teller into the village on his shoulders, just like a chief!

Even the other missionaries liked to hear these tales and sometimes, during Conference, after a long and tiring day someone would ask, 'Have you heard a new story lately, Brother Burton?' The younger ones would be openly hilarious as they heard about the reed buck who made his horns grow forwards instead of backwards, just to be different, and even the older, staider ones had difficulty in suppressing a chuckle at the tale of the young water buck who had no ears.

Willie Burton told us how Aesop's fables were nothing more than the animal tales Aesop had heard at home in Africa, before being carried away to Greece as a slave, adapted to the Greek language and to the animals known there. In the same way, 'Uncle Remus' carried them with him in his slave-ship and adapted them to American life.

It is difficult to list all the books, booklets and pamphlets Mr Burton has written. How he could find the time to turn out such a prodigious amount is a mystery. He wrote many of his books about the Congo work during very busy furloughs, and much on board ship, travelling between Cape Town and England and America. He wasted no time, planning every moment carefully.

His published works were of three main kinds: his thrilling missionary books, his scholarly treatises on the Congolese people – their lives, language and customs, and his detailed and thorough studies on Bible doctrine. The following outline will show something of the scope of his written work and the breadth of his interests. Some of his books have run through several editions and all have had a wide appeal. There are no shelves of unsold copies and many are out of print.

His Bible study books were the result of early morning's reading of the Word for two hours before the day's work began, though he did much arranging of the material in a form suitable for publication while on furlough. He was also a contributor from time to time to *Redemption Tidings* of Britain, *The Comforter* of South Africa and *The Pentecostal Evangel* of the United States. Many other papers throughout the world copied the articles and he was glad for them to do so; in later years much of his material has been used on various radio stations in Europe and the United States.

His brainchild was *The Congo Evangelistic Mission Report* (now called *Contact*), the magazine which grew out of eight years of his occasional newsletters, which were printed mostly by the Apostolic Faith Mission of South Africa. Willie Burton wrote much in the early issues; it wasn't easy to get newsy articles on time from distant stations but his fluent pen always made up the difference. Sometimes he sent a runner who had to wait while the flustered and harassed missionary scribbled something of what God was doing at that particular time. He often contributed anonymously, or sometimes under the nom-de-plume of 'Kapamu', but his vivid style always showed clearly who wielded the pen. He continued to send us articles long after he left the Field – almost to the end, in fact – as well as to supply sketches on demand.

The first missionary book was *Missionary Pioneering in Congo Forests*, put together by Max Wood Moorhead of Rochester, New York, and described as 'a missionary mosaic composed of letters, printed reports, newspaper and magazine articles and a few hitherto unpublished papers from Mr Burton's pen'. It was printed in England in 1922 during his first furlough, and contains the full story of 'A Luban Pentecost.'

In 1933 there appeared a larger volume, *God Working With Them*, being the official history of the first 18 years of the Congo Evangelistic Mission. Then followed four books that were very popular, all in the mid-1930s. First *When God Changes a Man*, the life story of Shalumbo the redeemed slave, pioneer to his own tribe the Bekalebwe, and right-hand helper of F. D. Johnstone and other Kipushya missionaries. Then *When God Changes a Village*, the story of Bunda, where there is a thriving Pentecostal work to this day, and where the Chief became an outstanding Christian. Then *When God Makes a Pastor*, the account of the conversion and outstanding Bible ministry of Elias Letwaba of South Africa, and after whom a large church at Mwanza was called. And finally *When God Makes a Missionary*, the life story of Edgar Mahon, founder of the Mahon Mission of South Africa.

About the same time *Congo Sketches* was published, a large book with beautiful pictures in colour and black-and-white, with written sketches of Bantu life, missionary work and changed hearts. There followed *Mudishi, Congo Hunter*, a well-received book; constant demand necessitated a further edition some time ago; then *Where to go with your Troubles*, which had a wide appeal, and a children's book, *How They Live in Congoland*, based on talks he had given to his nephews and nieces; finally *What Mean Ye by These Stones*. Most of these were published by Victory Press.

Various presses in South Africa printed an assortment of books, notably *Signs Following*, containing his own testimony of an authenticated healing of cancer of the colon, with X-ray photographs before and after. Also *Gospel Nuggets* with three editions in English and one in Afrikaans – fascinating Gospel stories, one edition having many fine illustrations by the author. Then *Honey Bee*, the thrilling story of the life and ministry of the first convert in 1915 who is still alive, preaching the Gospel (1973). This was followed by *Teachings from the Word of God*, which had earlier appeared in Congo in the Kiluba language and in Kisongye, and was now available in English, French, Swahili and Afrikaans. Missionaries all over Africa and in India asked for permission to translate it into their languages, Vemba, Nyanja, Shona, Ndebele, Zulu, Sesuto, Pedi, Yoruba, Otetela, Shangaan, Xosa, Luganda, Tamil and even Neo-Melanese for New Guinea, while for Europe translations were made in Portuguese, Romanian, Czech and Russian – 24 so far with others in preparation. He himself financed editions in many missionary languages.

In South Africa his book on *Safe Eternally* was written and published as were two sets of Bible Studies of about 50 each, some of several pages, some with charts and illustrations. These studies represent a lifetime of careful study and are in great demand.

Booklets of 8,000 words down to four leaf tracts poured from his pen with titles such as: *Babylon, The Promise is to You, Concerning the Promised Return of the Lord Jesus, A Missionary's Call and Qualifications, The New Birth, Three in One and One in Three, Preaching Power, A Word to the Evolutionist, Snares, Hell and Immortality, The Scriptural Order of a Local Assembly, A Talk to Men and Boys, God's Sent-Ones, Please don't call me Reverend* – and many more.

Mention should be made of his two scientific books on the people to whom God sent him: *Luba Religion and Magic in Custom and Belief*, and *Proverbs of the Baluba*. Both were published by: *La Revue Juridique du Congo Belge*, and were exhaustive on the subject. There was also his children's book of Congo Fables, *The Magic Drum*, published by Methuen.

Among William Burton's papers is an interesting letter of thanks from the Smithsonian Institution, or U.S. National Museum, for information they had requested concerning the significance of various objects collected among the Congolese people. He also supplied information and tribal objects to the famous Royal Museum of Tervuren in Belgium, while there is a 'Burton Collection' of photographs, pottery and other relics of Baluba and pre-Baluba people in the Witwatersrand University Museum, Johannesburg.

This indefatigable worker wrote with ceaseless energy to the very last, and no fewer than three books were found in various stages of manuscript form. The first was the English edition of the biography of Rosalie Hegi, Swiss Pentecostal missionary, and for very many years pioneer worker on the British Assemblies of God Field in the then Belgian Congo. A book entitled *Mine*, composed of much-appreciated convention ministry (My Church, My Spirit, My Son, My Wrath, My Silver and Gold, My Handmaids, My Word, etc.) was almost ready for printing, while a further volume called *Anecdotes on Hospitality* was unfinished.

His books were read widely, and were not only read by many who had never met him, but were sometimes used to their conversion.

When he was in New Zealand in 1955, it had been arranged that, after speaking at a town on the Eastern seaboard of South Island, he was to speak the next night at a place on the West Coast; this meant crossing the Alps, as there was no time to go round them. This posed something of a problem, however, as there was no public transport. He prayed about the matter and mentioned it to his host. 'No problem,' he said, 'I'll take the day off tomorrow and drive you over by car by a short route, the only one that will get you there on time.'

Burton was humbled by this dear brother's sacrificial offer and thoroughly enjoyed the glorious scenery and snow-capped peaks, gorgeous waterfalls and wonderful forests of planted pines and of Kauri, Tawhai and other local timbers, interspersed with smiling farms and green fields in the valleys. It was midday when they saw a peaceful-looking homestead on a hillside. 'Let's call on these folks, they'll give us a refreshing cup of tea.' Willie Burton remonstrated. 'These lonely farmers are extremely hospitable,' replied his friend. 'They'll be glad to have a chat.'

True enough, they were warmly welcomed. During conversation, which turned to spiritual things and the need of the human heart for God, the lady of the house said 'Strangely enough, my husband and I were ordinary decent-living people but hadn't realised our deep need of God until some time ago a book came into our hands – a sort of missionary book about some hunter in Central Africa, *Mudishi, the Congo Hunter*, it was called – I'll fetch it just now to show you – and, you know, our lives were changed! We believed on the Lord Jesus Christ and now we're so happy in Him and read His Word each day. The author's a man called Burton.'

'Are you ill, sir?' she suddenly cried anxiously, as she saw one of her visitors turn white. 'N-n-no,' he stammered, choking on the words, 'I-I'm not ill – I'm Burton!' And he was moved as he thought of the mercy of God, and of the wind of the Holy Spirit blowing the seed of testimony across the mountains of New Zealand to find a lodging place in the hearts of the folks on that lonely farm.

13
Bible teacher extraordinary

Apart from being one of the best-known Pentecostal missionaries in the world, William Burton was certainly known more than anything else as a Bible Teacher, an exponent of the Word of God. He lived in the Word of God, every day, all day. The Word of God was his constant diet, his perpetual delight and the subject of ceaseless discussion. He was a missionary solely to give God's Word of salvation to the lost, a minister to expound the Word of Grace to the saints and a disciple to witness to the Word of Truth to all who would hear.

In an age when there was a clamour for brighter and shorter sermons, and when it was claimed to be old-fashioned to give a 'Bible Reading', he could hold any audience of God's people spell-bound in quiet dignity for an hour or more with a message that consisted chiefly of a long string of verses of Scripture which developed some doctrinal theme. He avoided histrionics, abhorred 'apt alliteration's artful aid', and completely ignored the sermoniser's essential firstly, secondly and thirdly.

How, then, did he hold the crowd? Why did they constantly ask for more? Firstly, he prepared for them good, satisfying spiritual food; secondly, he was provocative in his presentation of doctrinal truth. He was forthright, clear and plain in his delivery, beginning arrestingly and finishing emotionally. He was always practical and down-to-earth in his application of his message and made his Bible talks come alive by his careful use of vivid, gripping illustration. Indeed one sometimes felt that his illustrations 'made' his message. Last but not least his diction was good, his choice of words exact and his English perfect.

He was undoubtedly a master speaker, though he did not possess a good or powerful voice; indeed, he often expressed his great regret that he did not have a deeper or stronger voice. He tried to keep it below its higher registers and, though he did not always succeed, he always spoke with such deliberate care that everything he said was clearly heard.

Like any great speaker, he saw to it that everybody heard what he wanted them to hear. Nothing was lost through careless or hurried speech; every word was used to the best advantage.

His illustrations were of three kinds. Many were from the Bible itself; his knowledge of the Word of God was encyclopaedic and all sorts of odd characters, obscure customs and bits of background sparkled afresh in striking application to Gospel truth or believers' doctrine. No-one who ever heard him speak of Epaphroditus who 'gambled his all for God' (Phil. 2:30) or of the 'blue ribbon' of the border of the High Priest's garment, or of 'boring the ear of the willing slave to the doorpost', will ever forget his graphic word-pictures and moving appeal.

James Salter once said that he and Willie Burton were 'bees that gathered honey from all flowers'. And when one listened to the way Burton applied tales of yesterday and today, things he had read in books and things he had heard about in everyday life, one wondered why others hadn't seen them in the same fascinating way that he presented them. For instance, 200 years ago an old Dutch pioneer, Woltemaad, saved 14 lives from a storm-tossed wreck off the South African coast by swimming his great, strong horse out to sea seven times and bringing back two men each time; but he perished himself in the effort. The noble statue of this hero in Cape Town gripped William Burton's heart and he saw it as a picture of the servant of Christ, who would rescue lost souls even at the cost of his own life.

Another story he told with great effect and with an original twist was that of St. Patrick and the King of Connaught. Looking and praying for some illustration of 'Three in One and One in Three', Patrick's eye lit on a shamrock leaf at his feet. Flourishing it before the assembled counsellors he cried, 'One leaf or three?' Some said, 'Three,' others, 'One'. 'Surely three in one,' replied Patrick, 'and so is the Eternal God Three in One and One in Three.' 'True! true!' cried king and counsellors. 'And,' to quote Burton, 'the old king tottered from his throne, and taking the missionary by the arm, he said, "Come on Patrick, to the river and put me under, I'm going to be a Christian!"'

He was quick to pick up stories from conversations. Once he was asking me about my home town and I told him that my mother knew John Mackintosh, founder of the great toffee firm, and had bought toffee from his basket as he stood at the corner of the street. His wife had made it in the kitchen copper that she used for boiling the clothes. This poor man gave his tithes to the Lord and rose from poverty to be the largest maker of toffee in the world, and gave vast sums of money to missionary work, supporting a whole Mission Station in China anonymously. I told him, too, of the weaver John Crossley who, with his

Quaker wife, knelt on the stone floor of their cottage, promising to give the tithe of all they earned to God's work if He would bless their one loom. From that humble beginning they became the town's greatest benefactors, and their carpet factories the largest in the world. He wrote at once to Mackintoshes Ltd. and to Crossley's Carpets to verify these stories, obtained further details and used them with telling effect when speaking on Christian giving.

The third type of illustration was from his own observations and experiences. Who but he could have observed from the railway carriage window that the big tree in the middle of the garden of a ganger's cottage that straddled the boundary of Zaire (Congo today) and Zambia was as much on one side as on the other? Or realised that, seeing the railway ran along the ridge of the watershed dividing the Congo water system from the Zambezi tributaries, raindrops could trickle off one side of the tree to the Luapula River, to the Congo and thus into the Atlantic, while the drops on the other side could run into the Kafue River, then into the Zambezi to the Indian Ocean? 'And so,' he would explain, 'two lives begin together, hear the same Gospel. One believes on Jesus and goes to life eternal; the other rejects and goes to everlasting punishment,' adding, 'My friend, on which side are you?'

For an illustration of God's provision, Willie Burton would tell of the time when he was travelling from Mwanza to distant Kipushya, 15 days' journey away, on urgent Mission business. He fell sick with fever, too ill to walk or cycle, so he had to be carried in a hammock. Food had long since run out, and the next village lay miles ahead in the unknown. 'Lord,' he prayed, 'please provide meat for my hungry men, I have no strength left to hunt.' Just then the hammock men stopped. One of them whispered, 'I can just see an antelope standing in the tall grass. It moved its head, do you think you could shoot from the hammock?' They stood perfectly still as the sick man slowly raised himself up and aimed with fever-blurred eye at the two horns just visible above the grass. They vanished only to appear again. He was a dead shot and normally could not miss. 'It must be this fever,' he muttered as he fired carefully a second time. Again they vanished only to appear a third time. He mustered all his remaining strength, steadied his shaking arms, fired again and sank back exhausted. The horns did not reappear this time so the men ran forward to find-not one antelope but three! They dropped on their knees crying, 'God is real, God is good. He has answered prayer!' Jehovah-Jireh had provided abundantly.

More moving still were tales of heathen converted, witch doctors turning to Christ and cannibals being completely changed on believing on the only One who can save from sin. There seemed to be no end to the real-life illustrations that constantly illuminated his Bible talks, bringing a breath of adventure, a glimpse of God's power and fresh light on His Word.

He was extremely thorough in his Bible study. I once rather proudly told him that I had listed forty points in the life of Joseph which typi-fied the Lord Jesus Christ. He replied, 'Keep going, so far I have found over a hundred!' He left piles of his old Bible notes and studies, some yellow and worn with age, all in his very small yet beautiful script. One study has 145 points – more, I think, than even he could give in one evening! Many are neatly set out and paged. Others are hastily written, almost microscopically, on any handy scrap of paper or on the back of an envelope, hot from the anvil of his inspired thinking, ready to be worked up into a fuller study. He was generous in giving others his studies, never afraid that they might preach his sermons, but rather encouraging them to use them if they were of any help. Busy as he was, he often jotted down several scriptures in his letters to friends, giving the precious thoughts that had come to him that very morning. A brother-minister showed me a letter written three months before he died in which he jotted down two beautiful sets of verses: one on 'Our nothingness' and one on 'His fullness'.

He held strong views on certain aspects of doctrine and was fearless in expressing them and justifying them with extensive quotations from the Scriptures though his views were not always accepted by other Bible teachers. What he saw was the Truth! It was written there plain for all to see! He was a protagonist of the views he held, from public platforms, by written books and pamphlets, in discussions with all who would take part, and through ceaseless correspondence. He went so far as to pay for the publication of one book of which he sent free copies to friends and ministers of the Gospel all over the world, so convinced was he of the scriptural truth contained in it and the urgent necessity of the deepest consideration of the doctrine set forth.

Whether other Bible students agreed with him or not, all had the utmost respect for his honesty, forthrightness and deep concern for the Word of Truth, as well as for his vast knowledge of the written Word of God.

14
Tramp preacher

The City Hall in Cape Town was crowded. Claude Cooper, then a famous campaign evangelist, was holding a very successful series of meetings. This particular evening, the meeting opened with enthusiasm; the singing was wonderful. Then came a moment of quiet before the proceedings were committed to the Lord. The evangelist's quick eye spotted a familiar figure right in the middle of the audience. He whispered to Congo missionary Leslie Wigglesworth who was beside him on the platform, 'Isn't that Brother Burton down from the Field?' 'Yes, it certainly is!' was the excited reply.

The evangelist rose. 'This evening, dear friends, I see we have a most distinguished visitor with us,' he said, 'an intrepid explorer-missionary from Central Africa, a famous preacher, a great linguist, an authority on African customs, a map-maker who has trod those lonely tropical forests where no white man has been before, an outstanding man of this generation – in fact a modern Livingstone or Stanley. I am now going to call upon the Reverend William F. P. Burton to lead this service in prayer.'

The large, dignified gentleman slowly rose to his feet. Dead silence. Then in that slightly piping voice of his, he said very deliberately, 'My dear friends, I am not famous nor great, neither am I a modern Livingstone, I am plain Willie Burton, just a tramp preacher willing to tramp the Congo forests for Jesus. Now shall we pray...' Then he led that hushed audience to the very presence of God, directing their thoughts and hearts to Jesus, the One who shed His blood to save them from their sin. 'Only a great man could have done that' the evangelist said quietly and feelingly at the end of the prayer.

'Tramp Preacher' was always his favourite title. He did not like to be called 'Pastor' for that would limit him to one flock and his hackles rose if men called him 'Reverend', since he believed this to be unscriptural. He just liked to be considered a 'tramp preacher', without capitals. However he was obliged to submit, with obvious pain, to the unscriptural title in the case of government documents, as the Roman Catholic government of the then Congo could not conceive of designating any full-time religious worker and preacher by any title other than an ecclesiastical one, especially when he had to sign the papers for Mission lands or be issued with a permit of some kind. Officials were often puzzled by the evangelical's use of 'brother'; to them a 'Brother' meant a Catholic lay worker, and to their orderly minds a 'Brother' made furniture, laid bricks and taught in school, while a 'Father' took services, prayed and preached. They were confused by Protestant missionaries who did any job that a 'Brother' did but preached in church and in open village, prayed fervently for the sick, married and buried their believers and yet did not wish to be called 'Father' or 'Reverend'. They did not mind wearing overalls but apparently did not care for special gowns or collars.

Willie Burton often explained why he liked to be considered 'just a tramp preacher'. He reminded folks that it was said of Jesus that 'he went about doing good'. That meant to say, quite literally, that Jesus tramped around preaching, helping, healing. A humble job, a useful job. And so he wanted to be nothing more than his Lord, a humble tramp preacher. He remembered, too, that missionary Paul was very much the same. Like Jesus, he was of 'no fixed abode', but tramped up and down those Mediterranean lands preaching Jesus and establishing assemblies.

Being a man of strong personality and presence, it wasn't always easy for him to be humble. He made tremendous efforts to overcome what could have been, and often was, a dominating manner. Dominating, but never domineering, for he was always the Christian gentleman. He often did the most menial tasks to overcome the natural ego and knew great victory over self. 'Not I but Christ' was his life-motto, as it was the Apostle Paul's. Paul, too, must have had the same trouble with his own powerful, dominating, personality. And as Paul pushed forward the somewhat reluctant Timothy, so Willie Burton encouraged the dormant qualities in others and placed responsibilities upon them.

Jesus left no worldly goods, save the cloth in which his body was laid in the tomb. Paul, too, had just what he stood up in, plus a cloak he had left behind in Troas but now needed in the cold Roman prison, and a few books and parchments. The disciples of the Lord Jesus were sent out tramping and preaching the Gospel throughout Judea and Samaria and to the uttermost parts of the earth. They obeyed and went out, sowing the seed of the Word of God, and left behind them a crop of growing, living churches throughout North Africa, across Europe, in Asia and Bithynia, and even in India and China.

They were all tramp preachers, sent ones, apostles. Willie Burton was a tramp preacher, a sent one and an apostle too; not that he ever referred to himself as an apostle, but all the missionaries who worked with him considered him to be one. Every apostle is a missionary but every missionary is not an apostle. He was a sent one, a pioneer of new fields, a founder of churches, the 'signs of an apostle were wrought among you (the Baluba and Basongye) in all patience, in signs and wonders, and mighty deeds' (2 Cor. 12:12). Among ourselves we often referred to him as 'the Bishop', but knowing his revulsion towards titles we did not address him in this way. We did not then know that in their earlier years both he and Jimmy Salter addressed their letters to their leader and teacher, Thomas Myerscough as 'dear Bishop', such was their respect for him.

It was in 1911 that William Burton resigned his profession and went out with five shillings in his pocket as a tramp preacher, and began to refer to himself as such. He wrote in his book, *Where to Go with your Troubles,* 'My wanderings have taken me over considerable parts of Europe, Africa and America.' And, one may add, Australia and New Zealand. Most of his life, however, was spent in Congo.

After he was married he found it necessary to improve his hut, which developed over the years into a beautiful home, though all the furniture was home-made. It remained basically simple, retaining the original sun-dried brick walls and thatched roof, though additions were made, burnt brick walls added to the exterior, and, in typical missionary fashion, bits of the veranda enclosed to make extra little rooms. Later he cast some lovely fluted veranda pillars in concrete to replace the rotting wooden ones, making his own core and mould in his carpenter's shop.

When Mrs Burton became older and almost housebound, he painted some beautiful bunches of luscious-looking grapes on the wall of her room as a birthday surprise. 'Every grape,' he said, 'will tell you "I love you" while I am away on my treks.' On his return, his wife smilingly said, 'While you were away I counted all these grapes, so I know now how many times you love me!' 'Ah that is just the beginning,' he replied – and painted in a few more!

From this home, he regularly shot off in all directions. On foot, by bicycle and, in later years, in a motor car, on the Lord's business, preaching, testifying and teaching everywhere, till a thousand villages became as familiar to him as his own home town. He was still very much the tramp preacher, the apostle, working from a base.

After his dear wife died in 1952 he gradually became less tied to his essential base, and travelled more. Following the great evacuation of 1960 he left the Field at 74 years of age and once more became exclusively a tramp preacher, living from a suitcase. In 1962 he was back on the Field for three months, during some of the most difficult times of troubles and bloodshed, and taught daily in the Kamina Bible Training Institute. The rest of the Field was cut off. In 1967 his airfare from London to Congo was paid, but trouble flared up again and his visit had to be cancelled. He planned once more to go back to the Field in 1971, when he was called home. He had his passport and visa in order, and all documents prepared, and we felt that he had it in mind to get back to Mwanza before he died so that his body could be laid to rest beside that of Mrs Burton. But God willed otherwise. So he went on tramping and preaching and teaching wherever he could, and doors were opened to him everywhere.

If Jesus had nothing but a shroud and Paul a cloak, Willie Burton boasted of little more. He had no house of his own and no furniture. He travelled with two suitcases, one for clothes and one for books and correspondence. He had a third in his 'pied-à-terre' in Johannes- burg and shared someone else's post box for the delivery of mail. Truly he could say 'I'm but a stranger here, Heaven is my home'.

He could have had plenty of homes. Scores and scores of people all over the world would have gladly given him a comfortable, even luxurious, lodging. He was such an easy guest to entertain, happy and content with everything. He had a way of making his hostess feel that everything that she set before him was exactly what he wanted. Mrs Burton's nephews and nieces in South Africa begged him to stay with them and were disappointed when he would spend only a few days, then move on. He loved them all dearly but did not wish to be a burden to any; rather, he wanted to keep on tramping as long as he could.

For the last six years of his life he had a small room with the Fischers in Johannesburg, which was very convenient and central for him in his travelling, and where he left his spare suitcase. They and the mem- bers of their Assembly realised the privilege they had of entertaining him and of enjoying his ministry. He loved their beautiful garden and the wooded valley behind, a quiet retreat where he could study the Word and the glories of nature, and paint a little; it was a veritable sanctuary for the golden oriole and green pigeon, for the waxbill and sunbird, birds he had been used to at Mwanza. However, he was only there between preaching tours. Twice in that time he toured the British assemblies and he travelled far and wide in South Africa, Rhodesia (Zimbabwe) and Zambia, and also paid a visit to Kenya. He gave several series of Bible Lectures at Bible Training Schools in Belgium, South Africa and Nairobi.

It was during those last few years when he made those two last extended tours of Britain that so many people began to call him 'Uncle Willie'. These were mostly comparatively new friends who took the mature, kind, helpful, considerate, spiritual and humorous old gentleman into their hearts and homes. This 'Uncle Willie' cult was a rather startling though most pleasing aspect of his many-sided character to those of us who had laboured with him and known him as our respected leader through many long years. Hitherto only his nieces and nephews had ever called him 'Uncle Willie'. The little children on the Field called him 'Uncle Burton' and none of the older missionaries called him 'Willie' except for Fred Johnstone and Teddy Hodgson. To everybody he was 'Brother Burton', and more often 'Mr Burton', and no familiarities were ever taken with him. He was the director of the Mission and respected and honoured as such.

So it was beautiful to see his totally relaxed latter years, all responsibilities gone, trekking – now by plane, train and other people's cars – from place to place, doing nothing but preaching and teaching the Word. He had always been so very correct, even Victorian, in his attitude to others but now it was evident that he enjoyed this new relationship and the widening of the circle of his spiritual 'nephews and nieces', and it seemed that he felt a tinge of regret that this surprisingly sweet familiarity had not been exercised a little earlier. He had always been a 'tramp preacher'; now he was the beloved tramp preacher.

15
Inasmuch...

William Burton was indeed 'the succourer of many'. A whole volume would be needed to describe his generosity, his gifts, his help to countless friends, fellow-workers and loved ones. So much of this was quite private, just between him and the needy one and God. Living practically in a suitcase, travelling from place to place, the tramp preacher had few needs of his own. Since his dear wife went to glory, and having no children of his own, whatever came to him by way of income from his paintings, or from a few of his books, or personal gifts for his own private needs, all this was readily available to help those whom he considered to be in greater need than himself.

Few people knew how others had been helped, but many knew that their own need had been met in a wonderful way. He always felt that he was a steward and what he was able to give was from the Lord, not himself. He was never any man's debtor; whatever he received from others he endeavoured to repay quietly and privately but in abundant measure.

On two occasions we replaced the Burtons during their furlough, caring for their station at Mwanza during 1931 and again in 1937, the second time for a year. We tried our best to do the many jobs that Burton could probably have done better – repairing doors and windows, making a new set of gates, replacing sections of galvanised ant-proof coursing in the walls of the Mission House, and many similar jobs. It was all in the course of normal care and upkeep, but he noticed it on his return. Some time later he found out that I was particularly fond of a certain type of book. In due course, a large parcel arrived and to my amazement there was a complete set of twelve large volumes! It was a 'Thank you'; it was to him 'more blessed to give than to receive'.

Every station in the CEM has been helped in its hour of need. Every missionary in times of trial or testing has benefited from his kind assistance if he has known about their need. Soon after I arrived on the Field, the missionaries at far off, lonely Kipushya lost everything in a disastrous fire. As Burton read out to us the sad letter that came by special runner from Mr and Mrs Rupert Thomas and Miss Toerein, tears began to flow. Brushing them aside he rushed to the workshop and began to make plans for some strong but very light furniture to be made, suitable for transportation. We all contributed a shirt, trousers or frock, whatever we could spare. In a matter of days, carriers set out on the 12 to 15 days' trek with their loads of cleverly-designed chairs and tables and other essential supplies.

Willie Burton took a special interest in the Printing Press and Mrs Burton's brother-in-law, Edward Saunders, and his family contributed largely to the fine building put up at Katompe by Fred Ramsbottom and Emil Hartmann as well as to some of the machinery; in fact, it was called the Saunders Press. On one occasion, there was a dire need for a small engine to drive the main printing press, as it was a killing job in tropical heat to work the machines by hand and some by foot. Burton shared the burden in prayer and wondered how he could help. Just then he had to go to South Africa and decided to take some paintings in case he could sell any en route; mission funds were very low and we needed money for missionaries' support.

Lubumbashi – then Elisabethville – the provincial capital, did not seem to attract the usual interest in his work. He got on to the train rather despondently to continue his journey south. But just before the brass horn blew for departure, a man came panting up and swung himself aboard. 'Burton here?' he cried. 'Yes, right along the train.' 'Hello, where have you been? Have you any paintings with you? Good! Then I'll take the lot. Yes, I've got my cheque book with me. Hurry, the horn's blowing, I'm on the north-bound train. Thanks ever so much!' Without mentioning a price a cheque changed hands. Willie Burton opened his suitcase, grabbed his paintings and handed them over to this old acquaintance who dropped off the train, the pictures under his arm, as it began to chug out of the station. Only just in time, but nevertheless on time.

A still somewhat dazed Burton got off the train two days later at Bulawayo, and was directed by a friend to a man who dealt in engines.

'Just the thing here,' he said, 'It will cost you £60. Where did you say it was for? Congo? Then I'll just check the transport costs. Let me see – that will be just another £15 and nothing for the packing. How much have you got, sir?'

It was exactly what he had received for the paintings. The printery was saved and Brothers Hartmann and Ramsbottom got their engine.

CEM missionaries have always shared and shared alike, from the oldest to the youngest, so Burton had no advantage over any other. Neither could he personally, according to the constitution, allocate any mission funds; this was done by the Executive Field Council. The only way he could help was by earning the money through the skills that God had given him. Every station could testify of help in this way for special projects, family needs, church buildings, mission houses and the like. Money, of course, was by no means always available but when it was there, it was used.

The Africans too were helped tremendously, far more than they knew. Once, when there was a great demand, Bibles were being snapped up by better-off believers who had ready cash. Willie Burton found out that many of our full-time workers were still using torn, worn-out copies because they could not afford new ones, so he started to paint pictures in all the spare time he could manage, prayed for customers, got them, ordered a whole shipment of Bibles and eventually was able to supply a free copy to all full-time workers. This took a lot of time and a lot of money, for these workers numbered several hundreds – but oh, the joy with which they were received! They did not know the sacrifice and hard work involved, nor did their father-in-God wish them to know.

It was not only in the Congo that his help was given but in all sorts of places, among relatives and friends alike. Many are the testimonies to William Burton proving himself to be a 'friend in need'; sometimes it was by money obtained from the sale of his paintings, sometimes by advice, or by prayer, faith and service. For instance, once when my wife and I were very run down and needed a rest, a letter arrived saying, 'I want you to break your journey to the Cape at a Christian Guest Farm near George, on the south coast. I will arrange for it and the dear friends will be happy to entertain you without charge.'

We were rather nervous about going but were met at the railway station and taken to 'Carmel' where we had one of the most restful holidays of our lives. Jack Edkins took me one day to see the fine new water-pump which supplied the needs of the happy crowds of believers, young and old, who came here for fellowship, convention meetings and spiritual uplift. 'I want you to know how glad we are to have you,' he said; then he added 'and I should like to tell you how we got this abundant supply of water.'

Apparently, when Burton had stayed there on one particular occasion, he appreciated the difficulties they were experiencing with a totally inadequate water supply. Without plenty of pure water, their vision of this ministry for the encouragement of believers, especially the young ones, and the salvation of souls, could never be fulfilled. Professional water-diviners had worked over every square yard of the farm, but not a sign of water could be found. Burton shared this burden with them in prayer. Though the situation seemed hopeless, he was supremely confident that water was there or God would not have given them the vision of a Convention Guest Farm. The next morning he said, 'Let us try just once more, I believe God will show us the place.' So they tried, and sure enough they reached water in a most unexpected place, ample for all their needs. Then God in a wonderful way supplied the necessary pump and equipment.

It was never beneath his dignity to help. When he visited our assembly at Halifax during his first furlough in 1921, we young folk were thrilled by his graphic stories of missionary conquest in Congoland, equally by his fascinating expositions of the Word of God, and were altogether somewhat overawed by the great man. Coming home with him from a house-meeting one evening in pouring rain, we saw a car stuck on a hill. To our surprise, he at once hurried forward to give a hand and soon we were all pushing it over the crown of the hill till the engine started. Before waving goodbye, he witnessed to the owner, telling him we had helped him for Jesus' sake.

When the Mantle brothers visited the Field they were struck to see such a gifted man so humble. They arose one morning at about four o'clock to make an early start and, in the half light of dawn, they saw a figure busy stowing away their baggage in the station-wagon – none other than Willie Burton, helping again to give them a little more time for breakfast. He was always doing this sort of thing, for black and white alike.

Bricks were made and stacked and stones gathered in heaps for the building of a new church near Mwanza. The Christians soon got tired of the hard work through the long dry season, and felt they could do no more. No amount of exhortation from the local pastor could stir them from their lethargy. The rainy season approached; storm clouds gathered. The sun-dried bricks would be softened into a soggy mass and the whole work ruined if the job was not completed and the building thatched. Missionary Burton heard about it. Next morning, about six o'clock, a believer arose to beat the drum for morning worship and heard a noise among the heaps. He looked – there was a white man loading a barrow with heavy stones for the foundations. He must have been at it for some time by the look of things – why, it was Bwana Burton! He turned to his drum and excitedly beat a different call. 'Kapamu is here. Kapamu is here. Men, men, come quickly, come quickly. Work, work, work.' Men came pouring out of their huts and, when they saw what he was doing, they too seized the heavy stones, working with a will, shamed by the humble example of their leader. It was enough. The church was built before the rains broke.

During a visit to Britain, Burton was invited to minister the Word in the Shetland Isles. He stayed with an old fisherman who lived in a cottage by the shore, no longer able to go with the younger men to sea. One morning he was repairing his humble home and the visitor found him trying to lift a large stone slab for a new doorstep. 'Stop' cried Willie Burton, himself an old man in his middle seventies, 'I'll do that for you!' And he did, not only lifting it for him but cementing it into position. 'Your servant, for Christ's sake.'

His very last gift, as far as we know, and it must have drained his final resources, was a Landrover for Mwanza Station which he had opened in 1915. The senior worker there, Otaniela Yumba, was the President of our 2,000 churches as well as supervisor of Mwanza District. How fitting that he, a lad of ten when the pioneers first arrived, should be thus equipped to carry on the work of William Burton.

16
To live is Christ

William Burton always lived with his eyes looking towards heaven. In fact he usually prayed with his eyes open and looking up. When he took evening prayers at Mwanza, or on another station, he would comment on the passage of Scripture in the normal way. But instead of bringing his remarks to a conclusion and then announcing prayer, his remarks just merged into prayer. One moment he was talking to us and the next moment to God. One moment he was on earth, the next in heaven.

I can see him now, commenting, illustrating; then a faraway look would creep into his upturned eyes and his pronouns would change. He was no longer talking about the Lord but to the Lord. He had moved smoothly from preaching into praying. I have never known anyone else quite like that. We all felt the same; after a moment or so we would glance at one another, one with a blush, another a smile, then bow our heads and close our eyes. His head remained up and his eyes open and when he stopped praying and we opened our eyes he would still be looking into space and we had to make an effort to refocus to earth.

He lived so near to God, heaven and earth were so close to each other, that he turned from one to the other naturally, easily, with no hesitation at all. He seemed to have discovered the secret of a timeless eternity: time did not exist between him and God. Distance did not count. He slipped easily into another dimension on the wings of prayer. He lived in the realm of 'nothing between'. No veil existed, no barrier of unconfessed sin. His life was transparent. If there was even the shadow of a misunderstanding between him and another, he would go the length of our Congo Field to put it right.

'Have you been to the lemon tree yet?' was a famous remark often made by one missionary to another, sometimes half humorously, sometimes enquiringly. It meant, 'Have you yet had a heart-to-heart talk with Brother Burton?' There was an old lemon tree at the end of the garden near the carpenter's shop and it was Burton's habit to invite some young missionary who was in the need of a bit of fatherly help, advice or correction, or perhaps some older worker involved in misunderstanding with William Burton or with some other worker, to 'take a little walk as far as the lemon tree.'

Often after Conference evening prayers he would ask one or another 'to stroll in the garden along by the lemon tree.' So he would try to help, advise, tell what the Scriptures had to say about the matter, reprove, ask pardon – in short, do as Paul advised Timothy to do in 2 Tim. 4:2. 'Preach the Word, be instant (urgent, diligent) whether you are ready and the moment is opportune or not; reprove, rebuke, exhort, with all endurance and teaching.' His one desire was to please the Lord and have a band of fellow-workers who loved each other, worked in harmony and so also pleased the Lord. He succeeded to a remarkable degree, even though at first some were rather embarrassed when they saw him approach with that 'lemon-tree-look' in his eye!

William Burton always tried to live in such a way that at any moment he could meet his Lord with joy. But that is not to say that he was too heavenly to be human, too spiritual to be natural. Far from it! He was naturally spiritual and spiritually natural. He could romp with the kiddies, black or white, chat with his old village cronies about their everyday lives, and talk with Congolese fishermen, European scientists, old washerwomen, young teenagers, anybody and everybody with familiarity and friendliness, using their language and sharing their interests.

He was especially happy with the children. He often comforted Mrs Burton by saying that their heavenly Father had taken away their only little one to give them a love for everybody else's children. Many an unresponsive village, hardened against the Gospel, has been won by his attitude to the little ones. When younger he would run and play with them and he always, right to old age, played conjuring tricks with them. In no time he would have a crowd, and then he would tell them about Jesus.

Often his fame would go before him and the youngsters would cry out, 'Please show us how to make the money grow like you did at Kabango!' These Baluba were all very good gardeners and so he would challenge the children to make money grow. They would each make a row of little mounds in the earth, like the big ones they made when planting manioc. He would plant a franc in one, and hey presto! out would sprout francs from every one of his heaps, but they would try and try in vain! This all helped to establish a friendly relationship and many a fine lad, attracted in this way, stayed to listen to the story of Jesus and became a Christian and a witness for Him.

He had many of these tricks, the most famous one being the Peanut Trick. He learnt it by watching an African conjuror in Adderley Street, Cape Town, who had won a championship prize with this original trick; few could copy it. One single peanut was rapidly manipulated till peanuts seemed to be coming out of ears, nose, mouth and everywhere. They then gradually disappeared till only one was left on his hand. He blew and it vanished into thin air! Modifications of that trick have fascinated countless families of children in homes where he has been entertained throughout the world, as well as in hundreds of Congo villages. The tricks led to stories, usually animal stories told round African campfires, then tales of Jesus and the way of salvation, made so simple that a child could understand.

He used every means to tell others about his Lord. One of the most moving was only revealed by the piles of correspondence he left. No-one, it would seem, knew of this particular ministry. It seems that in the last year or so of his life he made a special effort to make contact with friends he had lost touch with since his earliest years. His physical strength beginning to wane, and travelling becoming more of a problem, he hit upon the idea of writing to all who could be traced, to ask about their spiritual condition and to witness to them of Christ.

He even traced some of his old friends from St. Laurence College, Ramsgate, whom he had not seen for 65 years or more. Replies came from business men and bishops, scientists and archdeacons; they even referred to each other by their school nicknames, such as 'fatty' or 'fossil'. 'Fossil,' of course, was Willie Burton and one old friend referred to his unrivalled collections of fossils, coins and birds' eggs. Another one said that Willie was one of the most practical and efficient persons he had ever met and amazingly thorough. He adds, 'I am as keen a Christian as I was 60 years ago.' Some were saved men, one referring to the Torrey and Alexander Campaign in London in 1905. Others, though probably not Christians, were grateful to him for bringing to their notice these eternal verities.

People wrote to him with all kinds of spiritual needs. A teenage girl from South Africa wanted to know how salvation could be personal, because he was her idea of a super-Christian. He replied with patience and understanding. He was always on the lookout to witness to people who needed Christ, and he could do it because he lived so near to God. Willie Hacking told me that he and Fred Watson of Blackburn took the latter's hard, ungodly brother to Preston to call on Thomas Myerscough and Willie Burton, who was just home from the Congo for the first time. After a little general talk, Burton sized up the situation and politely asked the young man if he would care to see some of his Congo curios. It seemed but five minutes later when they were back in the room; the young man with arms outstretched and tears coursing down his face, rushed to his brother crying, 'Oh, Fred, what will my dear old mother say, I've given my heart to Jesus!' From curios to Christ! With consecrated skill Willie Burton had done the impossible and drawn the sinner to where he himself stood, with the Saviour. Such cases could be multiplied.

He lived so near to God that when he was struck down with abdominal cancer in 1944 and was given six months to live, he was quite happy to go or to stay. He was ready to 'be with Christ which is far better', but felt that, if it was God's will, it would be more helpful to the Congo church 'to abide in the flesh', as he had left certain work unfinished. He was 'in a strait betwixt two' but wanted, like Paul, that Christ should 'be magnified in my body, whether it be by life, or by death' (Phil. 1:20-26). A caecostomy operation had been performed in Johannesburg, but, a year after his return to Mwanza to die, his natural functions were restored, and in 1946 the hole in his side was closed up by surgical operation in Luanshya, Zambia, and he returned to normal life, being more active in later years than most men of his age. The whole story, with X-ray photographs, is told in his book, *Signs Following*:

We have just recently returned from South Africa and from interviewing three of the five doctors and one hospital sister who were present at a double operation performed on me in May and June, 1944. I would like you to follow closely the circumstances.

In February 1944, terrible pains gripped the left side of my abdomen. At first I thought it was a swollen spleen from malaria but when it became unbearable I went to Manono tin mines where the doctor took X-ray photographs of my colon with barium. All the negatives showed plainly the horizontal and descending sections of the colon seriously constricted by disease, so that the food was almost unable to pass and had clogged into a great mass in the ascending colon. I had been anointed by the elders of our Congo church as soon as the first onset took place but no improvement followed.

I was advised to go with all speed to the best man possible. I could not have found a better – a brilliant surgeon of international reputation and a lecturer at Johannesburg medical school. Further X-ray photographs in Johannesburg hospital showed how rapidly the growths in my colon were developing. Thus in May a hole was opened in my right side (a caecostomy operation) allowing my waste products to discharge there, and a month later the whole abdomen was laid open for a thorough examination.

On my return to consciousness they told me that the obstructing growth had been removed. This was untrue, however, and was only said to comfort me, as they admitted to me later that they could not possibly remove it and had just sewn me up, leaving me to die. The surgeon and hospital authorities called my wife and informed her that the whole horizontal and descending colon were choked with cancer. They said that I could only live six months at most. A month later a running abscess appeared in my left side, right over the place where the growths had been located.

My brave little wife took me from the hospital as soon as I could be conveniently moved. The hospital register says "Mr. Burton was discharged from the hospital at his own request in a dying condition."

We were given loving hospitality in the home of my wife's sister and her husband, both earnest believers, and many came to pray for me. Also I was again anointed with oil in the Name of the Lord. In the Congo thousands of believers were crying to God continually to spare my life.

The weeks that followed were a time of extreme weakness but instead of sinking I became stronger, until in January, 1945, six months from the operation, we returned to our missionary work in the Congo. I had gladly submitted my future to my Lord's will, as instructed in James 4:15, ready and happy to go to Him if He wished, but yet with a feeling that my missionary work was not yet done, I asked God to allow me for my wife's sake and for the work's sake to continue a little longer. For over a year after my return to the Congo I continued to wear a cup and rubber bag over my side to receive the waste products from my body. The running abscess in my side gradually dried right up and by May, 1946, my natural functions of elimination were so far restored that I visited a hospital in Luanshya, Northern Rhodesia (today's Zambia), where further X-ray examination revealed no evidence at all of cancer. My side was sewn up and I returned once more to normal life – a whole man and more active than most men of my age.

The X-ray photographs surely give all the scientific evidence that could be asked for as proof of this healing. When later (1948) I visited the doctors who opened up my body and saw the condition of the colon, they looked at me as though I were one raised from the dead, but all of them were men big enough to give God the glory and to admit that He had performed the miracle.

Many signs and wonders glorified Christ through the laying on of the hands and prayer of this modern apostle. In his preaching he was careful to quote cases that had been authenticated, often writing for medical proof years after the healing to be sure that it was permanent. For example, in 1908, while still an electrical engineer, he was called to pray with a girl of 18 who was not expected to live till midday. The manager gave reluctant permission for him to leave his testbed. He rushed to the dying girl, who was a member of his choir; the doctor said she had been coughing up blood and bits of her lungs and could die at any moment. Willie Burton placed his hands on her in the name of Jesus and prayed, then hurried back to work. She stopped coughing at once and was soon up and about. Later she married, and 57 years after her healing she wrote him as follows:

> Dear Mr Burton, you asked me to have an X-ray. I have had one and am sending it to you, trusting it will be to the glory of God. I was eighteen when the Lord healed me and I shall be 75 this month... He is the same yesterday and today and forever... I never forget to pray for you.
>
> Yours in Him, Alice Eccles (Rossall).

The certificate was from Manchester Regional Hospital Board and said, 'Thank you for your co-operation. You will be pleased to learn that your chest X-ray was satisfactory on 27th April 1965.'

When the time came for him to go, he was ready. He had always lived close to the Lord and was happy to go whenever Jesus said, 'Come'. He was not even at his pied-a-terre when the call came; he was on the move again. He had accepted an invitation to stay for a week or two at the home of Mr and Mrs H. Robertson of Stirling Farm, Delmas, near Pretoria. Mrs Robertson was Phyllis Heatley, the daughter of Mr and Mrs Charles Heatley, whose home had been his base of operations during his year in South Africa before going up to the Congo. As a small girl she had sat on his knee while he told her stories of Jesus.

The Robertsons were getting the car out to take him for a run, and he went to fetch his camera from his room across the garden; on his way back, the call came. His spirit soared away and the angels laid his body gently down among the gorgeous blooms on the edge of the veranda. No cry, no bruise. The physician said that he was gone before his body touched the ground.

It seemed most wonderful and fitting that he should end his days in the home of the family who had opened their home to him when he arrived in Africa way back in 1914. The cycle of his African service was complete.

In 1972 a number of the ZEM/CEM (now CAM) family who now work in the Johannesburg area gathered for an anniversary meeting, and saw the place where he fell.

We almost felt the softly swishing wings of hovering angels. A few yards away was the 'rondavel', or round house of stone with thatched roof, where he sat and painted his very last picture, the veranda and the flowers among which he was to fall. Just beyond was the meeting hall where William Burton had preached each evening of his last week on earth and where he had won his last souls to Christ. We enjoyed a sweet time of fellowship, song, prayer and the ministry of the Word with the large crowd of black and white friends who gathered, and rejoiced that the end of his earthly ministry came just as he would have wished.

When it is finished

Lord when Thou seest that my work is done
Let me not linger on with failing powers
*   Adown the weary hours*
A worthless worker in a world of work
*   But with a word just call me home*
*   And I will come.*

So quoted William Burton several years before, and this is a reproduction of the verse he kept pinned over his desk. And as he wished it, so it was. Active to the end, a worthy worker in a world of work; then God called him. He hadn't far to go, for he always lived in His presence, but the time had come for the tired body to be put aside, that he might serve Him in spirit.

17

The Congo Evangelistic Mission

The CEM was often referred to as 'Burton's Mission'. He deprecated this, but as he stood head and shoulders above the rest it was inevitable that such an expression should be used. He always gave others the maximum of praise, at times to their embarrassment. Once when taking over some office from another brother during the latter's furlough he said, 'I can never fill Brother X's shoes but I'll do my best to rattle around in them!' No-one was deceived.

His greatest influence was, of course, on the Congolese Church itself, called 'The Pentecostal Community of Congo', an indigenous church, whose first member was saved in December 1915, which had 985 assemblies when he left the Field in 1960 and now in 1973 has snowballed to over 2,100 assemblies. The faithful sowing has brought forth an abundant harvest. Throughout his long years on the Field – 1915 to 1960 – except for furloughs, his base was at Mwanza, so naturally his influence is most clearly seen there and in the 60 or more assemblies of the area.

I have two letters that were written to him by the elders of the Mwanza district, men who were won by him to Christ, trained by him and now doing the work that he once did. One was written on 10th April 1964: 'We can never forget you; day and night we mention your name and the great work you did among us in the Lord. We are your field that you have cultivated and today there is fruit in abundance. You planted during your 45 years amongst us and we water but God gives the increase. We don't know where you are just now but we pray that God will bless you and bless the work that you began in Congo. God be praised. Many people are now coming from far beyond our borders to seek the baptism of the Holy Spirit so we are able to help them and pray with them.'

The second was signed by eight senior overseers of the district and written on February 23rd 1968. Here are some extracts: 'We want to tell you how God is blessing the work you left behind among the Baluba and Basongye peoples. Many are being saved, many filled with the Holy Spirit and many healed in the Name of the Lord Jesus. We thank God and the church at Preston for sending you to give us the Gospel and especially for giving us the priceless Book of God. We want God's children over there to continue to pray for us that the Word of the Lord shall have free course everywhere and that the Holy Spirit will work yet more signs and wonders in our land. We have just had a great gathering which was attended by all the Chiefs in the Territory and several government officials to celebrate the 50 years since you started the work, and God gave us a tremendous blessing.'

After many details of the development of the work they add: 'We should like you to come back again to Mwanza to complete your work on earth so that we could bury you alongside Mrs Burton. If we could see again the face of Kapamu-husband-of-Kyamutala our tears would turn to joy. We should love to hear you preach again.'

When the news of his translation to glory filtered through, great memorial services were held in various parts of the Field. There are no longer any missionaries at Mwanza, or at most of our stations, so the memorial service there was arranged entirely by the brethren who wrote the above letters; two or three of our missionaries made the 250 mile journey from Kamina to Mwanza for the occasion.

A crowd of 3,500 people gathered under the huge mango trees on Mwanza Mission hill, exactly where Burton and Salter pitched their tent on September 1st 1915. They came to remember Kapamu, a beloved leader and friend. Various veteran preachers spoke of the first time they saw him and how they were saved. Next a troop of old ladies came forward, wives and widows of pastors, and one-time girls of Mrs Burton's rescue home. Then a man came carrying a brick and brick-mould, followed by two sawyers, a long pit-saw across their shoulders, then two carpenters with their tools and basket-workers with a cane chair, and finally women with plaited strands of papyrus reed, showing how they made mats and carpets. All these were believers who had been taught by Mr and Mrs Burton and who, in their turn, now taught others.

A pastor announced, 'All these useful crafts were taught us by our own Kapamu – they were unknown before he came – but the very best thing he taught us was the Word of God. Let us hold up our Bibles and sing "Lama Mukanda".' And so, their arms aloft, holding the precious book, the great crowd sang 'Cling to the Bible, tho' all else be taken... ' with increasing fervour, over and over again, finishing with a tremendous shout of 'Hallelujah! Hallelujah!' Here was a completely indigenous church raised to the glory of God. Fifty-six years before not one of them had heard of Jesus; now they were mature, independent Christians, and this vast crowd was but a small section of an ever-growing movement of Bible-loving, God-fearing believers that has doubled during the last ten years.

18

The mission he helped found

It is perhaps appropriate, as we have marvelled at the life and work of an outstanding missionary and man of God, to glance back and see him in the wider context of the mission with which he was associated.

The official name of the Mission, until 1919, was registered as 'The Pentecostal Mission', and was part of the 'South and Central Africa Pentecostal Mission'.

William Burton and James Salter had come to Congo in 1915 together with two of 'The Pentecostal Mission' workers. Despite this association they maintained their personal liberty and the right to trust God for their own support. Their plan was to help found the Pentecostal Mission work at Mwanza, then to move out to some other equally needy area to found their own work and apply for separate Government recognition, while retaining the bonds of close fellowship and mutual assistance.

However, seeing that George Armstrong died before reaching their destination, and Joseph Blakeney, the official 'Legal Representative', returned home a month after the party arrived at Mwanza, William Burton as deputy leader (*représentant légal suppléant*), was obliged by law to be responsible for the work and fulfil the obligations imposed by the conditions of the Mission's acceptance; hence he automatically became the recognised director. He and James Salter were willing to continue in this way until the Pentecostal Mission could send a suitable and qualified man to take charge. To this, George Bowie, leader of the South and Central Africa Mission, fully agreed, though no man of this calibre was ever available. Ladies were sent to help and did a wonderful job, but usually had to leave through ill health after a limited period of service.

The Apostolic Faith Mission, a large denomination in South Africa, came into being in 1910, chiefly through the ministry of John G. Lake and Brother Bryant of the United States and their own Jack Armstrong, son of 'Daddy' Armstrong. This movement gradually absorbed much of the American work, while becoming more national in character.

They supplied many of our early missionaries, and the CEM can never forget how much it owes to South African leaders in its formation. Revered names spring to mind: 'Father' Le Roux, Dugmore, Welsh, Hooper, Beetje, to mention but a few, and later Brothers Vermeulen and David DuPlessis.

Soon after the AFM was formed, the Full Gospel Church of South Africa was created and Archibald Cooper, an Englishman who became its leader, was a great friend of William Burton and the CEM. This Church also supplied valued workers to the Congo Mission.

Interest was widening in the Congo venture, particularly in the British Isles but also in other parts of the world, resulting from Burton and Salter's newsletters. When William Burton went to South Africa in 1918 to recruit more workers, a meeting of the Pentecostal Mission was held in Pretoria at which the leaders discussed missionary policy. They turned over all their interests and claims in the Congo work to him and, while remaining in fellowship, recognised him as the Director of that Field. For his part, Burton offered to pay a sum to them personally *in lieu of debit accounts* but the brethren generously declined to accept this.

By this time the Pentecostal Movement was spreading rapidly in the British Isles. The assemblies for the most part were independent churches, missions and house meetings, maintaining fellowship together mainly by means of great conventions held in Sunderland, London, Bradford and other centres. Some assemblies grouped together under the title 'Church of God', while in Ireland, George Jeffreys had formed the 'Elim Evangelistic Band' in Monaghan, Northern Ireland in January 1915, at first purely for evangelism and the spread of the Full Gospel. James Salter was with them in those early days before sailing for Africa.

These conventions were tremendous times of fellowship and ministry. People travelled great distances from all over the British Isles to receive blessing and to take it back with them to their scattered assemblies. They slept and ate anywhere and anyhow – anything rather than miss the glorious fellowship. Hospitable believers received the visitors with open arms and hallelujahs and packed them in, like sardines in a tin, turning none away. Women filled the bedrooms and men slept downstairs on the floors; all helped happily in the work so that as many as possible could get to the meetings.

The Annual Whitsuntide Convention had moved from All Saints Church, Sunderland to Kingsway Hall, London during World War 1. James Salter was in England just in time for the Wigglesworth Easter Convention at the northern centre of Bradford. He then went on to London for the Whitsuntide Convention and, concerning this, Donald Gee writes in *'The Pentecostal Movement'*.

'The outstanding memory of Kingsway 1919 was the missionary

message of James Salter, just home from the Congo for his first furlough. For nearly two hours he held the great audience spellbound as this large British congregation heard the thrilling story of how God had worked with William Burton and himself in establishing the church at Mwanza.'

'I can see Brother Salter now,' he continues, 'a slight figure, standing almost motionless while speaking, and gripping the audience in rapt attention by the sheer dynamic of his personality and his witness to the unchanging Christ.' He told how, after burying "Daddy" Armstrong, the steamer was kept waiting because it was expected every minute that he would die also, and be buried in the same grave, but God raised him up. Six times he was raised from a deathbed. On the last occasion a sheet was laid over him, and he was left for dead. A faithful Christian sobbed his heart out at his side in fervent prayer. The sheet moved, and James Salter was able to start his convention on time!

'We could have listened for hours! No wonder that young men and women all over the land felt a longing desire to join the intrepid couple, and the British Pentecostal Movement took the Congo Evangelistic Mission to its heart forthwith, and the convention made an indelible impression on many lives.'

The Congo work was now fully accepted in all British Pentecostal circles because something had been accomplished. Those young men had proved themselves and had suffered to found a church to the glory of God.

Donald Gee adds that later on there arose an insistent urge to adopt some form of distinctively Pentecostal organisation and that, as regards missionary work, this was seen in the Congo Evangelistic Mission. Furthermore, he states, in 1922 steps were taken tentatively towards an organised fellowship. He adds, 'W. F. P. Burton was home for his first furlough from the Congo in 1922, and his itineraries revealed to him the widespread need and desire. Before returning to the Field he used his influence to secure the necessary preliminary steps.' Eventually the Assemblies of God of Great Britain and Ireland came into being in 1924 through the leadership of J. N. Parr and A. H. Carter and later, when James Salter was the CEM Home Director, he was several times elected chairman of the conference, and for years was a member of the Executive Council of the Assemblies of God.

We may have been 'organised' but not in the sense of being directed and controlled on the Field by a Home Council whose members lived thousands of miles away. Such a system was felt to be unscriptural. Our founders felt that the Field should be run by its own missionaries, senior and experienced brethren holding executive office. A Home Council was, at the same time, essential for help in the propagation of news among the praying assemblies, for the interviewing and recommending of possible missionary candidates, and for dealing with financial matters and comity with other groups. The Mission would look to God for the supply of all its needs. We were from the beginning, and still remain, entirely a Faith Mission with no guaranteed income, and up to this present moment the Lord has met our needs according to His promises. Donald Gee writes 'There has always been something delightfully scriptural about the relationship with the home assembly at Preston from which these servants of God went forth "being recommended by the brethren unto the grace of God".' Every successive CEM Home Office Secretary and Treasurer has been an active member of this church, the first, Thomas Myerscough (till his death in 1932) and the present one, Thomas A. Billsborough, being pastors. The Myerscough family, Thomas, Philip and Edith, and later J. W. Jolly, P. Heaton and J. D. Parker have done yeoman service in this office.

In line with all this, and with the formal separation of the Congo work from the Pentecostal Mission, William Burton asked James Salter to form a Home Council in England, not to control but to be a Reference and Advisory Committee. This communication reached James Salter during that Whitsuntide Convention in London in 1919. Well, no time like the present! Most of the British Pentecostal leaders were right there on the platform, and at his request several of them agreed wholeheartedly to serve, and did so with conspicuous ability, usually till death or old age.

This Advisory Committee included: Thomas Myerscough who was already acting as distributor of newsletters and forwarder of funds, and considered by both Burton and Salter to be their 'father in God'. Joseph Walshaw, a Halifax solicitor, was named President. He was a remarkable figure with flowing white hair and long white beard which likened him to 'Moses' or 'Elijah'. His wife, 'Granny Walshaw', a renowned Bible teacher, was also included in the number as was John Nelson Parr, personal friend of Willie Burton and founder of Bethshan Tabernacle in Manchester. Finally, there was E. W. Moser, the well-known Bible teacher from Southsea. Later George Jeffreys, founder of the Elim Movement, F. Watson, Tom Mercy, T. J. Jones and George Atkinson served for many years. As these have gone to be with the Lord, other equally valued brethren have always been willing to fill their places. In addition Home Reference Councils were formed in New Zealand and Australia while the Executive Councils of the AOG of France and Belgium and of the FGC and the AFM of South Africa, acted in this capacity.

When the Burtons returned to the Field, after furlough, in 1922, James Salter assumed the Home Directorship of the rapidly expanding Congo Evangelistic Mission on a permanent basis but with regular, and sometimes extended, visits to the Field. William Burton continued as Field Director. Mrs Salter, a most active and practical firebrand, was Alice Wigglesworth, daughter of evangelist Smith Wigglesworth. As a young woman, she had been a missionary with the Stober Mission in Northern Angola, then married the Rev. S. Smith, the British and Foreign Bible Society's representative for South America and worked with him in that continent till he died. She was a wonderful recruiter of young missionaries and was always full of practical advice when they sailed from England's shores. She was a dynamic speaker in missionary meetings, blending pawky humour with spiritual challenge. She loved every missionary and they loved her.

The Mission gradually began to arouse worldwide interest and the Salters often accompanied Smith Wigglesworth on his overseas campaigns. With him they visited the United States on several occasions and also Canada, New Zealand, Australia, South Africa, Scandinavia and many European countries. Among the 181 missionaries who have served us in Congo for varying periods up to 1972 we have had workers from England, Scotland, Ireland, Wales, America, Canada, Switzerland, South Africa, Rhodesia (Zimbabwe), New Zealand, Australia, Holland and Germany.

William F.P. Burton has run his race, he has finished the course with great honour and acclaim as a faithful servant of the Lord Jesus Christ, but in addition to that, he has left behind him a vast number of men and women, boys and girls who on that day will rise up and call him blessed.

Missionary Pioneering
in Congo Forests

1
My conversion and call to Africa

Both my Father, Mother, and their parents before them, were children of God through faith in Christ Jesus. From them and from my uncles and aunts, as well as from the children of God who visited the home, we constantly heard the gospel, so that I cannot ever remember a time when I did not know God's plan of salvation. As soon as we could understand what was said to us, my two brothers, two sisters, and I were gathered about Mother's knee for prayer at night and in the morning. Sunday was a special day. Always called 'Holy, happy Sunday' (despite the fact that, on that day, we had cold meals so far as possible, to enable the servants to attend a place of worship, if they would). Mother did her best to make us enjoy the day. At tea table we would go round the table with an alphabet of gospel texts. The first would say A – 'All we like sheep have gone astray, etc.' Then the next would take it up, B – 'Behold the Lamb of God who takes away the sin of the world.' And so on to Z. We were encouraged to vary the texts. But X always had to be 'Except a man is born again, he cannot see the Kingdom of God.' And Z was always either 'Zaccheus, come down' or 'Zealous of good works.'

Father was in command of a vessel which went around the world every voyage. Often we would see him only for two or three weeks in five or six months; but on Sunday evening, punctually at 6 p.m., was 'the time of father's prayer.' Mother then gathered us together, and reminded us that, wherever father was, on land or sea, and whether the time might be night or day, at the place that he was in, corresponding to 6 p.m. in England, father was with us in spirit at our Heavenly Father's footstool. And there, in front of each other, we were encouraged to pray just what was in our hearts, and knew that father was praying too.

Often when my mother was asked to go off to some convention, or to take part in some mission, she would reply: 'No, God has given me a sacred charge in my five children. They are five bright little arrows to be shot out into the world for His glory, and I must not neglect them for what lies farther afield.' Or she would quote the passage in 1 Kings 20, 39-40, where the prisoner was allowed to escape 'While thy servant was busy here and there.' Mother would remark: 'I am not going to be busy here and there, and let the precious children whom God has given me be neglected and go to hell.'

When I was still a wee boy of three or four years, a Christian lady visiting our home in Redhill, Surrey, brought a missionary picture book, showing Mtesa, and details of Bishop Hannington's labours in Uganda. As a result, from that day forward I would always say, when asked what I was going to be when I grew up, 'I'm going to be a missionary.'

My mother and grandmother delighted to have God's children in their homes, and an event of importance was the coming to my grand-mother's house of an old African, named Thomas L. Johnson, who had been a slave in USA from birth till 28 years old, but who afterwards became an evangelist.

Old Bro. Johnson had been poorly and so we had the joy of nurs-ing him up and entertaining him. Though at first afraid of this black man, I soon grew to love him, and cried bitterly when he left. I cannot have been older than six, but I well remember the old fellow placing his hands on my head, and asking God to send me to his people in Africa.

It was clearly in mother's mind that I should one day be in the far off wilds. She referred to it frequently, and made arrangements for us to go to a carpenter's shop during holidays, to learn the use of tools. She loved to have our minds stored with scripture, saying: 'One day you may be lying sick and too weak to read, so hide God's word in your hearts.' After much prayer mother selected a set of scriptures to link with the name of each of her children. My texts were:

W   'Whosoever will, let him take of the water of life, freely.'
I   'I am the way, the truth, and the life; no man comes
      to the Father but by Me.'
L   'Looking unto Jesus.'
L   'Looking for that blessed Hope.'
I   'I am with you always, even unto the end of the world.'
E   'Endure hardness as a good soldier of Jesus Christ.'

Another incident which early showed God's plan for my life occurred in New Zealand where I was staying for some months with an uncle, who was a doctor, when I was 14 years of age. My uncle and I one day walked out into the country to attend to a godly old farmer who was suffering from cancer in the lip. After the visit, the old man walked down to his farm gate with us and, in saying goodbye, laid his hand upon my head and prayed, 'Lord, save this lad's soul, and send him out to preach Thy gospel.' Then after a pause he added: 'And I have a strong presentiment that it will be in Africa.'

At 17 I went into work as an electrical engineer, and soon got into sin and sadness. However, conviction deepened, and I knew my need of a Saviour, so that it was only lack of decision which prevented my taking the step then of receiving God's salvation.

In those days God's ministers more often preached the pure full gospel than today. I knew well the truth of the Lord's coming to call away His saints, and of the eternal doom in hell awaiting the impenitent. Thus I would awake in terror at night and, hearing all things so still, would fear that the rest of the family had been caught up and that I had been left to a Christless eternity.

I would be much relieved an hour or two later to hear a cough or someone getting up, and to feel that so far I was safe. Or again, sometimes I was afraid to sleep at night, knowing that if I died before morning I would open my eyes in the flames of hell. At last, when I was 19 years old, about August 3rd, 1905, I knelt in the afternoon by my own bedside in Batley, Yorkshire (where I was working on tramway construction), and claimed the promises in John 1, 12; Rom. 10, 13; John 6, 37. Well do I remember the prayer which I prayed: 'I am only a lost undeserving sinner, O God, but I take the Lord Jesus to be my Saviour, and please take me to be Your servant. I ask this in Jesus' Name.'

If I had died as I knelt down by my bed I should have dropped straight into hell, but I arose from my knees saved, rejoicing and on my way to glory.

I immediately got into touch with some of the African missionary societies and began to learn all I could of Central Africa. Also an evangelist, James Gilchrist much helped to confirm my faith in God's Word.

Having obeyed God's word in baptism, I at once united with a company of people who acknowledge one Head – the Lord Jesus – and who desire to be known by no other name than those given in the Bible: Christians, brethren, children of God, saints, believers, etc.

For eight years after this I could not consider leaving for the foreign field as I had a sister and an invalid mother who might be dependent upon me, as well as a father whose health was failing. 'If any provide not for his own, and especially for those of his own house, he is worse than an infidel, and has denied the faith' (1 Tim. 5, 8).

It was very tender of our heavenly Father to allow this consideration to keep me at home, and to make me at this time so hungry for something – I did not know what. The Scripture said: 'You shall receive power after the Holy Spirit has come upon you' – and I searched for that power with insatiable longing at Keswick Conventions, at 'Holiness Meetings', etc. until at last God satisfied me in February 1911, by enduing me with power from on high, when He poured out upon me His Holy Spirit, and I praised His exalted Son, the Lord Jesus, in a new tongue, which I had never learned.

I also praise God for putting me in touch at this time with our beloved Brother Mr Myerscough, of Preston, at whose feet I, with many more young fellows, was privileged to sit. For five years continuously, and then intermittently ever since, he has helped to build me up and confirm me in God's word; and from the little company at Preston missionaries have gone out to North and South America, Australia, India, China, and Japan, to many parts of Africa, and to several countries of Europe – filled with the Holy Spirit, and preaching the whole gospel, healing the sick, and glorifying the Name of Jesus. As it was with Paul and Timothy (Phil. 2, 22), so it was with Bro. Myerscough and myself. As a son with the father, I was permitted to serve with him in the gospel.

I remember – while I was still working at electrical engineering and enjoying evenings of Bible study with Mr Myerscough – stopping one day in the street and talking over the future with a young Christian lad. I said to him: 'Jimmy, did you ever think of God's command to go into all the world and preach the gospel to every creature? And did you ever consider Africa's need of the gospel message?' Little did I think that this would be my faithful companion some years later in the heart of the Congo forests. We have lived together, preached and studied and prayed together, worked and tramped and camped together; in tropical blazing sun, and tropical torrential rain Bro. Jimmy Salter has been by my side. I have nursed him back from the gates of death with fever, and he has done the same for me. We have shared our last meal together, and our last franc piece – not knowing where the next would come from. He has been my counsellor in perplexity, and my comfort in trouble. And I can never sufficiently thank God for calling so loyal and consistent a Christian friend to my side as a result of that chat that day in the street at Preston.

During the time of waiting, the impression became more and more strong that the door was about to open, allowing me to step forth into Central Africa. Often in the night, in my own room, my pleadings in the Spirit for the heathen became almost intolerable. Sometimes a sad African, with a yearning look and a white growth over one eye, drew near my bed as I lay longing and praying. He gazed so long at me and looked so beseechingly that I could not mistake the meaning of the vision. At a later date I saw this very man in the flesh, sitting listening in one of our meetings in Africa.

At last on June 5th, 1914, God took away the last remaining barrier, and I was able to sail for Africa with a heart filled with joy. It was still, however, to be a year before our beloved Brother Salter came out to join me. How can I sufficiently praise God for the waiting time?

We in England know very little of the problems of mission work. But in South Africa I was privileged to have the help and advice of a fine company of Spirit-filled men and women, who had been born and brought up among Africans, and whose zeal and love was matured and balanced by a rich fund of experience and insight into their character. Thus I am sure that our Congo work was saved many mistakes and difficulties through the advice of Bros. Dugmore, Le Roux and others.

Then when our beloved Bro. Salter arrived, and all the necessary outfit was ready, we travelled northwards and stepped on to Congo soil, in Jesus' Name, on July 1st, 1915.

2
A year in South Africa
Outward bound – Basutoland-Johannesburg

Notes from an address by Mr W. F. P. Burton in Sion College, Thames Embankment, London, on the evening of March 14th, 1921, shortly after the return of the Missionaries to England from Africa, after Mr Burton's absence from the homeland for nearly seven years.

"I would like you to see me starting off from Fenchurch Street Station. There were several dear Christian people to see me off. I got into the carriage, and nobody else got into the same compartment, and all the way down the river I was able to have a compartment to myself for prayer, and from that time onward I was never left alone by the royal escort all the way to the Congo. My Heavenly Father sent His angels to look after me every step of the journey, and at every turn I met other Christians.

I got on board the ship – all absolute strangers – did not know a soul – but before we had been there many minutes a lady sat down at the piano and began to play a gospel hymn. It was her little testimony to show that at least one on board was a Christian, and a group soon gathered round her. We shook hands all round, but we did not discover one brother who was on board. When we got further out our numbers decreased; one after another turned pale and went down. Of course, I am an old sailor, so I did not get seasick.

The next morning it was very rough. I got up early and went on deck before the rest of the people were about, and I thought I would have a nice little time alone with God before anyone saw me. I was strolling up and down the deck singing a hymn, and I think it was 'I shall know Him, I shall know Him,' when who should lurch up against me but a big dark man I had seen sprawled across the deck the night before – sick. I could see that he was fearfully ill, and he said in a broad Scotch accent: 'Is that true what you are singing?'

I said: 'Praise God, I shall know Him'; and he said: 'So shall I,' and we shook hands with one another. I said: 'Brother what about this, don't you know the Lord healed our infirmities and carried our sicknesses? Come along down to the cabin, and let us have a word of prayer.'

So we went and had a word of prayer, and before we had said 'Amen' the seasickness had gone; and although we had rough weather afterwards he was never sick again. He belongs to a company of people who were strongly opposed to the teaching of Divine healing, but wherever he goes he testifies to how the Lord took away his sea-sickness in answer to prayer.

Well, we had a pleasant little time. The Captain was good; he permitted us to hold our open-air meetings (or open-sea meetings) every night of the voyage, excepting one, just where the first, second, and third classes could all hear, and it was not long before one or two souls were converted.

One after another the Christians on board would come up and ask us to pray for another, until, before the voyage was over, we wished it could be longer.

We were gathered on the last Sunday to break bread, and one man wanted to be baptised. This was on the vessel going as far as Cape Town, and there I changed ships, and went on to another vessel going to Durban, and it was not very long after the vessel sailed when we went down to have a meal, and I noticed a lady opposite me bow her head and say grace. I found her to be a bright Christian; we also found one or two others.

There I set foot in a strange land in the Name of the Lord, and started for Johannesburg, and in the train, in the same compartment as myself among other passengers, there was a blaspheming, cursing, godless actor, and every sentence or two he would come out with an oath, and take the Name of Jesus in vain, and it hurt me so that I said to him: 'My friend, supposing someone should insult your mother, what would you do?' He said: 'I would hit him.' Then I said: 'Do you know you are insulting One who is much dearer to me than my mother?' and he said: 'I beg your pardon, sir,' and ceased doing it. I noticed an old man sitting over in the corner, and he nodded to me. I thought – another of them. We shook hands, and I found him to be a dear brother in the Lord, and he travelled with me as far as Johannesburg where I had friends to meet me at the station.

My Heavenly Father sent His children to accompany me all the way. I do praise God for a year in South Africa before we set out for the Congo. During that time we were able to minister to the Dutch, English and Basuto people."

Bro. Burton spent three months in Basutoland among the people there. He was not able to speak much of the language, but can point to one soul who professed conversion. In a Basuto village there was a farmer's wife who could speak both English and Sesuto, and since he could not speak the Sesuto language he asked her to interpret for him, which she did. Seeing a woman with a little baby on her back he took her as an illustration and talked of Hagar and the way she was driven out by Abraham, with Ishmael on her back. She started out for an unknown land, when God revealed to her the well of living water. A few days later, quite a distance from that village, when wandering on the hill with a precipice below, a man called up and said: 'I heard what you said, and was interested; and God has shown me Jesus, the well of Living Water – and so you can imagine how happy I am.'

The following letter from Johannesburg, Transvaal, is addressed to Mr Thomas Myerscough, of Preston, Lancs:

"God is still proving Himself in a most wonderful way the God of Deliverances to me. I believe that I told you they were anxious to detain me in Basutoland (today's Lesotho), but that had I remained two days longer I would have been taken prisoner by De Wet, who stopped the train following the one in which I travelled.

Of course there is any amount of work to be done. I often give three or four Bible readings a day: one every morning at 8 a.m. at Jeppe, for the workers, in which I take up more advanced subjects. Last night there were 30 present. I am living in daily hope that things may sufficiently settle for me to move off again among the local people. Yesterday afternoon one of the evangelists came along to the house to have a talk about church authority. Apparently he has had some difficulty with his flock; but at the Leribe Conference I had a long talk with him on law and grace, with the result that recently he has been experiencing a wonderful revival. A large number of this man Elias's converts speak in tongues as they come out of the water, and I believe that they genuinely receive the Holy Spirit. They want to be and do right, but lack steadfastness and aim. A Brother Oldfield some time ago was sent to write a report against this work, but was convinced of its heavenly origin, filled with the Spirit, and is now very hungry for the Word.

I am making some headway with the Zulu language though not perhaps as accurately as the Sesuto language, for I have not the same opportunities for continual intercourse with the people here. Moreover, the Zulu spoken is not pure but what is known as 'Fanikalo.' However, I have been invited to a Zulu mission station on the border of Swaziland. This will be a blessed experience for me, as I understand the newcomer makes a lot of bungles, which are apt to cause much trouble afterwards. Consequently it will be better to gain experience from other people's bungles than from my own. News is to hand of about 300 African believers in Gazaland, which is inland from Inhambane, Portuguese East Africa (Mozambique today). A few were converted at the mines (Shangan speaking people) and have gone back to their people with the Gospel message. They have now sent a message to ask for a white teacher. It would be a very difficult task to tackle, as the Ethiopian spirit (which at the time proposed a teaching of 'Africa for the black man') invariably creeps into unsupervised evangelism, and consequently the missionary would be expected to shoulder all responsibility but to exercise no authority.

I possess a photo of a leg on which sores had been running for 13 years. Professor Koch – a man of international repute – said they were caused by taking quinine and never could be healed. The quinine problem is a tremendous one, and none but those who have been on the field can understand its seriousness. The Angola Mission point to twelve graves of those who refused quinine. The Apostolic Faith and Pentecostal Mission have 33 graves of splendid men and women who refused quinine and died. One recognises its evil effect. Yet I am confident we must maintain an open mind with regard to this subject. God, however, healed the leg at once in answer to prayer, and the black marks are just scars. A woman came to the house last night, a nine years' martyr to rheumatism, but was straightened out before she left the house. Yesterday, a Rhodesian (today's Zimbabwe), from 140 miles north of Salisbury (Harare today) came for prayer for bad eyes – combined effect of malaria and quinine. He said his eyes were much better, though not quite right, when he left the building. I had a nice little open-air service with boys and girls last night, including a lot of little Jews and Jewesses, who soon learnt 'The blood of Jesus Christ, God's Son, cleanses us from all sin.' "

From Basutoland (Lesotho today):

"I am getting on much better with the language than at first. As I feel I am not getting enough conversation and as I have no one to help me, I must speak my needs in Sesuto or else go without. Oh, what a crowd I had this afternoon. I picked up a cheap banjo in Johannesburg, and feeling a wee bit lonely, I took it up on to the rocks, and had a little strum. A great part of the village turned out to listen. I long for the day when I shall be able to translate some of our old Preston favourite hymns into Sesuto.

I was at a heathen graveside the other day and it was terrible. The relations were frantic – almost drunken – with grief. One cannot wonder at it, for they know nothing of resurrection. The little piles of stones below each village tell of those for whom we are already too late, and every extra month that I take in mastering Sesuto, is adding to the number. They have a vague idea of something after death, but cannot tell what.

The night before last, the war summons was shouted from village to village around the hills, and several thousand assegai-armed horsemen went off post-haste to the capital. Apparently four of the chief's grandchildren had been killed, and certain parts of the entrails extracted for wizards to make 'medicine', i.e. charms, with. The murderers were surprised in the act of burning the rest of the bodies over a fire. Some days ago a woman was missing at Thaba Bosiu (some distance to the south) and after a long search they found her blanket with a few cut up parts of a woman's body in a wizard's cave, up the mountain side. Yet so great is the dread of these wizards and so terrible are their threats that they are not always brought to book."

From Johannesburg:

"I had last week one of the narrowest escapes from a frightful accident. A Christian 'Compound Manager' on one of the mines was anxious that I should have a talk with a doctor, and so made up a party to go down a gold mine at Benoni (about 30 miles away). Hearing that the doctor was interesting when discoursing on geology, I got him to discuss the mineral of the reef. I was examining the face of the rock with a naked acetylene flame, when suddenly a black man shouted and snatched me back. My lamp flame was only two inches from the end of a fuse attached to a heavy charge of dynamite which had been placed in a big hole drilled in the rock, and had failed to explode on the previous shift. Another two inches, and it would only have taken a second or so to turn us all into mangled corpses.

I need scarcely say that this afforded an excellent opportunity for speaking of Christ's power to deliver. The doctor's wife came from somewhere between 'Withy Trees' Preston and Broughton. She had heard me preach on Preston Market, and could recall what was said. Little did we imagine that our Preston testimony was reaching the remotest corner of Witwaterstrand Gold Reef. They were all evidently very much affected but tried to laugh it off. A man was saved the night before last in the open air, and a woman in a little mission last night. We are now having a Bible reading at 6 a.m. We have been going through the Levitical offerings, and had a most delightful time this morning on the 'Sin Offering'.

April 11th, 1915. We have just come to the last night of a most glorious Convention. At least 40 or 50 have been filled with the Holy Spirit, scores have been saved and healed and baptised in water. In the midst of this, however, my head is heavy and my heart also, and it is as though

Congo pioneer: William F. P. Burton

Right: William Burton and his beloved wife, Hettie, during their first furlough in England, 1921.

Below: Burton on the rock at Kayembe Hill, Mwanza, where he and James Salter used to pray for the villages across the plains below.

Above: The first four pioneers – *(left to right)* James Salter, William Burton, George 'Daddy' Armstrong and Joseph Blakeney.

Below: Burton with a warthog's head – part of the 'Pentecostal Pork Shop'.

Above: Burton and Salter overseeing the loading of goods into their boat as they journeyed up the Congo River.

Below: The funeral of 'Daddy' Armstrong. James Salter was so ill at the time that the grave was left open as he was also near to death.

Above: Five early evangelists; Abraham Nyuki, the very first convert, is 2nd from the right.

Left: Abraham Nyuki *(right)* at 70 years of age, with one of his first converts, Beseka Yumba, the then President of the Pentecostal Church in Congo.

Left:
A Luba
witchdoctor.

Right:
A secret society
dancer, hundreds
of whom have
been saved.

Above: Carpenters trained by the mission at work in Mwanza.

Below: Luba village life.

Right: Miniature huts were placed outside the door of a man's home to accommodate the spirits of his ancestors. A small fire would be lit and food placed in the doorway.

Below: Portable idols, objects of great respect, were often carried in procession around the chieftainships. They were given food and fire to keep them warm, and devotees would pray to them early each morning seeking protection and blessing for the day.

Above: Travelling between villages during the rainy season.

Below: Burton conducts an open air meeting under a wild fig tree.

Above: Early morning Bible study at Mwanza.

Below: William and Hettie Burton at their home in Mwanza.

The Missionaries in Conference at Kabongo in August 1954.

The Field Executive Council and the Home Director

Back row, l to r: C. Yesson, F. Ramsbottom and W. W. Hall.

Front row, l to r: H. Womersley, W. F. P. Burton, J. Salter (Home Director) and E. Hodgson.

Below: Mr and Mrs Salter and William Burton *(right)*.

Above: *(l to r)* Harold Womersley, James Salter and William Burton.

Below: *(l to r)* 'Teddy' Hodgson, William Burton and James Salter.

WILLIAM FREDERICK PADWICK BURTON

"PIONEER MISSIONARY"

FOUNDER-PIONEER OF THE
CONGO (ZAIRE) EVANGELISTIC MISSION

BORN ENGLAND 24TH MAR. 1886
DIED PRETORIA 23RD JAN. 1971

MARRIED TO HETTIE H. TROLLIP,
BEACONSFIELD FARM, CAPE.
23RD MAY 1918

GAVE A LONG AND USEFUL LIFE
FOR THE GOSPEL IN AFRICA.

"AN ABUNDANT ENTRANCE INTO THE
KINGDOM OF JESUS CHRIST."
2. PET. 1:11.

SUMMERLEE
PERCY BERNARD

Above:
William Burton

Below:
Burton went to be
with the Lord on
January 23rd 1971,
at the age of 84.

**Barium X-rays of William Burton's colon (large intestine)
before and after he was healed by God**

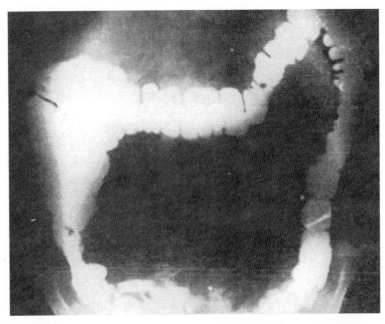

Above: Taken in 1944, showing the diseased colon constricted by cancer. Burton was given six months to live by doctors.

Below: Taken in 1947, showing the now healthy intestine.

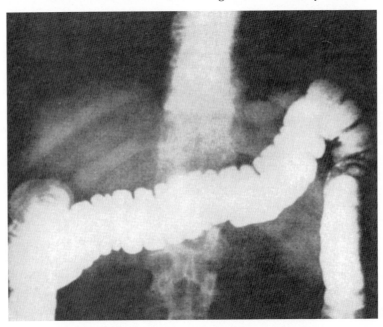

I were in a maze. With one and another I have been fighting the devil and malaria for days. Brother Oldfleld had a comparatively slight touch of malaria. But it struck him so suddenly that he dropped like a stone as he was crossing the veldt, and was very near meeting death by sunstroke. Brother Bowie, the leader of the Pentecostal Mission, is still between life and death, with a temperature of 104°F. A brilliant young schoolmaster, and one whom I love as my own soul, was also suddenly attacked with it. I helped his wife and sister to nurse him. We prayed and rebuked. We did all we could. I fed him, washed him, prayed – yes, fought in prayer – for hours, kept him in bed when he was delirious – spent nights and days, fanned him for hours; 600 or 800 Spirit-filled saints prayed for his deliverance, and then, O brother, I cannot unburden myself to many, but feel I can write to you. I have just come back from preaching the Gospel to the crowd gathered around his open grave. He was faithful to the end. He wouldn't touch a drop of anything medicinal. I and five other brothers carried him to his last resting-place, and I feel just heart-broken over it all. I feel it was all a horrible defeat.

He was whole-hearted, athletic, 27 years old. A brilliant interpreter of English and Dutch. He leaves a sweet little wife. They had intended to go out and preach Christ. I cannot believe God wished to take him home. I wrote Jimmy Salter (who later joined W. F. P. Burton in the Belgian Congo – today's Democratic Republic of Congo or DRC) a long letter about the fever, as I felt he should know what he is coming out to.

The 'Pentecostal Mission' death roll is terrible. Nine have recently died, refusing quinine to the last, and confident that God would raise them up. Four on one station in Swaziland since Miss Taylor died there. One man's temperature went up to 110°F, and his life practically burned out. Another faithful preacher is a delirious maniac in hospital, and his condition is most precarious. For myself, I would gladly go into any leprous fever stricken hole in the Name of Jesus; because 'greater is He that is in you than He that is in the world.' Brother, if the power of God was not upon me, I would acknowledge it, and humbly seek the cause of failure. But people are being continually saved and healed. The day before last a brother was seriously ill. I was directed to visit him, and rebuked the disease in the mighty Name of the Lord Jesus, and immediately he went off to sleep. Shortly afterwards he awoke completely healed.

The Lord has been kind enough to use these poor, weak, unworthy hands for the healing of numbers during the Convention. If I were allowing anything between myself and God, this would not be. But now these malaria victims are dying, and of course some of the Spirit-filled missionaries are taking quinine, and they don't die, and they ask me which gives God most glory? To take this stuff and live, or refuse it and die? They declare that man cannot live up north without the quinine. When I look at the little tabloids (which they use) I laugh, as I consider such a thought as that God is supposed to be unable or unwilling to support us without that. Also I would rather die than disgrace His cause. Death is nothing to me. I would like to be with Jesus. But then there are these millions of dark heathen who don't know Christ, and I must live to carry the Gospel to them. Also I have my companion to consider and I must not be careless about my life, and leave him in the lurch. I am certainly up against facts, and want God's glory only.

A large number of Dutch people have been at the Convention who couldn't speak English, so my Dutch has been very useful, and has quite won their hearts, though of course it is extremely poor and stumbling, and is much laughed at. Last night we had a glorious open-air meeting. The spot selected was near a railway station, and a considerable number of people were so gripped by the Word of God that they lost their trains. One woman came and testified that for four months she had been in constant pain, and the doctors said that the only possible hope of her recovery was a serious operation. But a few weeks ago she was instantly healed when we laid hands upon her in the Name of Jesus. We are also having blessed cottage meetings.

A woman in a suburb of Johannesburg was in a fearful condition with rheumatism, and unable to move her head or lower limbs. She was given my little tract on divine healing. She said: 'Lord, it is written 'He sent His word and healed them.' This is your Word. I take it for a poultice in the Name of Your Son Jesus the Christ.' And laying the tract upon her neck and limbs, she was immediately healed and filled with such an exuberance of life that she arose, dressed and went to lay hands upon a dying man next door, whereupon he also leaped up, healed and singing,

'Arise, my soul, shake off thy guilty fears,
The bleeding sacrifice on thy behalf appears.'

Yesterday, I was asked to visit a boy who was suffering agonies with a disease which attacks the faces of children here (A swelling of the eye, ear and throat glands). We prayed before I went, and when I got to the place, he was perfectly healed. The Lord Jesus had removed the disease at the time we prayed."

Shortly before his leaving Johannesburg for the Congo in a meeting, a woman came in with a little boy whose foot had been twisted since his birth, and he had to have a special boot for it. When Brothers Burton and Salter prayed for him, the Lord gave the assurance that he would put the foot right. Soon after, the little lad began to cry and say how painful his foot was. The boot had to be removed from the foot, because it was found to be the wrong shape for it. God healed the foot by taking the twist out of it, causing it to take the normal shape. The brothers were called to pray for a man in a dying condition, whom God at once healed, and today he is strong and well.

The last night before the Brothers left for the Congo, at the close of a meeting when coming out of the rooms, the lady of the house nodded towards a little bedroom and said: 'My daughter is in there. She can no longer go to school. She was at play with the children, and while crossing the street, a motorcar ran over her, and now she is crippled for life. The doctors offer her no hope.'

The little girl was fast asleep, but slipping into the room they asked God to heal her, and laid hands on her in Jesus' Name. They never heard of her again until a number of years afterwards, when Brother Burton was introduced to a fine, bonny looking young woman, and was asked: 'Do you know who this is? She is the girl who five and a half years ago was crippled, and you prayed for her; the next morning she got up strong and well, and as soon as her new clothes were ready she was able to go back to school.'

3

Pioneers in Mwanza

On the evening of June 30th, 1915, Brother Burton, in company with Joseph Blakeney, set out from Johannesburg to reach the Belgian Congo (today's DRC). Their objective was a district 20 miles west of the Congo River, 27 East Lat. 7.5 South. They were able to travel five days' journey to Elisabethville (today's Lubumbashi) by train. The other two members of the party were James Salter, lately arrived from Preston, England, and George Armstrong, a man in late middle life, a carpenter by trade, familiarly known by the younger brothers as 'Daddy Armstrong.' The two last mentioned started a week later than their brethren. Brother Blakeney's and Burton's object in going ahead of the other two was to see their goods safely through the railway and customs, and to attend to official business with the Belgian Administrators.

Living in Elisabethville was expensive, and thus considerable saving was effected by the other two members of the party following later and joining Brothers Blakeney and Burton at Kambove. As independent missionaries might expect difficulties in settling in the Belgian Congo, the party entered nominally under the Pentecostal Mission, which is incorporated in the Transvaal.

Several weeks before Brother Burton had started north from Johannesburg, he had set aside enough money to land him in the Congo. In an opportune time a substantial gift arrived from Preston, enabling him to purchase part of his outfit at a sale. The provisions taken included a supply of lentils, flour, Bovril, tinned butter and jam, etc. He also took with him a bicycle and a camera.

A letter to Preston runs thus:

"There were about 150 people on Johannesburg station to see us off, and such waving and cheering, crying and handshaking! I can see that we are up against some terrible problems, but I believe that God's Word has a solution to everyone and, if we walk in the Spirit, we shall be more than conquerors.

We shall be in wireless communication with the outside world through Kikondja.

Jimmy's ministry was evidently much appreciated in South Africa, and I am glad that he stayed a while there."

Elisabethville, July 11th, 1915:

"At last we are through our official business. It would take me a long time to record all the ins and outs of formality and regulation necessary, but suffice it to say that God gave us great favour with the Belgian Officials, Vice-Governor General and his Assistant Minister of Justice, State Secretary, Minister of Finance, and Minister of the Interior. We have had to make application for a legal representative, for legal recognition, for land, etc. The Belgians were very kind and as informal as possible. This morning the Minister of Justice and the Assistant to the Vice-Governor General, have been showing us round the Roman Catholic school of manual training.

We are guaranteed leave to settle at Mwanza Kajingu. We will be less than 50 miles from a store, 50 miles from the Belgian post at Kikondja, in a more or less healthy country, and the Governor General tells us that it is very thickly populated. There will be about 10,000 at our doors, i.e. within two miles, and nearly a quarter of a million unevangelised heathen within a radius of 37 miles. I am pleased to discover that through Kikondja we shall be able to maintain uninterrupted postal communication with the outside world: overland till the rains come, and then by river. There are many points to remember for missionaries starting work in this land, and we propose to keep these on record for future use. If we had bought our foodstuff here instead of getting it up from Johannesburg, we would have saved £2 10s. 0d. though possibly our supplies would not have been so fresh.

Hearing that an influential trader from up country was in Elisabethville, we went to ask his advice as to route, etc. He told us that two people groups were at war and that we should have to go half the journey by boat.

By way of showing us official favour, the Vice-Governor General presented us with a special permit to shoot all animals excepting elephants. This saves us £8 and gives us the privilege of a £15 licence each. Then the railway construction line for about 80 miles is now complete, and should have been handed over to the Government by the contractor last week but, owing to some hitch, it will not be handed over till next month. If it had been the Government's line, that journey, with our goods, would have cost us £15 and more. But the contractor's manager is in favour of foreign missions and is running our truck through free.

In this way God has set His seal on the start of the work up here in sunny Congo, and shown 'Wonders in the land of Ham.' By the above-mentioned items, and a few more of similar nature, we are now able to see our way paid through to the journey's end, and to hire into the bargain our cook for the journey. What a great loving God we have!"

Kambove, July 27th, 1915:

"Another hitch in our official business has just cropped up. It is very blessed to know, in these times of perplexity, that we are being upheld by a band of faithful worshippers at home and, better still, to know that our High Priest is in constant intercession."

Bukama, August 21st, 1915:

"Just about to take the boat down the Congo River. Life is so entirely different from that at home that it would be quite impossible to describe all the scenes, people, food, etc. But I can only emphasise that we have the very same Jesus. On the journey through, after leaving the railway, we tramped for eleven days through the forests, and two of our party got dysentery through drinking impure water, but God healed them in answer to prayer. Now just as we are about to start off down the river poor old 'Daddy' Armstrong has been attacked with malaria fever, but we have prayed for him, and he is much better than he was. When we arrived the officials told us that they couldn't take us in the boats as a lot of government goods are to be transported by boats; but at the last moment God has answered our prayers. Some of the government loads were delayed and we are able to move off after all.

Then we only had just money enough to pay our boat trip and land us at our destination. We needed both meat and meal for food, and also some condensed milk for 'Daddy' who is poorly. I took the rifle early yesterday morning and went off into the forest with Jimmy Salter to kill some meat. After tramping some miles I saw a move-ment in the thicket a long way off, and fired. Then seeing an animal move in the grass nearby I shot at it. When we ran up we found two big wild boars just kicking their last. These wild pigs are generally full of tapeworm, so I turned to Jimmy and said: 'What's the good of pig to us? We will leave them.' But on second thoughts we fetched local people to cut their heads off, clean them out, and bring them into camp. But God overruled our misfortune, for as soon as the pigs were carried in the Africans crowded along with meal, arrowroot, groundnuts, and money, asking for a bit of pig. So we set up a 'Pente-costal Pork Shop' and did a roaring trade till all the pig was exchanged for more wholesome food. Thus God provided us with meal, etc. Last night the lions were heard roaring for the first time."

Excerpts are given from a Report dated September 4th, 1915, printed in Johannesburg.

Mwanza Kajingu Mission, Kikondja, Katanga Province, Belgian Congo, 4th September, 1915:

"I have been nursing our beloved Jimmy in camp, in a dirty poky little village among the palms, swamps, and banana groves, about a day's march from the Congo River. You will grieve to hear that he is between life and death, right on the borderland. 'Daddy' Armstrong failed with malaria about a day's journey down the Congo from Bukama and, after a week's hard struggle, blackwater fever set in and he died in 18 hours.

We buried him there under a solitary palm, away among the marshes with no human being for 40 miles around: nothing but hyenas, elephants, and hippopotami and herds of waterbuck and buffalo. There was no wood for a coffin, so we sewed him in his blanket and covered him with a Union Jack while the boatmen dug his grave, and then they lowered him into it on their paddles. For the first few days Jimmy affectionately nursed 'Daddy.' I took night duty, as in the daytime I fed practically the ship's crew by shooting antelope. On the fifth day Jimmy also went down with fever. He is a most unselfish, contented, patient fellow to nurse.

After the service at the graveside Brother Blakeney also practically swooned, and was rowed back to the river steamer in a high fever. I could also feel it gripping me, for, of course, as night nurse I was constantly exposed to clouds of mosquitoes. But I continually cried to God, for I dared not permit the fever to master me since two other lives as well as my own were dependent on me. On arrival at Mulongo, Brother Blakeney was very weak, but there were white men who let us have eggs, tinned fruit, etc. We had been very short of nourishment. Also the chief 'Mafingi' sent along some vegetables and a goat to make broth. So Brother Blakeney pulled round and is now all right again. We had to bring Jimmy 22 miles in a machila, a sort of hammock with an awning over it. He seemed fit at the end of it, but the strain was evidently too much for him. He is now very weak, and with pulse down below 40 to the minute. I believe that God will raise him up. 'Jesus the same today.' He shows a remarkable gift for languages, and I think he catches the thoughts of the Baluba more quickly than I, and is most diligent in putting down words and phrases. Of course, Brother Blakeney's Zulu is a great help too, as there is a similarity in all these 'Bantu' languages.

Now as for our sphere and plan. A large part of the Congo is only sparsely inhabited. The tsetse fly 'palpale' spreads the sleeping sickness along the big lakes and watercourses, and so the only survivors are little isolated villages, practically unknown to the world outside. For the rest, the people have congregated around a few strong leaders. Mushidi's successor Mwenda is a capable, progressive man, whose sympathies are toward the Gospel, and the 'Brethren' have a large school and mission there at Bunkeya under Mr and Mrs Last. An earnest young man, Brother Zentler, of German extraction, had worked as a 'Brethren' missionary down there but, on pushing up here to evangelise, he came upon such great hordes of absolutely unevangelised heathen that he determined to settle among them, so he started to work at Mulongo, Mafingi's capital. It is only 22 miles from here. This was against the advice of the 'Brethren', as they consider it too far out of reach, and too unhealthy. But his work was owned of God. But being of German extraction he has been made a prisoner of war and taken to Stanleyville (today's Kisangani).

When we arrived at Mulongo a young man came to greet us, and brought about 20 bright lads and young men with him. He said that in the absence of Mr Zentler he was carrying on the work. An African missionary standing alone! The lads brought their books, and we found that they could read very creditably. He tells me that six of them gather round the Lord's Table every Sunday.

Now after an uninhabited belt of 20 miles from Mulongo a new chieftainship commences of which Kajingu, an old conservative simple man, is the chief, and Mwanza Kajingu is the chief's district. From here for miles in every direction one can see the huts, banana groves, etc. This people, however, is not progressive. Mafingi came to greet us in a neat cycle suit, and was an intelligent man; but old Kajingu came with just a piece of cloth round him, a hippo-tooth fetish round his neck, and his hair shaved, except for a pad at the back like old-fashioned ladies wear, done up with beads, and a pointed stick stuck in to scratch himself with when the flies tickle.

These people resist oversight and rule, and hate taxation, etc. When the Administrator came to collect the tax a few months ago, in a village a day's journey north of this, they would have surrounded him and killed him. He had to send a runner for help and fight his way through. The inhabitants are armed with spears, bows and arrows, and axes; and excepting for a few inches of cloth, skin, or beads, they are naked. The Baluba people have not an absolutely uniform language. There is no doubt, however, that the Luba-Sanga testament translated by Dan Crawford, and given us at Koni Hill, will be most useful. Now that Mr Zentler is at Stanleyville (Kisangani), Mr Dan Crawford, at least two or three weeks' journey away, is our nearest white Protestant missionary, so far as I can discover.

Mr Bowie and others took a trip through this land last year with a view to discovering the best spheres for mission work. At his instructions the people set to work to build a house for the white teachers. On arrival, however, we find that the only substantial thing about the house is the price we have to pay the labourers. The roof isn't watertight; one can see the sky through it. The walls are bulging into all sorts of shapes, only five inches thick, and so cracked that you couldn't find enough solid wall to lay this sheet of paper on. Many cracks show two inches of daylight through them. However, we quite expected to have to build a permanent house, and doubtless we can fix up the temporary one as a school or carpenter's shop. The old chief came to greet us yesterday. We told him our business, and so this morning he and his village came up to hear the words of life, and he has invited us to come to his village this afternoon to continue. Imagine how helpless we feel, only having been here one day.

Now as to our plans, they are vague. God said: 'Go into all the world,' and so we are going. Within about 37 miles we have approximately a quarter of a million souls without a pastor. I believe that this offers field enough for ten white missionaries and 30 African evangelists, but circumstances make me a little uncertain as to whether Jimmy and I should stay in another part of this district, or take up the central village in another of the almost equally thickly populated areas within a few days' travel from here.

The people are ready and open for the first thing that reaches them. If the Full Gospel, it is well; but, alas! Roman Catholicism has grasped some. Up here it is the barest idolatry, and not the half-disguised thing which one sees in civilised England and South Africa. Beloved, it lies with us, God's Spirit-filled children, to fill these villages with sound doctrine at once. A wide-open door awaits us, and I feel that no sacrifice is too great in order to bring the Gospel to those who sit in darkness. I believe that many have heard God's call to the Congo. Oh may they fulfil God's highest purpose for them."

The following notes have been preserved of a public address in London by Brother Burton, adding further details of the earliest experiences of life in Mwanza:

"The whole of the country is one vast forest. Here in England we are used to woods and in every one you can come out on the other side; but in the Congo there is no other side. Just forest, forest, day after day, as one journeys. But in many of these forests you find little clearings where the people build their huts and make their gardens.

The Baluba people have a signal drum and whatever news there is to tell is passed from village to village by means of it so that, long before we arrived, the news had come that the white man had come to bring the words of God, and immediately the drums began to beat. At first we did not know what this meant. I was the last to arrive, and there were the men beating on the drums and shouting their peculiar noise o-o-o-o-o-o.

How strange it was to see them crowding around us, quarrelling as to who should get near us and greet us first. A crowd of youngsters preceded the Chief, who welcomed us with profuse bows, bringing a present of fowls, bananas, eggs, sweet potatoes, etc.

On Sunday morning they came in crowds. I do not know how we managed to understand. With a lot of chatter in between, they 'signed' to us that they wanted to hear about the words of God; but we could only sing a hymn or two in a language that they could not understand. We felt from the first, if we could say nothing else, at least we could say the Name of Jesus.

Day by day we picked up more words, and kept putting them into use. We did not understand the construction of the language; we were strangers to that and everything else.

After a while the people were tired of bringing us presents, and we were pretty short of food, and we did not know what to do. We sent a messenger to the chief, but he wanted the food for himself and would not sell us any.

On the Sunday morning, Brother Salter said he had a word for the people and, as he had been making the language out, a bit at a time, he thought the people would understand it. I said: 'What are you going to preach about?' 'Well,' he said, 'the message on my heart is Pontius Pilate.'

I thought that was rather a difficult subject to take, but I let him go on, I thought – we will see what he makes of it.

The chief and his people were only too glad to gather together and offered us a drum to sit on. Brother Salter and I, after having sung a hymn, waited a minute, and then he started his sermon on Pontius Pilate. The word for chief or ruler is 'Mulopwe' and he wanted to tell them that Pontius Pilate was a bad ruler, so he said several times 'Chief-bad man' 'Mulopwe-muntu mubi.' Here was the chief sitting beside us, and Brother Salter was saying 'Chief bad man' meaning, of course, Pontius Pilate. When the chief of a village wants to show his displeasure he grinds his teeth, and he has a knack of grinding his teeth so that he makes quite a noise. I am sure the noise this chief made could have been heard by all present.

We came to the conclusion that Brother Salter had said quite enough to displease the old chief, so he finished his sermon, and we dismissed them; but I could afterwards see that God gave him the message on Pontius Pilate, as it did us a good turn.

The chief evidently gathered his people together, and they no doubt thought that Brother Salter had called him a bad man because he had not been doing his duty towards us, and so, shortly afterwards, up came chickens and goats and other presents: he was going to show us he wasn't such a bad man after all. So God takes even our mistakes and turns them to account.

Word by word we picked up the language and were able to say more to the people. I remember the first time I had a really good Gospel talk to a young man. We had been cutting down a tree for our house, and this fellow offered to help. I tried to tell him about the great and mighty God. I did not think that he understood very much, but I found out months afterwards that he had understood quite a lot of what I had said.

I do not think that the language need be a great hindrance if we have a heart full of love to these people; we will make them understand somehow.

They soon got to know that we had not come to get something out of them; we had not come to trade like the traders did. We had only come to give to them, not to get from them, and they knew that the great message that was burning in our hearts was about One called Jesus.

We were praying very much that God would bless precious souls, and we would watch the smoke coming up from the various villages and, looking away across the forest tree tops, would ask God to bless, so that when the time came for us to preach the Gospel to them they would be open hearted.

The first convert was a lad called Nyuki – what joy he gave us. I had had some talk with him while thatching our little house, and a few evenings later, as we were praying for the salvation of these people in the villages around us, Nyuki came on to the veranda and announced that he desired to receive the Lord Jesus. Oh how Brother Salter and I rejoiced, and as Nyuki went off back to his village, rejoicing in Christ his Saviour, we took each other by the hand and, with tears of gratitude welling up, we said: 'Surely it was worth while to come out from England, if only to save this one precious soul.' "

4
Foundation building

A few weeks after arrival in Mwanza, Joseph Blakeney's return to the south made it necessary for Brother Burton to take the position of 'legal representative' of the mission – an office required by the Government. He made a survey of the whole district and a scale drawing for the government, thus gaining an intimate knowledge of every stream, path, hill, village, and group of huts, and saving the expense of a surveyor. The language he found to be different from the nearest written languages, and he decided very soon after his arrival in Mwanza to formulate the grammar and translate the Scriptures. A few years later the laborious work of constructing a written language and translating the four Gospels and Acts into the Luba language (Kiluba) was completed chiefly by Mr Clarke of the Garenganze Mission (Open Brethren); and in 1921 the cases of books printed in Kiluba by the British and Foreign Bible Society were sent out to young Christian Churches in Lubaland, which in 1915 were not yet born.

(The latest news from Mr Clarke [1921] is that he has completed the New Testament).

Concerning the printing of these precious Gospels and the Book of Acts, Brother Burton in the July 1921 issue of the British and Foreign Bible Society's periodical, writes as follows:

"A momentous event is just about to take place in the giving of the four Gospels and Acts in their own tongues to the Baluba people – one of the largest Central African ethnic groups. Sections of the Baluba living between Lake Mweru and Bunkeya already possess an excellent version of the New Testament in Luba-Sanga translated by Mr Dan Crawford; while to the far west, on the Kasai River, over 400 miles from Lake Mweru, the American Presbyterians have just completed a version of the New Testament and part of the Old in Luba-Lulua, which is now published by our Society. But lying between these extremes are many hundreds of thousands of Africans who, while able to understand something of one or other of these two translations, could never enjoy, from such sources, the fullness of the Gospel message. The Baluba are intelligent people, expert in fishing, trapping, basket making, and agriculture. They weave their own cloth from raphia fibre; they smelt, forge, temper, and even oxidise their own iron-making knives so keen that one can shave with them. They adapt themselves with wonderful rapidity and ease to new conditions of civilisation. Fifteen years ago the vast majority of them had never seen a white man. Today the opening of the largest copper mines in the world, the building of the beautiful southern Congo Capital – Elisabethville – with its modern dwellings and organisation, and the completion to the Congo River of the Cape to Cairo Railway, have all brought modern thought and luxury to the doors of Lubaland, finding exceptionally intelligent people open-armed to receive all that comes from white men, both good and bad. Thus one finds enamel ware and Lancashire cotton goods in the cannibal villages of the Luvidjyo River, and cast-iron saucepans, scented soap, and Singer sewing machines in the mountain hamlets of the great Kibara.

The intelligence of this race is evidenced by the fact that they have a vocabulary of some 15,000 words compared with 7,000 which is the usual number in a Bantu language. Though the Kiluba tongue has only been reduced to writing in the last few years, the Baluba are exceedingly rich in the oral literature and folklore, using hundreds of proverbs in everyday conversation, displaying a profound philosophy, the more surprising since it comes from the mouth of a black forest dweller, living in a wee grass hut, and dressed in a skin, or simple loin cloth."

The letters dated October 11th, 1915 and December 6th, 1915 contained in this chapter were addressed to Mr Thomas Myerscough.

Mwanza, October 11th, 1915:

"Our temporary house is falling to pieces. I have propped it up, but the first heavy rains will bring it down. Then we have no money to pay for labour to build a new house. These and a lot more are the odds in front of us, but I feel they are glorious opportunities for testing God, and that we are wonderfully privileged in being permitted to stand in the battlefront for Him.

Jimmy and I preached to the people on Sunday for a few minutes in their own tongue – one month from arrival. I feel that we will come through triumphantly. We shall have to do the building ourselves and leave the walls in such a way that we can put an ant-proofing course in next dry season. I would not like you to be 'clerk of the works' when we build, but of course we must do the best we can to get a shelter till the rains are over, even though the architecture be anything but brilliant. A little distance down the path a handful of lion's fur was found, which the workers said was scratched off this morning. I was within 60 yards of the spot this morning, without any protection at all, looking for a place to dig a well. Also the 'Capita' – a sort of foreman of the chief – says that there are many elephants tramping the gardens – ten were seen together. If I met them it would be a case of who could cover the ground in the shortest time. We have just one house worker to do cooking, washing, bedmaking, etc. And we have been praying much for him.

Jimmy had an adventure today. He went with the helper to stop a woman who was chopping up the best of our timber. She turned and went for them with the axe, and gave the youth a nasty cut between his toes. However, Jimmy got her axe. I have a mahogany carpenter's bench nearing completion. Wouldn't the folks at home consider this a waste?"

A Report letter dated 24th October, 1915, and printed in Johannesburg:

"Brother Salter has been very near to death's door, but now he is once more in robust health. All glory to Jesus. He has walked 24 miles in a day, and can chop down a 14-inch diameter tree in half an hour; so, praise God, the recovery is complete. Then, though we cannot report definite conversions, yet the Gospel is evidently making an impression. A little boy was poisoned some days ago, and his body swelled terribly. We went to his hut and prayed for him, laying on hands in the Name of the Lord Jesus, and God healed him. Yesterday the head chief of the whole district (old Kajingu) came with a very bad head, the effects of drinking too much 'malwa' (local beer) the day before. I didn't know what to do, when he also asked prayer; but the verse came to me 'He healed all that came to Him.' So we laid hands on his greasy plaited hair in the Name of Jesus and asked the Lord to heal him. Immediately the headache went. Of course, I told the old chief: 'God is not mocked; and what you sow, you will reap. You must not drink malwa till you get a bad head, and then come to God to get rid of it.'

Some weeks ago, when out for food with my rifle in the forest, I came across a place where the 'Bakasanji' (a secret society among the Baluba) had been holding a feast. There were human bones on the ground. A few days later, hearing that a Belgian was prospecting a tin deposit in the hills a few miles away, we went to visit him. We found the poor fellow so lonely, and longing to see a white face. He said that a few days previously the people had eaten a dead man within twelve yards of his camp. Even then Brother Salter was a little incredulous as to these people being cannibals, so last night he called in a lad from the village and asked him : 'Do those people eat human flesh?' He said : 'Mingi, mingi,' (lots and lots). 'But,' I asked, 'is that good?' He answered: 'Eyo kyakudia kiampe,' (Yes, it's very good meat). And the gleam of his eyes and teeth were so inexpressibly horrid that poor Brother Salter could scarcely sleep through the night for thinking of them.

Very few of them are cannibals. These are confined to a secret sect. These are people God has brought us to labour amongst, and upon whom God is going to pour out His Spirit in answer to your prayers. He says, 'I will pour out My Spirit upon all flesh,' so the Baluba are included. Also the redeemed around the throne are to be 'from every tribe'; so that Mwanza Kajingu will surely be represented. The precious Blood of Jesus, and the mighty healing virtue of His holy Name, avail everywhere, and for all. How excellent is Your Name in all the earth.' "

Letter to friends in Johannesburg – Mwanza, 26th Nov., 1915:

"Truly I wish you were here to help me build. Our beloved Brother Jimmy does the gardening while I build. But working with unseasoned trees in the rainy season (when one gets alternately half a day of raining 'cats and dogs' and then half a day of boiling sun) is not satisfactory. I cut down trees for the wall plates, sawed them from end to end, and trimmed them with the adze. Within the last month I have trimmed the wall plates from growing trees, mortised them every four feet to upright posts (four feet in the ground and twelve feet out), dove-tailed in cross-beams for the inside rooms, and mortised those also on to uprights, roughed out about 14 windows and six doors, half-notched roof principles (every six feet along the building) and mortised cross-ties into them, fitted veranda posts all round, and a score of other jobs, as well as 'bossing up' a gang of 18 workers to bring in beams, bamboos, and mix mud (for bricks), etc. I think that Jimmy and I will content ourselves with a little house about twelve feet square, in which we can live and study until the rains are finished. Of course we have to economise in nails here, so a lot of the house is tied together with rope made from the bark of trees, and we have to have a lot of other makeshifts. But from an engineering point of view it is substantial.

How do they receive the Gospel? They gulp it down without stopping to chew, and then come for more. Really, if I were fluent in Kiluba,

I could get audiences for eight hours a day, and seven days to the week. You see it is all new to them. Never a whisper has reached them before. The resurrection of Christ is the great theme. They love to hear about it. Since my vocabulary is short, my gesticulation has to be correspondingly vivid. They already understand there is a God, but so mysterious and far away, that it is quite a new idea that we can approach and speak to Him in the Name of Jesus. They already believe in angels and have a local name for them. Being filled with the Spirit will be no hard thing for them to understand, for every day they can see their own witch doctors under the possession of demons. They naturally expect to see supernatural manifestations accompany the Gospel, and this is where we have the key to the whole situation.

In Mark 16, 15-18, the word 'signs' might be termed 'credentials'. We carry our 'credentials' with us. We are not afraid of snakes. We eat palm nuts which it was thought the witch doctor had poisoned, with no ill results (though, of course, we did not do this deliberately); but above all, again and again, we lay hands on the sick in the Name of Jesus and they recover, whereas the witch doctors' fetishes could not, in some cases, heal them. So you see, Christ had a very strong reason when He said, 'These signs shall follow them that believe.' And the father of lies has also a strong reason for trying to stop the signs following. Of course as might be expected this also has weight with them, the fetish man charges goats, francs, cloth, chickens, etc. for his charms and we charge nothing for our prayers. We cannot see at present what difference the Gospel will have on the people, but we shall see, for it is going to make a great big difference.

I believe that healing in the Name of Jesus is the very foundation of pioneer missionary work. 'And whatever city you enter into, and they receive you . . . heal the sick that are there.'

Luke 10, 8-9. So when we hear of people being sick we go and pray for them indiscriminately, in the Name of Jesus. And God heals them as a testimony to the village of the power which He has vested in His risen Son, whom we preach."

The following letter was written on December 11th, 1915, from Mwanza to a friend in Johannesburg by James Salter, Brother Burton's yoke fellow:

"May grace, mercy and peace be your portion from His presence, from beneath whose throne flows the stream of life. I do indeed praise God with all my heart for the prayerful sympathy of the saints of the Apostolic Faith Mission Assemblies. I feel confident that it is the prayers of God's people which have carried us through so far. We are here today. Why? Is it because of strong constitutions, big faith, or being acclimatised? I answer emphatically, No! What we are and where we are is a living testimony to the faithfulness of God, and to prayer answered on our behalf. Still can we cheerfully say:

'Though all around our soul give way,
He still is all our hope and stay;
On Christ, the solid Rock we stand,
All other ground is sinking sand.'

What a privilege is ours: to declare Christ among those to whom He was not previously known. To proclaim and practise the Gospel of God's grace to the poor benighted heathen. The disciples' commission was not only 'As ye go, preach', but also 'heal the sick', etc., etc. To the Church of Christ these are the days of glorious privileges, but also great responsibilities. The words of that hymn are true today as perhaps never before.

'See o'er the world wide-open door inviting,
Soldiers of Christ, arise, and enter in;
Christians, awake, your forces all uniting,
Send forth the Gospel, break the chains of sin.'

The Lord still appeals, 'Who will go for us?' Who, with a heart open to God, immersed in His love, with a divine compassion for lost souls, will say, 'Here am I, send me'? With an open Bible, open lands for His word, open hearts and outstretched hands for the Gospel, God needs 'a man.' The only qualification required, but it is an absolute necessity, is an 'unction from the Holy One,' and a life abiding beneath the anointing.

'Power to heal the leper,
Power to raise the dead,
Power to fill the empty pots with oil,
Is waiting for the worker
Who in Jesus' steps will tread,
And leave his life of ease for one of toil.'

In our parish, which at the present is one of about 200 miles radius of the Mission Station and 400 to the north west, there are no other Protestant missionaries. We are up against sin in its vilest and most hideous forms. The name 'Baluba' means the lost people; and one may say a more fitting title could not have been adopted. Lost, morally and spiritually: naturally speaking, especially to one who knows a little of their inner life, there is nothing to attract one to them, but rather an inclination to avoid them. Yet, with a love which is heaven born, we are willing to spend and be spent for them, daily yielding ourselves to God a living sacrifice on their behalf. What a holy enthusiasm grips one, as the opportunity presents itself of speaking to a company of them of the wonderful, the only and glorious theme, Jesus. How, as one kneels in prayer with them, a deep sense of the presence of God and a mighty wave of intercession sweeps over us, whilst at the close of these soul gushings, they usually respond with a fervent 'Amen,' which word they have learnt from us.

Going to Mulongo, a place about 22 miles distant, I had to stay at a village a day and night owing to continuous showers of rain. The people soon crowded to the hut where I was sheltered, and I had the chance to tell them of Jesus. Then I went and sat in the doorway of some of the huts, and again we talked of Jesus just before turning in for the night. Standing in the centre of the village, I had to tell an enquiring group of our wonderful Jesus.

It was too cold for me to sleep that night, as I had neither bed nor bedding with me, so I found joy and satisfaction in my Saviour and the blessed privilege of declaring a little of the unsearchable riches of our Lord Jesus Christ. We are day by day gaining the confidence of the people, and now it is a regular thing for them to come for prayer when ill. Some of them, including the chief of the village, have been healed in answer to the prayer of faith. We are confident that the 'medicine men' and witch doctors will soon have to seek employment elsewhere, and are looking expectantly to our God for Him to infuse His word with a mighty soul-saving, healing, and baptising power, that the Gospel may go forth, not in word only, but in the mighty power and demonstration of the Lord the Spirit. We are here called to be the reflection of our God, and by His Grace we will contend for the faith, continuing in the Apostles' doctrine, and awaiting not only a repetition of Pentecost, but the promised greater things."

Mwanza, December 5th, 1915:   '

"The Belgian Government demands that any religious or philanthropic body settling in the Congo be duly incorporated. Consequently, unless I desired the trouble and expense of incorporating my own mission, it was necessary to link up with someone. So, hearing that two 'Pentecostal Mission' men were moving North, I joined in with them, maintaining meanwhile my personal liberty and right to trust God for supplies. Two sisters from Johannesburg say they were led to come and fill the gap occasioned by the departure of Brother Blakeney. To give them their due they are a plucky couple, but though, as you know, I strongly believe in being led of God, yet I cannot understand their coming up here when we have no housing or accommodation.

The country is now a vast swamp. The rains surpass everything that one can conceive of in England. There are scores of rivers from inches to yards deep. It is the wet season. The food is wet, the ground is a puddle, and one's clothes get mouldy in a day. One can wash them in an hour or two, but I have had underclothes drying, in the shelter, for 16 days and they are not fit to put on yet. I had no time to stop these Sisters as they came with full authority of the Pentecostal Mission. They are now somewhere within 200 miles of here, plunging through the long drenching grass and dripping trees.

I have obtained for the Pentecostal Mission an excellent grant of 200 acres of land. It includes splendid garden land, fine timber, a good clear spring, a stream (for dry-weather gardening) and a high hill, as a healthy site for the mission station. Moreover, there are at least 20 or 30 villages and thousands of people within an hour's walk. I am now director and legal representative. So the Government Administrator ordered me to cut a road round the ground. Our exchequer was done, so a brilliant thought struck us. We paid the workers with our blue mottled soap – and got the road two and a half miles long cut for about a quarter of our stock of soap.

But now the two Sisters were to arrive within a few weeks, and there was no house, when money, long delayed at the Banque du Congo Belge (Bank of the Belgian Congo) arrived. We needed food and stores, but resolved to put up a house first. Consequently we have an excellent house nearly completed. But while we have had to pay 19 workers to help in the building (and have had to put our bottom dollar into a building which we shall probably never use) Jimmy and I have been on short commons, and this hurt me more than I can say. Personally, you know, I can stand more fatigue and privation than most people, but when returning from Mulongo (22 miles away) Jimmy and his worker had to go into the forest and grub up roots for food on which to walk that distance. While I don't mind for myself, I do mind for Jimmy.

But now we are in the middle of Equatorial rains, and I have spent all our time on the Sisters' house; we have neither time nor money for our own house. We have no shelter. A few times gifts have come from England and South Africa, but the greater part has gone to paying the workers to hurry on the Sisters' home. But as Jimmy and I have sat on our camp bedsides, and looked at the empty money bag, we have encouraged ourselves in God knowing that while we were providing for others our faithful God was caring for us. So now that news comes of the kind gift from Preston we can have a nice wee house – price £2; two men to clear garden land – price £2; and an additional £5 for food. This is the realisation of your faithfulness and our trust in God. Hallelujah!

The language here is going well. I have a vocabulary which must have about 1,500 words, and we can make ourselves understood on many points. I find there is a salt spring at Kiambi, eight days east from here across the Congo. To some extent we can use salt instead of money and, by sending helpers to Kiambi, I believe we can reduce our food bill by at least one-third. We have already got our first stock of Kiambi salt. Owing to the war we can get no more flour and no more matches, but we have a big stock of matches, and hope to sow wheat and rice shortly. We have both ready for putting in.

The old chief came up last Sunday morning with a present of two fowls, and wanted to know more of the resurrection of Christ. But he is awfully bound by the wizards, who are consulted by the people and give out solemn utterances, interspersed with shaking, grovelling and muttering. They make a fat living at it, but are terribly emaciated physically. One of the chief's sons is a soothsayer (there are six in Mwanza village) and, in his horrid paroxysms of grovelling and possession, he has dug with his fingernails a hole in the ground big enough to bury a furniture van. Oh what a stir there is going to be when these demons get cast out in the Name of Jesus. Pray continually that we may be faithful to all the great commission delivered to us."

Mwanza [undated]:

"Mrs Richardson, whose husband laid down his life in the Congo a year ago and who had years of missionary experience in British East Africa, and Miss Hodges, who has had some experience in Zululand, arrived a few weeks before the completion of their big airy house. So we left them the old house while we went into tents, and at the same time commenced a small temporary house for ourselves, allotting the big nearly completed house to the ladies. Towards the end of the building I became very lackadaisical and tired, but did not realise that it was a low fever until all my strength went, and Brother Salter and I went down with fever on the same morning. Fortunately my fever was at its height at night, and I was a little bit able to superintend Brother Salter during the day. During this time the Sisters moved into the big house. Our fever soon dropped and we were just getting our legs again when, one evening, a man came running to us during a thunder storm, and shrieked in terror something about the ladies' house. We at once ran to see what was wrong, and found that the lightning had struck the ridge of the roof and the house was in flames. However, we managed to get most of the goods out without a great deal of damage, and then we stood watching my three months' work go up in flames. Two days later I started a new temporary house for the ladies. But we had only done a day's work on it when the inhabitants of a village six miles away raided our villages, killing two men and wounding four more. One of the killed and one of the wounded were fellows who had been working for us in the building. Now all the population have gone off to defend their villages, and our building is once more at a standstill. There have been other minor inconveniences: the collapse of our kitchen, the raiding of our house by 'driver ants,' and so on. But I must confess that in all these things God has kept us in perfect peace. Satan seems to be exerting his utmost efforts to hinder our work, but 'if God be for us, who can be against us? In all these things we are more than conquerors through Him who loves us and cares for us.'

On the day that we left Johannesburg for the Congo a farewell prayer meeting was held. One old lady prayed: 'Lord, find the brothers some faithful believers to help them there in the Congo.' I remember thinking 'My good woman we want to go where Christ has not been named. There can be no African Christian helpers.' But I was mistaken, and God wonderfully answered that old sister's prayer as follows:

Some 30 years before, the great tyrant chief Mushidi (also known as Msiri) had gathered vast districts under his sway, and unruly subjects were often sold as slaves. In this way many of the local villages about Mwanza were raided, and young fellows were taken into captivity and sold to the Biéans down in Portuguese West Africa (Angola today). There the good news of salvation through the Lord Jesus reached them through the faithful ministries of Messrs. Tucker, Lane, Saunders, etc., and many hundreds of these slaves have been saved. Later, the Portuguese abolished slavery, and the Baluba were given their papers declaring them free, and they at once determined to set off back to their homes in Lubaland with the Gospel message.

A few months after Bro. Salter and I reached Mwanza we were sitting on the rocks near the mission one day, preaching to the people, when we heard a well-known Sankey tune in the distance. I said: 'Jimmy, listen ! We've never taught the believers that tune. Who can it be?' Presently a party of about 30 travel-stained men, women and children appeared singing hymns and with tears of joy trickling down their faces. They brought letters of commendation, passes, etc., which showed that they had left Bié, Angola, and set out for Lubaland just at the time when that old Sister was praying in Johannesburg. They were full of joy at reaching the end of their 740-mile tramp, and finding white missionaries in their villages.

So keen were these dear people to spread the Gospel among their fellow villagers that they neglected their gardens, with the result that, after some time, they found themselves in dire straits, and indeed on more than one occasion they were without food for two or three days at a stretch before we discovered it.

So at last I said 'Come on! I'll go into the forest and see if I can't find you a buffalo.' We set off before light in the morning, and tramped many weary miles, but the undergrowth was so dense and the animals so wary that I could not get a good shot and the only buffalo that I did hit was merely grazed, and soon sealed up his wound in a mud hole. This is quite common. God seems to have given animals the instinct to thus staunch the flow of blood. Next day we set out again, tramping all day through the forests, but only obtaining a small antelope, scarcely the size of a retriever dog. We always kneel around the animal that we shoot, and thank God for the meat. But on rising from our knees one of the men said, 'Bwana, that won't go very far with all our hungry little ones.'

My feet were so blistered and legs and arms so cut in the forest that I could not go out again. We must have covered 50 miles in two days. An old necromancer in the village laughed at one of the Christians saying 'Look – your teacher prays to God, yet you've got no more meat than I could obtain by calling upon the spirits of the departed.' We could say nothing, and so perforce left the old fellow to sneer.

That night a somewhat unusual sound awoke the stillness of the evening. The roar of a lion – and of course the people would see to it that their hut doors were well fastened, and their fires burning well through the night. But that lion did us a good turn. He must have got into a herd of buffalo and scattered them, so that some took refuge in the gardens. The result was that a woman came running up the mission hill early next morning in a terrible scare, to say that she had discovered some buffalo in her manioc plantation. I seized my rifle, and with two lads was soon following the footprints. Before long a bullet went home and we stood rejoicing over a fine fat buffalo. The Christians soon came with baskets and knives to carry off the meat. But first we knelt around the buffalo and thanked God for the meat. Many people, hearing shots in the neighbourhood of the village, gathered to see the results, and on rising from our knees there stood the old sorcerer, who had twitted us about the antelope, looking on with the rest. So the Christian who had been the butt of his jests on the former occasion now stepped to his side, saying 'See how good God is. Had we shot a buffalo away in the forests we should have had a long weary journey to carry home the meat, so God has sent us a buffalo quite close to the village.'

The following Sunday we preached from the text 'Be sober and diligent, because your adversary the devil as a roaring lion goes about, seeking whom he may devour,' etc. The interest was intense and after the meeting about 60 people followed us. A few did not seem in earnest but had apparently merely come to look on, so we sent them away, and with the rest – perhaps 50 in number – Bro. Salter and I went very carefully over God's plan of salvation as they sat around us upon the veranda of our little home. Finally claiming God's promise 'Whoever shall call upon the Name of the Lord shall be saved' (Rom. 10, 13) – we started to pray with the people, but so eager were they to be saved that they could not wait for each other, and before very long the whole company was praying together, and shouting, and pleading, and finally one by one the people seemed to gain assurance and a sweet peace and spirit of praise settled down upon all.

Brother Salter and I could do nothing. We felt that the meeting was in God's hands, and all that we could do was to look on, and praise Him, as the tears of gratitude flowed freely.

It is impossible to count numbers. Suffice it to say that, while a few have not given evidence of changed lives, many of those who received salvation that day have gone steadily on ever since, so that we have not even yet come to the end of our lion and buffalo story."

5
Beginnings of revival

The first anniversary of the Brothers setting foot in the Congo was indeed a blessed day, for on that Sunday morning at the meeting some cried to the Lord for salvation, two of whom were specially definite, and Brother Burton was encouraged to believe that a quiet but real work was progressing in several hearts. The cook had made a half-hearted profession of conversion some time before, but the reality of a deep work of grace in his heart was called in question. To the great joy of the Brothers they now found him bearing testimony and exhorting others to come to Christ.

Letters dated August 20th, October 9th, November 10th, 1916, and January 1st, February 12th, April 16th, and May 15th, 1917, were addressed to Mr Thomas Myerscough, of Preston. The letter of July 10th, 1917, was a printed circular letter.

Mwanza, August 20th, 1916:

Letters often are a great comfort to me, both in the writing and in the receiving of them. God has given us earthly companionship. Even the Christ of God, despite the fact that, in Gethsemane, He was able to see His Father's face in prayer, nevertheless He sought the fellowship of His earthly friends, Peter, James and John. And so, tho' I praise Him that I have rolled the burden upon Him, I feel like letting you know it too. Jimmy is in a poor state of health, and some devilish thing has gripped him which I cannot locate. His heart is good, and appetite is fair, but each few days he sinks in absolute lassitude and weakness.

I am kept pretty hard at work with the new brick building, and Jimmy has not had strength to do more than check the bundles of grass that come in for thatching – even this seemed a burden almost more than he could stand. Today the weakness is creeping over him more than usual.

Last night (Saturday) I went to the village and had a good talk to the

Chief and headmen. The consequence is that today's meetings have been fine. The power of God gripped the big crowds that gathered both in the morning and afternoon. But, tho' Jimmy spoke a few words this morning with some effort, he was unable to do so this evening. He accompanied me to the village and gave out a hymn, but I could see that even that was too much for him. I am praising God that at the time of writing I am in splendid trim. But it would be just like the enemy of souls to try to hinder us through illness, for the interest is becoming tense, and I've not the slightest doubt that we are in for a big revival. Our Christian young men are praying for it, and we are expecting it. You in the homeland are backing us up in prayer. It's bound to come. Each day the wave of interest rises. The singing of hymns specially moves the people, and today the Chief and several leading men were visibly moved. One great massive old councillor said, 'Bwana, we didn't know, and we've been silly enough to invoke fetishes, but our hearts are turned round and, as for me, I'm going to pray to them no more. I'm going to pray to God.'

But tonight Brother Jimmy was almost too weak to get into bed. It's a long time and a long way ere you get this letter, but I know that tonight, even as I write, God will put it on your hearts to pray through with me.

Did I tell you that, in Johannesburg, a mob came for me, to a new little chapel which Charlie Heatley opened in one of the suburbs. I was taken outside, on to a vacant lot of land, and they threatened to scrag me, etc. But God kept me in perfect peace, and I was able to testify to them of Christ. Only having a little harmless pushing around – well, I've just heard the sequel.

Two fellows who were the ringleaders have been born again and one of them has received the Holy Spirit – and some of them have sent us £5 for our work in the Congo. So hallelujah! 'The wrath of man has once more been turned to good account.' "

Mwanza, October 9th, 1916:

"With a heart full of praise I write of our precious Jimmy's miraculous and complete recovery. Victory came absolutely, instantaneously, and he is now as fit as ever.

At present my rifle has supplied most of our food for some weeks. Last week I dropped two fine reedbuck quite close to the path, and we have salted some of the meat. The Christians from Bié have nothing until their gardens begin to yield, so that most of my meat goes to them. At present grass is short and shooting is easy but in a few weeks the forests will be almost impassable, and the ground marshy, so that we shall have to fall back on our gardens and our goats. If any of the saints in the little upper room have wholesome garden vegetable seeds to spare, they will be most welcomed here."

Mwanza, November 10th, 1916:

"In the photographs sent last week I marked one fellow (in the picture of rolling the log to the sawpit) 'very near the Kingdom.' Well, he and a young friend have just yielded to the Gospel and received the Lord Jesus. He is one of the first of these villagers that I ever spoke to of Christ's claims, and he has been the object of much prayer. So, with very full hearts, we raise our song of thanks to God.

There are several matters in which God has wonderfully provided. The people here have very little idea of work, and after a few weeks they get tired and stop. Thus on the sawpit I've trained about a dozen fellows to cut planks, but after a week or so they said, 'Bwana, it's hard work. I'm going to sit in the village.' So they stop work. But, bit-by-bit, I got enough planks to make a little furniture and, at the time of building our new house, I had four short and two long planks unused. I had very little rope for scaffolding, but we prayed God to supply every need, and the planks in hand were just enough to permit me to work on a platform without a scaffold. God saw to it that we had enough. And, now that I have moved into the house, we shall need wood to season, so that in a few months' time we can make doors and windows (for at present we've had no doors and windows since arriving in the Congo. We've shut up nothing, and never had privacy). Hence God has sent me two trained sawpit workers who were taught by a Portuguese man 700 miles south west. It is still hard sometimes to get chickens, but we've had enough."

Mwanza, January 1st, 1917:

"Brother Bowie has just forwarded £14 from you, and I desire to thank you all very much for this most opportune gift. Our stock of matches, baking powder, sugar, etc., has been running very low, and your timely gift will now enable us to get in a fresh stock. There is no grocer's shop round the corner, and we have to allow quite three months from the time we send off the order to the time we receive the goods, for our supplies have to travel from Elisabethville – over 300 miles journey – and for much of the distance they come by African carriers and boat. How we praise God that He so mercifully cares for our goods. Some of our letters get lost. Some months ago we had no answer to a letter, and have only now discovered that the canoe in which it was carried was overturned on the river; the carrier escaped only with his life. Your gift of seeds also has come to hand. This is fine. We do enjoy our vegetables. Even if we are unable to shoot buck, or get African fowls, we can always have a good feast of turnips, beans, green mealies, (maize), mustard and cress, radishes, etc. A good garden is half the battle here in the Congo.

We are having happy times in witnessing for Christ, and are on the whole in good health (though with occasional slight recurrences of malaria).

The Roman Catholics are exerting all their power to undermine our influence and, today, I have discovered that their African catechists have even been secretly visiting our own villages here, and bribing the chief. What a blessed thing it is to know that they cannot thwart God's purposes. Those who don't want the truth will believe the Roman Catholic lie, but those who hunger and thirst after righteousness shall be filled.

We have just made application for a grant of land for a second station at Ngoimani (area including today's Lwamba) – two days distant from here. The villages along the Saboi River are very numerous, and we had a blessed week of witnessing there during Christmas week. I was the first white man who has ever been in one village, and in many they have never heard the Name of Jesus.

At present we are undermanned here at Mwanza but, if I put up a small rest house over at Ngoimani, one or other of us can go over for a few weeks occasionally and preach the Gospel, with a view to placing either an evangelist or white workers there later on. Now, beloved, it will be scriptural if you pray with us for more workers for this great needy land, for He has told us to ask that more labourers be sent forth.

> '*I am free, I am free,*
> *Jesus paid all my debt on Calvary;*
> *And the blessed Holy Ghost*
> *In my heart is now the host*
> *Hallelujah blessed Jesus,*
> *I am free.*'

Big congregations continue and at almost every service some express their intention or desire of leaving the life of sin and trusting in Christ. On Sunday morning we had 158 at the Gospel meeting (8:45 am.), and in the afternoon at the village there were over 100 gathered in the shade of a big hut to hear the Gospel. The old chief granted the freed slaves from Bié a liberal slice of land on the borders of our mission, and they are already fitting in well and helping us to tell out the Gospel message in all the villages around. There are five men, six women and 19 children – 30 in all. The leaders carry splendid letters of commendation from the missionaries.

About three months ago, a big, hardy, athletic man arrived at Mwanza from a village away in the swamps, four days' journey south east. He applied for work and, after a few odd jobs, I gave him work on our sawpit. From the start he evinced a strange affection for me. He was very silent, and always listened most intently to the Gospel meetings in local villages. This morning (Lord's Day) several of my lads undertook to hold Gospel meetings in local villages, so I was free to slip off on my cycle to Lubinda and Kikose to carry them the news of Calvary for the first time in the memory of man.

I didn't like to command anyone to run with me for so long a distance, but Ngoi-wa-Kana, when he heard my intentions, asked to go. He had never made any profession, but I was very glad when, at Kikose, he started in, and preached briefly and well. Then as we sat under a great spreading forest tree, sharing our dinner of green mealies, he opened his heart to me: 'Bwana, I have two wives and four children away on the Pungwe marshes. I wanted God, and when we heard that real teachers (as distinct from Roman Catholics) had arrived at Mwanza, I started with a friend to come and hear your words. My friend turned back. I have heard your words, and have today seen that I too can tell out the Gospel. Tomorrow I would like to return to my people and let them hear how they may be saved.' Beloved, you may imagine how my heart runs over with praise at God's way of working. Excepting for a few months at the end of the dry season it would be courting death for us to venture out into those fever infested swamps. But right here God has been getting ready His own missionary for the job. Hallelujah! Ngoi-wa-Kana says he wishes to return later and receive the Holy Spirit, but is anxious about his home. Pray for this dear fellow.

I might say that we had a most enthusiastic reception at Kikose and Lubinda. Such deafening shrieks and drumming and shouting. Also deep interest in the Gospel message. I left a Christian at Lubinda to answer questions and burn up idols, at the chief's request. The journey to, and arrival at Ngoimani was not without interest and excitement. The Lungui River was so swollen that little Matokembadi was nearly washed away. He had to tiptoe across with water to his chin, and then nearly one half-mile of mud and slush varying from ankle to waist deep. We found Ngoimani and Kiungu (villages miles apart, on opposite sides of the same valley) on a war footing, and young men with big quivers of poisoned arrows watching for an opportunity to kill anyone from the opposing village. During the night the Kiungu men got up into the bushes above Ngoimani and shouted a rather amusing defiance at their enemy, declaring that they would stamp the village flat, and take old chief Luambi's head back with them.

Our helpers have worked well, and have nearly completed the boundary around the land which I have selected for a government grant – cutting a roadway through the bush, and planting slips of the quickly growing Kaswamasenge tree.

Yesterday a terrific thunderstorm rolled upon us almost without warning, striking a clump of trees quite near the tent. The wind and rain were so violent that I had a lively five minutes tightening the pegs as they pulled out, praying, and hanging grimly on to the rattling swirling, bulging tent fly, while two of the men held the tent poles lest they should snap. Now I'm sporting round in a muddy pair of pyjamas and my mosquito slippers, with scarcely a dry rag in the tent, and apparently more rain to follow. These are times when a song seems to relieve the situation – 'I sing because I'm happy, I sing because I'm free; His eye is on the sparrow, And I know He watches me. Hallelujah!' "

Mwanza, February 12th, 1917:

"I take opportunity during a very rainy day to let you know how God is answering your prayers. Speaking of his preaching, Paul says we are unto God a sweet savour of Christ in those who are being saved and in those who are perishing (1 Cor. 2, 15). In other words, Paul says – My preaching not only has an effect on the heathen, in saving or condemning them, it also affords pleasure to God, ascending to Him as incense of a sweet savour. Now, I rejoice in this aspect of Gospel preaching. Irrespective of its effect upon the hearers, here in the great dense forests of Central Africa, in places where for centuries God has caught no sound of the blessed Name of His Son, the Lord Jesus, He now has the joy of hearing the Gospel (His own lovingly planned, eternally thought out Gospel), given out in the villages, passed from hut to hut, sung along the forest paths, discussed around the camp fires, and echoed abroad by whites and blacks alike. And God tells us that is a sweet savour to Him. Whoever else may think light of it, He enjoys it thoroughly. Hallelujah! What an honour! I am permitted to give real pleasure to the Eternal God, even if souls are not saved. But now, turning to the heathen-ward aspect of our preaching, we are beginning to see very definite results, and what I believe is to be the big wide-spreading tide of salvation rolling over this land.

Some 13 miles away an old chief, Ndala by name, was healed of asthma several months ago, and at that time the power of God was manifested, and people came running together to see. His idol was broken down, and we saw that he desired to trust in Christ. In the pressure of our work we were not often able to visit this old chief, and he grew cold and allowed a devil dance in his clearing, but later on, as some Christian friends were passing his village, he brought out his charms, fetishes, and the whole paraphernalia, to be burned publicly. Ndala's son, Chigala, has a large village three miles nearer here, and this son has now told Brother Salter that he wishes to burn his fetishes also, and to trust in Christ. In each case the action of these chiefs will have a mighty effect for many miles around.

But another case:

Right close to our mission, within a quarter of an hour's walk, is a big village, Kanguba, presided over by old chief Mwepo. His one object in approaching us has been to get presents and, when he found that he could not induce us to give them without his giving a fair return, he would neither listen to us himself, nor encourage his people to do so. In fact, he often organised hunts, dances, beer-drinks, and other counter-attractions on the Lord's Day, keeping his people from our services. Naturally this led to our focusing a good deal of prayer upon Mwepo and his village. Last Sunday week one of Mwepo's younger sons came up to our veranda, after the morning gospel service, with several other lads, to accept salvation in Christ Jesus. At the time I had not much confidence in his conversion, but I was evidently mistaken for he immediately went to Mwepo and said: 'Father, I cannot pour out libations of beer any more in honour of our dead relatives' (a heathen custom).

The same afternoon I visited Kanguba, and found the old chief sitting alone and very glum because of his son's change of heart. All his people were at a funeral beer-drink some miles away. I had a very blessed private talk with Mwepo, showing him the folly of his way and giving him a solemn warning. Toward the end of the conversation the eldest son arrived and seemed much impressed. On the next afternoon a messenger came along asking me to go to another small village, near Kanguba and tributary to it. The messenger said that Mwepo and his eldest son had together destroyed their charms and now the small under-chief and his people also wanted to know what it was all about. I went at once, and had a most blessed meeting, as the result of which the messenger came again today, asking me to return as soon as possible, for several want to be saved and have expressed a wish to have their charms and fetishes burned publicly.

Yesterday, the Lord's Day, Mwepo and his eldest son, Shimbishele, were at our morning meeting, sitting humbly among the people and taking a real interest in the message (I was talking of the cities of refuge from the avenger of blood, and a little lad fled for refuge to Christ). At the end of the service, Mwepo came forward and said: 'I was glad to come today, and I want always to come with God's people, for I am one of them.' I have not yet had opportunity to talk with him and find exactly on what his faith is based, and I do not want to have people think that baptism or fetish burning or any such thing is salvation.

'On Christ the solid Rock we stand,
All other ground is sinking sand.'

Another chief, Chembe, of Kilumba, a village eleven miles north, an influential man, has always shown himself friendly disposed to the Gospel and, though he has not at present professed conversion, yet he always welcomes us gladly, calls his people to hear, presides personally over our meetings, wishes to have a meeting house in his own village, and is manifestly very near the kingdom.

I have given prominence to the chiefs in this report, as it is around these that the people gather, but also we are having happy results among the other lads and men, and there is some evidence of a move among the women and girls also. It is a great joy to see the young converts earnestly and independently witnessing among their fellows. I have already mentioned in some letters to you that we propose opening a second station, two days' journey north west from here, in a great thickly-populated and prosperous valley. The people are restless, suspicious, fickle, and independent. They will not supply us with food, and in many ways the work will be difficult, but there are hungry hearts there, and so we are going right ahead as God leads the way. We already have Government permission for temporary settlement, and I propose going over there this week to cut the boundaries, and to prepare for our first building. Dear ones, continue to pray for us, to labour in prayer with us, that Christ may have many thousands of trophies from Lubaland.

One of our Christians has just returned from Ndala and he reports having had splendid meetings. Also at Chigala, on the way home, he was persuaded to stay the night, and ten adults, as well as children and young people, yielded to the Lord Jesus, bringing their charms and fetishes to burn. Hallelujah."

Ngoimani, March 7th, 1917:

"The rain is coming down in torrents. The ground outside is all 'on the swim,' and the tent in which I sit is waving and slapping as the wind catches it, and the noise of the water pelting on to my outer canvas tent-fly is like a great roar. Thunder is rolling and lightning is vividly flashing. During the dry parts of the day all the ropes and canvas are slack and limp but, as soon as the rain comes, everything soon becomes taut and rigid. I got a lot of inspiration from these howling, rushing, crashing storms.

How often God's children get slack, lacking in energy, and lose the sense of the awful consequences of a soul dropping into Hell. They forget the grandness and completeness of God's salvation in Christ Jesus. What is needed is a heavenly storm, a tornado that turns things over and discovers the leaky places in the tent. It's God alone who can show us our own littleness and defects, but it is I alone who can allow Him to do so. Search me, O God, through and through. I want not one scrap of leaven, not one leaky spot in my tent, not one day's time to be burned up in wood, hay and stubble.

While Jimmy is holding the fort at Mwanza, I am putting the finishing touches to the temporary building, and spending as much time as possible scattering Gospel seed. I've caught more than one fish. Hallelujah! One fellow came to the tent about one hour ago with pains in head and body and, when prayed for, God healed him. The pains went at once, and he said he desired salvation.

It's hard for people at home to understand the needs and features of a work like this. A map is nothing to a great many people, but I send you a diagram sketch which will give you some idea of the great needs and possibilities around Ngoimani, and a little of what has been done. Of course to evangelise thoroughly one needs African helpers and a good cycle, and the best preaching can be done on a sort of circuit system, taking in about three or four villages per day. We have the cycles, and the local lads are just beginning to get keen on soul winning. As one looks across the valley (south east) there is a big range of hills beyond it. Also in that direction there are many large villages. Lubaland for Jesus! Set this country aflame with the Gospel by your prayers.

God is indeed blessing the work here in saving souls, though it has been said to me: 'You don't know the African character. You can't be sure that one of them will be a stable Christian.' For my part I want to give Jesus all the glory, so I'll give Him glory now for saving them and, when I see them stable, I'll give Him added glory for keeping them. I haven't any time for these timid, faithless, half-hearted methods. If I begin to doubt all that God is doing I'll doubt my own salvation next. I'd rather enjoy the grapes than knock my knees together at the giants.

I'm digging clay for the walls of the temporary house. We exhumed an old human skeleton. Many of my workers are afraid to continue the job. I wish they were as much afraid of sin as of an old lifeless corpse.

'Uphold me – free Spirit,
Then will I teach transgressors Thy ways,
And sinners shall be converted unto Thee.'

Yours in God's all sufficient grace.
'Waters to swim in'."

Mwanza, April 16th, 1917:

"Here I am down with another dose of fever, and a temperature of 102°F. However, I think the worst of it is over, and I want to write, if only a few lines, in acknowledgement and thanksgiving for your gift. How I praise God for all His care. I always endeavour to answer letters by return when dealing with money, but in this case I'm shaky, and my head is all on the swim, so that I feel the donors will not mind if I make the one letter do.

The two lady missionaries who recently arrived from South Africa are just broken down and weak, and so they leave the day after tomorrow for a few months' rest and change up on the high Tchilongo plateau, and perhaps they will go to South Africa. Also Jimmy is five days' journey distant, so that in two or three days the whole of the mission work and meetings, etc. will be on my shoulders for a while.

Jimmy had a heavy journey to Kabenga. Roads here are not what they are at home. He managed the distance in five days. At this time of year the little narrow twisting paths are almost hidden in the long soaking grass and forest undergrowth. Often they are worn down into mere gutters by the constant tread of feet, and now are filled with water. Jimmy writes, 'After leaving Kikondja I was going barelegged for two days, the 'roads' being flooded with the exception of a few yards here and there. The vile, evil smelling mud, oftentimes up to one's middle, was a sore trial. My legs are scorched with the sun. Yesterday evening, when turning in, my socks were stuck to the raw inflamed sores on my feet.'

However, he was rewarded, on reaching his destination, by finding a company of people waiting for his message, and he already reports some definite conversions.

Later: I have just returned from a four days' trip in the other direction. We had blessed meetings at some large villages, and our Christians rose to the occasion well. Some of the lads are becoming good preachers. During one meeting some iron workers from Mpianambayo were present. They heard the message for the first time and asked me to visit their district where, they say, there are several big villages up among the hills.

We have been having some very blessed waiting meetings. The other evening when about 20 were on our veranda, praying for the Holy Spirit, the power of God came down. Some had visions. The praise and adoration of these simple Baluba was blessed, but no one has yet been baptised in the Spirit."

Mwanza, May 15th, 1917:

"Just now we are experiencing the heaviest floods which have been known for years, and even the Congolese are ill. I have been down with fever more or less severe for the last six weeks, but am strong enough to get around a little and hold Gospel services. But Jimmy is in a critical condition. Just over two months ago I had a time of mighty blessing among the wild, lawless inhabitants of Ngoimani and Lubinda districts, two and three days' journey respectively from here. One chief was mightily healed, and in another village I put up a little temporary house, in order that we might go over there for a few weeks' preaching occasionally.

Lubinda is an influential chief whose arm was healed in answer to prayer and laying on hands in Jesus' all prevailing Name. He has sent, pleading for us to return and tell him more of God's salvation. As I was too weak with fever to take so long a journey, Jimmy set off about three weeks ago to follow up the work which I had started. Soon after he left, I became terribly burdened in prayer for him, and could only groan and cry to God for him. Later, news came that he was lying sick at Ngoimani in the little temporary house which I had put up. I couldn't forbear longer but sent one of our Christians to help him out. I heard nothing further for about a fortnight, when Jimmy himself came staggering in, in an awful condition. Some of the Christians went off and had a good cry, and I could hardly refrain from the same. He was pale and haggard, with eyes sunken, cheekbones standing out, face drawn and white, and limbs like sticks – a living skeleton. He had been too dazed to write, but had been living semi-conscious at Ngoimani for five days with blackwater fever. This is a most deadly African fever, and more than half the people who get it in this part of the world die within 48 hours. The Christian that I sent – a man baptised only a few weeks ago – on his arrival, neither ate nor slept but prayed through night and day to victory, and truly we owe Jimmy's life to him under God. But when Jimmy came round sufficiently to walk, instead of coming straight back in the hammock, he started off again (scarcely knowing what he was doing) with raging fever, and went with the tent and carriers preaching in village after village for about a 50-mile circuit away beyond Ngoimani, among some of the wildest outlaws and cut-throats in this dark land. At last, providentially, a young trader found Jimmy at Kachimpwe, which is three days' journey from here. He was horrified at his condition, took him to his camp for the night, and persuaded him to return home here without delay. Now Jimmy is piteously weak, his heart is evidently affected, and he can only walk just short distances. He rests most of the day in bed or in the hammock, and is gradually regaining strength. Thank God, my fever is now gone, and our goats are giving more milk, and the chickens more eggs than usual. All glory to El Shaddai. So that I think he will pull round with plenty of rest. I want him to go to South Africa as soon as he has strength to go."

Mwanza, 10th July, 1917:

"You will remember that at Christmas time we were surveying to establish a second mission station, in view of fresh oncoming missionaries, expected in answer to your prayers. As a result of this I made the necessary official arrangements in order to take up a grant of land, and in March I went to the selected spot to erect a temporary house.

March is at the end of a six months' rainy season. Violent thunderstorms preceded by the most furious tornadoes occur practically every afternoon, and often far into the night. The sight of the forest trees lashed into a fury by the frenzy of the shrieking winds, the incessant boom of heavenly artillery, the continuous flashes of extraordinarily vivid lightning, the deluges of rain, which in a few seconds turn the hillsides into rushing torrents and the level land into pools, all these are utterly beyond description. During the six times that I went that journey of 25 miles between our present station at Mwanza and the prospective one at Ngoimani, God in His faithfulness always held off the rain. It rained during other days almost incessantly, but not on the days on which I travelled. However for a large part of my journeys I had to travel barefooted through mud and water from a few inches to waist deep.

The building occupied a month, together with marking boundaries and cutting the necessary paths, and the diverting of a little streamlet permanently to irrigate the mission land. During this month I had some splendid services, and God graciously confirmed the word by stretching forth His hand to heal in the Name of the Lord Jesus. On my return I found the two Sisters suffering with fever, which has eventually necessitated their leaving for a complete change in South Africa.

At this time, the brother of a chief of a large village five days' journey to the south came to beg us to go and help tell out the Gospel in that place. As I was not strong enough to go at the time Brother Salter went, experiencing considerable hardship on the road, but great blessing at the end of the journey. To understand rainy season travel, imagine travelling in a ditch nine inches wide, and with grass anything up to twelve feet high sending down drenching sprays at every step. This until 10 a.m., after which add a scorching tropical sun to raise the standing water to uncomfortably near boiling point, and to blister the bare arms and legs of the traveller. When you have thoroughly gripped the above description, I trust that when you next mount a streetcar, or sit comfortably in a railway carriage, you will spend a few minutes asking God's blessing on His African missionaries on the tramp.

Owing to the long continued rains and the rising of the Congo River far above the usual level, there has been an exceptionally unhealthy season. Practically all our people have been down with malaria, and in the villages the wailing for the dead was almost continual, while even the wild animals were affected, and hundreds of thousands of fish died in Lake Niange.

During this time, attendance at our meetings increased by leaps and bounds. Our little chapel holding 150 has been packed, and scores have had to listen from outside in the tropical sun. People came in regularly from ten and twelve miles away, and I am often encouraged, when visiting villages at a distance, to find that some one or other has come to the service at the mission, learnt a hymn, and gone back to teach it (with variations!) to the rest of the village.

As soon as the rain ceased, having previously prepared moulds etc., we started to make the bricks for a big new church and school building, to hold 500 inside (with a squeeze), and a veranda which will run about four feet wide round the building.

One day as I was at work (Brother Salter having gone over for a stay at Ngoimani), I was surprised to see a Roman Catholic priest appear in long white robe and full regalia. I did not know at first what to do but, after a little upward look, I felt free to invite him to sit down and take a cup of tea. He then told me that he was on his way to Ngoimani, and wished me to resign all claims at that place. I told him I would sooner lose my life than yield an inch to him.

The priest left with many protestations that I was mistaken and that he actually was my friend, but later, in the villages, he warned people not to listen to us as our doctrine was false. Hence, when later he passed me and offered me his hand before all his following, I of course refused, explaining that under such circumstances I should be a hypocrite to shake hands. Whereupon, and I see how clearly God was in it, in his indignation at my 'insult,' he gave away his whole campaign. The Roman Catholics evidently are determined to encroach and encroach upon us until we have no free village left to preach in. For obvious reasons I cannot lay here all the steps I am taking to frustrate their designs, but we realise that the battle is not ours. The same Captain of the Lord's host who appeared to Joshua is with us – the Lord Jesus Christ.

Naturally these matters throw added responsibility upon us. The Roman Catholics are teaching youngsters a catechism, and then sending them out as 'catechists'. In this way, villages where the sick have been healed, fetishes have been burned, and a blessed work of God commenced, are likely to be taken from us. Thus we must train our Christians, teach them to read, put Testaments in their hands and send them out. The present situation argues the necessity for Congolese evangelists and a forward movement. We must carry on an extensive programme in other ways. A couple of months ago, I wondered why suddenly a considerable sum of money came to hand. More than we apparently needed. Now we see that every penny of it will be needed in our forward march for God, and we thank those in the blessed Name of Jesus who were so faithful in sending it.

Scarcely a week goes by without young fellows yielding to Christ, but alas, we have our disappointments as well as joys in these dear lads. Since we are busy on the building of the big church and school building all day, I do most of my evangelising at night. And very blessed happy times we have together, as a hundred or two sit around the crackling bonfires listening to the Word of Life, and singing the Songs of Zion.

A free rendering by Mrs Richardson of 'Shall we gather at the river' is a special favourite. The Congolese never tire of a song. They get up with it in the morning, and go to bed with it at night. They sing it as they carry in the timber for the mission building, and it comes floating up the hill, as I sit in the cool of the evening, from the villages all around. Our two beloved and faithful black brothers, Shakayobo and Shalumbo, with their wives, Napaula and Nasele, together with the younger man Shakitu, comprise a most estimable quintet. They are never weary in the work of God, going out continually when we are needed nearer home, telling with eager earnestness of 'this great salvation', and never so happy as when they were marching home with a handkerchief full of charms to burn. Often I am almost constrained to urge a rest, but they say 'Now we realise that war and famine are sounding out Jesus' coming, and we want everyone to know.' Their lives, their love, their prayers and their faithfulness are exemplary. We praise God indeed for these black co-workers, and trust they may soon meet their fullest desire, in being filled with the Holy Spirit. The land is very sunshiny, but hearts are, Oh so black!

A report comes to hand from Brother Salter in which he mentions praying for a blind girl in the village of Kalembi. After a little while the men came running to tell him with delight that one eye was already opened, and I doubt not that God will complete this miracle speedily, since this is one of the villages in which the priest has told the people to refuse to listen to us. Here also a man, who has suffered for nine months from a terrible bullet wound in his right arm and has tried all sorts of local charms, came to us with his wounds so putrid and foul that one wondered that the arm had not rotted off. We prayed for him and recommended pure water in liberal applications, with the result that God has beautifully healed up the arm, and though deep scars remain, they are perfectly sound, and covered with firm hard skin.

'Dear dying Lamb Thy precious Blood
Shall never lose its power.'"

6
The truth of divine healing
in relation to evangelism

*In a letter to a personal friend in the homeland Brother Burton tells of the
healing of the chief Ndala, which resulted in a pressing invitation to return
for a few days to preach the Gospel to the inhabitants of the chief's village.*

"I put up one night at the village of a surly disagreeable old chief
'Ndala.' My worker told me something of what the old fellow was
saying in Kiswahili, and it was not polite. So I went for a stroll along
the forest path while the tent was being straightened out, and the
green mealies (corn) were steaming, to pray for the chief. I noticed
that he had a terrible hacking cough, so I prayed for him, having
explained that Leza-Mungu, Who made the trees, rivers and hills,
had a Son Who died, instead of sinners, and rose again, and that if I
asked this risen mighty Son of God to take away the disease it was
bound to go. As I laid hands on him, oh how the power of God came
down. Villagers came out to look, so that, when I was through, I
had a crowd to whom for about one quarter of an hour I explained
the Gospel.

My carriers and helper quite entered into the business, explaining
matters, and showing that they themselves had grasped the details of
my faltering and informal talks, in a way which I little suspected.
Then the old chief came forward once more, just shaking with the
earnestness of his appeal to ask: 'Won't you come back through my
village and stop three days, or at least two, to tell us about this Jesus
Christ, the Son of God?' So I've promised [D.V.] to take the tent and
spend a week there soon with Jimmy, that he may call his villagers
together to hear the Gospel. Oh! that we may have the joy of baptising
him !"

*In a paper Brother Burton sets forth what the Bible teaches concerning a
truth which has a very practical and important bearing upon the service of*

the Missionary, namely 'The Truth of Divine Healing in relation to Evangelism.'

"'The signs of an apostle were wrought among you in all patience, in signs and wonders, and mighty deeds' (2 Cor. 12, 12). So speaks Paul of his divine credentials. The proof that God had sent (apostellô-ed [the Greek]) him was the accompanying signs (see also 1 Cor. 2, 4).

Gideon was quite right in assuring himself that the angel (literally – messenger), who was sent to him, came by divine authority, and so he asks firstly, 'If the Lord be with us where are all his miracles?' And later Gideon prays, 'If now I have found grace in your sight, then show me a sign that it is really you talking to me' (Judges 6, 13, 17).

God has at all times given his children credentials. When Moses approached Pharaoh God gave him signs (Ex. 4, 1-8). When Elijah confronted the prophets of Baal on Mount Carmel God gave him a sign (1 Kings 18, 38-39). And so it will be right to the times of the tribulation and the end, when God's two witnesses will accompany their testimony with the credentials of signs (Rev. 11, 6). Jesus Himself said, 'The same works that I do bear witness to who I am and that the Father sent me' (Jn 5, 36).

When Christ sent forth His first apostles He told them that they must heal the sick (Luke 9, 2; 10, 9) and this command has never been countermanded or withdrawn. The command against taking purse, scrip and money, which command had been given when the disciples were sent to the 'lost sheep of the house of Israel' (Matt. 10, 5-6) was abrogated later (Luke 22, 35-36) in view of the worldwide ministry. And whereas, before, the disciples had not been permitted to take a staff, now they might even buy a sword. But the command to heal the sick was not, either then or at any subsequent time, repealed. It still stands. In fact, when sending His disciples into all the world (Mark 16, 15-20) Christ's last words were: 'These signs (credentials) shall follow them that believe.' And, true to His promise, the Lord plentifully strewed their pathway as they went forth and preached everywhere 'with signs following'. Thus we see Philip at Samaria healing the sick (Acts. 8, 6-7), Peter at Lydda healing the sick (Acts 9, 34-35), and Paul at Lystra healing the sick (Acts 14, 6-10).

'Oh!' says someone, 'these were special men, unique men, extraordinary men.' And so thought the people of Lystra, for they were about to sacrifice to them. But Barnabas and Paul soon disillusioned them on this point by asking: 'Why do you these things? We are men of like passions with you' (Acts 14,15). Just ordinary, everyday men but with 'God also bearing them witness, both with signs and wonders and with many miracles, and with gifts of the Holy Spirit, according to His own will' (Heb. 2, 4). And this lasted up to the last chapter of divinely recorded Church History where we find Paul still healing in the case of Publius' father on the island of Malta (Acts 28, 8).

'Well,' says someone else, 'those were apostolic days.' Exactly! And we are still in apostolic days. 'God gave some apostles... for the edifying of the body of Christ, till we all come, in the unity of the faith and of the knowledge of the Son of God, unto a perfect man, unto the measure of the stature of the fullness of Christ' (Eph. 4, 11-13). Do we yet see the Church a full-grown and perfect body, in unity of the faith, etc.? No! Well then there must be apostles still, because apostles were given till then.

Much wrong has been done in this matter by a misapplication of the passage 'Am I not an apostle? Am I not free? Have I not seen Jesus Christ our Lord?' (1 Cor. 9, 1-2) from which it is argued that an apostle must be one who has seen Christ in the flesh. The foolishness of the argument is manifest, for there is no record that Epaphroditus saw the Lord, but he certainly was called an apostle (Phil. 2, 25), though the Authorised Version translates the same word – messenger. And this brings us to another point. An apostle is simply a sent one - a messenger. And a missionary is exactly the same thing, 'a sent one'. Apostellô is the Greek word meaning 'to send' and mittere (Latin) is the word 'to send' from which comes missionary. They both mean the same thing and, if a man is sent by God, he is an apostle, a missionary. But if God does not send the man, whatsoever he may call himself, he is neither an apostle nor a missionary, for he is not 'a sent one'.

Now Jesus never divided the Gospel age into two parts. He didn't say, 'You are going to have an apostolic age with signs following, and then a post-apostolic age without any signs.' No! He said, 'As the Father has apostellô-ed (sent) Me, so have I apostellô-ed (sent) you' (John. 20, 21). And He told His disciples to make other disciples among all nations (Matt. 28, 19-20. R.V.), and He said: 'Teaching them to observe everything that I have commanded you.' So, of course, since Jesus had commanded His followers to heal the sick, they must teach their disciples to do the same. And so we find Paul teaching his disciple to deliver the same things to others, that they may hand on these very things to others also (2 Tim. 2, 2).

Is it not clear that Jesus Christ, our risen Lord, started off the method of evangelism exactly in the same way that He meant it to proceed? And since 'into all the world', 'of all nations', 'to every creature', and 'always even unto the end of the age' are specifically mentioned in this connection (see Matt. 28 and Mark 16), are we not grievously to blame, if we take out the healing of the sick from our Gospel message?

Moreover, if people come with a message purporting to be sent from God, have we not a right to expect the credentials of 'signs following' as an evidence of their mission or apostleship?

We bless God that, from the very first, in Lubaland He has accompanied the proclamation of His word with 'signs following', so that many sick people, who have suffered for years and have been regarded as entirely beyond the help of man, have been blessedly and sometimes immediately restored in the Name of the Lord Jesus.

Moreover, while those healed in some cases remain unsaved to this day, yet both they and their heathen associates acknowledge the power of God and the authority of Jesus' Name in these healings, proving to them clearly that we have been apostellô-ed (sent) by God, since 'these signs follow'.

The following letters dated March 24th, 28th, June 10th, and July 4th, 1916, are personal letters addressed to Mr Thomas Myerscough, but matter dated April 15th, June 4th, and July 1st, 1916, are 'Reports.'

Mwanza, March 24th, 1916:

"Your kind letter is to hand in which I note that £23 is on its way. I read the news while sitting in the stifling heat of the little Belgian 'poste' (Government administrative outstation) overlooking Lake Kisale, and my eyes filled with tears at the faithfulness of our great God. I'm of the opinion that the officials thought I'd received bad news, but with stately Belgian courtesy they said nothing.

Three days ago Brother Salter and I had been talking of our project of leaving Mwanza Kajingu to the ladies from South Africa, and of the expenses which must be incurred in establishing a new station, and in moving our outfit again. We resolved to lay the matter before God, and definitely ask for our needs to be met before the rains cease, when we would set out. Your letter seemed like a beam of glory straight from the Father's throne. I believe I wrote last week telling you that I was still a bit weak from malaria. I praise God that 'to those that are without might He increases strength.' I'm just completing the last day's march of a 70-mile trip necessary for a Government transaction. In places the water was waist deep. Often the grass was 15 feet long, and for the first two hours of the journey each day we have been drenched with dew. Yet I have had no difficulty or over fatigue whatever.

This morning we passed the fresh 'spoor' (tracks) of elephants, bushbuck, lions, buffalo, waterbuck, wild boar, reedbuck, etc. The little Kisale children ran a long way to see me on the road, while, for fun, I occasionally chased them with the cow's tail switch which I carry to keep off the flies. At last they ran back with shouts of 'Enda biampe,

Bwana' – 'Journey well, sir'. At the Lovoi River the current is now so swift that the crocodiles cannot get up, so I and my carriers had a glorious swim. There are very many dear old bony, grey haired, shrivelled up women, who, with the children, are generally disregarded and made the drudges of the community. I always make a point of greeting these 'Eyo, mama, Wakamapo' – 'Oh yes, mother, you have health.' They give such a hearty grateful reply to such an honour as being noticed by a white man.

Lake Kisale (a huge marsh, about as big as Morecambe Bay, and bounded by mountains, with the Congo River flowing through) is governed by young Chief Kikondja and he receives royalty and a percentage of all fishing in the lake. I went to his village and met him yesterday. Dressed in good European clothes he is a fine stately fellow of about 23. He speaks and writes French, rides about in a hammock carried by six swift runners. His manners are faultless, but he refuses to sanction a mission station there because he has a huge number of wives (of whom he takes 15 or 20 favourites wherever he goes), and he knows that Christianity forbids this. However, there are dozens of villages about the lake, and I believe God will have His witnesses there even if He has to remove Chief Kikondja. (It is interesting to note in September, 1921, that God has removed this Chief, who was killed by an elephant; and the Chief who has taken his place is favourably disposed towards the Gospel. The Mission has now three evangelists and three schools among these great fishing villages.)

I think, however, this territory can be better worked by Congolese evangelists than by Europeans, as the mosquitoes are there in billions.

Mimpriss is a most useful book, but if you think it too ponderous to forward, then leave it. What about the Alford New Testament? Three or four volumes? Are they still in Preston and not in use? If so, is there any objection to our having them here? Of course, book post is one of our greatest boons, books being the one thing which can be got through cheaply. We've all but six chapters of Luke now translated, also bits of Romans and Revelation. Now that we are commencing translation work, I feel that we cannot be too careful to use all reliable information possible in setting forth the exact word of God.

Three or four times along the track to Kisale fellows came and took my hand and pleaded: 'Bwana, won't you let me come and lay table or cook for you, or keep the paths and gardens in order, or anything; for we want to know about Jesus Christ, the Son of God.' It is harder and sadder than I can possibly explain to say 'No!' to such appeals. Far and wide, village after village, district after district is open. The Administrator tells me of Mutombo Mukulu, a big densely populated district, some 200 miles south west of here where they are ready for missionaries to come. There is no one between us and there to preach Christ, and there are many villages on the way, so that if we can get the right people here an immense work can be done. People who know by practical experience the power of God, and have ministered faithfully and successfully at home, and who know their Bibles, and have God's seal of speaking in tongues as a sign that they have received God the Holy Spirit – people who are out for souls, God can use here. Oh! that I had a dozen such chaps as my beloved Jimmy here."

Mwanza, March 28th, 1916:

"Even here in the heart of Africa they are taking the men to carry loads to Tanganyika for those fighting against the Germans, and are also going from village to village buying up big quantities of chickens and meal, so that food is hard to get and also labour is getting more expensive, so that your generous gifts are a great help in furthering the work.

Central Africa is just now undergoing a big change. The older people wear a cloth around their loins made of bark or grass, but the younger ones wear cheap cotton cloth around them, or even trousers. The elder generation have their hair cut into pigtails. The younger generation have their hair cut short in European fashion. The older people live in wretched little round grass huts, dotted here and there in the forest. The younger make neat square houses with mud walls and veranda, and arrange their houses in two neat straight rows with a big open space in between. The older people fish with basket traps, but the younger with fish hooks and so on.

This sudden waking up of Africa to a new order of things is a marvellous, an unparalleled opportunity for presenting the realities of Christ, to take the place of their evil, cunning witch doctors. They are already casting away their fetishes and charms, and yet for hundreds of miles there is no one to point them to Jesus, so they will sink into drunkenness, immorality, and into the atheism of many of the whites of this land.

They are civilised people just as much as Europeans, but with a different sort of civilisation. We have many different tradesmen in the village who are very clever at their work. There is the blacksmith. He has a wonderful pair of bellows made of wood and skin, and his hammer and anvil are stone. He makes arrow heads, axe heads, hoe heads, spear heads, etc., out of iron which the people themselves mine and refine from the iron ore in the hill sides. Then the salt maker gets a wonderfully good salt from burnt reeds. The cloth maker makes cloth from palm leaves, grass, bark, or the papyrus. The basket makers are so skilful that they can make baskets tight enough to carry water in. The potters can make many kinds of pots and bowls which will stand the fire as well as our cast-iron saucepans, and vegetables cooked in them are much sweeter. The boat makers can make very fair canoes hollowed out of a single log. One often hears them chip, chip, chipping away in the forests. There is a tailor who sews with lock-stitch. I gave one man an old worn-out waistcoat. The tailor got it to copy from, and now there are about a dozen similar waistcoats about the village – blue, red, black, white, etc. Then there are village policemen who do everything but keep order. I mustn't forget to tell you of our wireless telegraph operator! He was probably working his wireless telegraph hundreds of years before we thought of it in England. How? Why? With drums! No white man has probably ever properly learned the code. But I can send a message 50 miles away in less time than I can write a letter. The drummer here hits off the message on the drum. The next village passes it on, and so it goes forward. On a clear night the drums can be heard 12 miles away. When the two Sisters were coming to join us, we knew of their departure from Tshilongo (which is 300 miles away) the same night – i.e., about a month before they got here. The news had come, from village to village, all the way on the drum.

The village doctors are consummate scamps. They make medicine from dead men's hair, dogs' blood, elephants' dung, owls' feathers, etc. The person who is sick does not swallow the medicine, but wears it round his neck. We have no barbers. Husbands and wives scrape each other's hair off with a piece of glass or local knives. They do not only say 'I'm married to Banza', but they say 'I shave Banza', which means the same. English people who have come up here have told me how stupid these people are, and that they cannot work. At first I thought so too. I brought with me spade, pickaxe, pitchfork, rake, felling axe, etc. But when I gave a man my pick and shovel to dig foundations for the house, he took five days to dig three holes. So I asked him if he would rather use another tool. He said: 'Yes, I'll bring my spade.' It was a little scrap of iron in the end of a stick, but he dug 15 or 20 holes a day with it. And in cutting down trees they struggle all day with my big axe, but with their own miserable little axes, they chip away and down topple the trees in no time. They bent the teeth of my rake, and broke the pitchfork, so I let them bring their own 'lubibo' – three bits of stick – and they rake up the grass and rubbish splendidly. So you see they are civilised, but with a civilisation of their own. But we want to bring Jesus to them in the midst of their own.

They are very polite. If one man comes into a gathering of a hundred or more, he says: 'Moyo' – how d'ye do – to each one, rubbing each shoulder with a little bit of dust each time.

It is very hard to know what is going on deep down in their hearts.

I sometimes think that they want to be Christians in order to be like the white man. But if we are faithful in preaching the right Gospel, I know that God will be faithful in giving the right results, 'God working with them and confirming the Word with signs following.' You know it says in Proverbs: 'As the cold of snow in time of harvest, so is a faithful messenger to those who send him, for he refreshes the soul of his masters.' How hot and oppressive it is in the hayfield. The sun beats down, and the hay reflects the heat, and one is tired through having got up early, and longs for teatime to come.

I think God the Father, Son and Holy Spirit are like that. They are tired of professing Christianity, and the sultry heat of battle and wholesale murder, of Christ rejection, and the disobedience of the Church. What can we do to refresh the mighty Godhead? We can be faithful messengers, and refresh the soul of our Heavenly Master. So I'm not responsible for appearances and apparent results, but in village and forest, before black and white, to individuals and companies, to the chief and to his slaves, to the village elders and to the wee children, oh God, help me to refresh my Saviour by being a faithful messenger. "

Mwanza, 15th April, 1916:

"Having occasion to go to the great Kisale Swamp and also on a three days' trip northward, I longed that friends at home might have been with me to 'look on the fields ripe unto the harvest.' The opportunities in this district are very great indeed. In one village I was able to pray for the old chief. His people gathered round as I laid hands on him in the Name of Jesus, affording me a fine opportunity for preaching Christ. He begged me on bended knees to come again for a few days, to preach Christ to his villagers. Naturally, in their fear of the white man, many people ran into the forests, but in other places numbers gathered round: the lepers, the people dropping asleep on their feet with sleeping sickness, the old tottering women, and great gaunt skinny old men of the vanishing generation, the lithe, free, supple men and tattooed women in the pride of life, and the shy, wee children peeping round from their mothers' loin-cloths, just as they hang to mother's skirts in the homeland. As I went up to the little groups and families, sitting on their grass mats in the shade of palm and banana trees, they would listen with perfect respect and attention to the Gospel message. There is an immense field waiting to be occupied. At Kilumba there is a group of about six villages, some of them quite large. They are just killing each other off. We saw huts falling into decay and fruit trees with no one to pluck the fruit. I rested at one of the Kilumba villages, and the chief and his people gathered in large numbers. I was too tired to have a proper meeting, but as my food was being prepared I sat on my camp bed and had a little informal talk. The chief was so interested that he accompanied us a long way on the road as we went on.

At Kabumbulu there is a very genial friendly trader. He proposes leaving his place shortly, and has offered us his whole place, houses, gardens and all – one of the prettiest, neatest trading camps on this part of the Congo River. He says that if we like he will just move out and let us move in free of cost. I climbed a precipitous hill only a couple of miles from this place to see if the population was large, and I could see villages stretching in every direction. Really a tremendous opportunity, though there are other reasons why it would possibly not be well to accept this offer. I found one of the local councillors ill. He was sitting on his mat in the shade, looking poorly and miserable. So I went to greet the old fellow, and he listened most attentively while I told him of a mighty Christ, who heals the sick, and who can wash the heart clean from sin. When I had fully finished, he said, 'Yes, Bwana, I understand what you say; but who is this Jesus, and where can I find Him that I may believe in Him, and that He may heal me, and wash my heart?' Almost the words of the blind man in John 9, 36, 'Lord, who is he, that I may believe on him?'

The rainy season is now practically finished, and next week [D.V.] Brother Salter is going up the river to Bukama – 150 miles south of here – to get our next six months' supplies, which should arrive there by caravan within the next few days. Every forenoon a local man comes to help me with the language study, and we praise God for progress in the language."

Mwanza, 4th June, 1916:

"It is Sunday evening, and we have just finished our little breaking of bread service. Poor Jimmy Salter is, I grieve to say, in considerable pain. He went off to Kabumbulu (a village some 19 miles distant) on the cycle on Wednesday, and on the road the pedal of the cycle struck a tree stump, and hurled him to the ground with the left arm beneath him. I am inclined to believe that the outer bone of the two forearm bones is damaged, and have made splints and fixed him up as well as possible, but naturally he has suffered considerably. He is a dear, patient fellow and does not say much, but I feel grieved to see him suffering. However, we have committed the arm to the Lord, and believe that He will fully restore it. How much we enjoy our Sundays here! It is indeed blessed to gather the people around us and tell them of Jesus. Today, I have been dwelling much on Paul's great sermon on Mars'

Hill, Athens. A marvellously fitting message for heathen people who do not know anything of God's plan of salvation. 'I see truly that in all things you are much given to invoking spirits' (Acts 17, 22-31).

Here one sees little grass houses, about 18 inches high, beside the huts. These wee houses are called 'nkishi', and are inhabited, so the villagers say, by spirits. Thus, when a man goes out hunting, he first asks his 'nkishi' to prosper his hunt, or if one is sick, the 'nkishi' is requested to drive the sickness away. In all things they invoke spirits, as the Athenians did. These people have strange ways of judging cases of suspected crime, called 'Mwavi'. The Government has forbidden the practice but it is undoubtedly in regular practice when the officials are away from the village. Some of these are:

(1) *'Mwavi wa kasolwa'* – Trial by axe in which the suspected person holds a heated axe head in his hand, and if the hand blisters, he is considered guilty.

(2) *'Mwavi wa mema asaluka'* – Trial by boiling water. Here the suspected one has to pick a stone from a pot of boiling water, and if the skin leaves his hand he is pronounced guilty.

(3) *'Mwavi wa bulembe'* – Trial by poison in which the suspected person drinks a gourd of poisoned water, and if the poison makes him vomit he is considered innocent, but if it has some other effect or makes him swell up and die then he is supposed to have been guilty.

Stealing is very rare, and the reason is not far to seek, for one may see people about the villages with the right hand cut off at the wrist. They are butts for the continual scorn of those who see them, or are pointed out with jesting – 'That man's hand was chopped off for stealing.'

Our house workers and a few of those about us seem to show a real desire after God, and we believe the long-desired outpouring of salvation and blessing is not far distant."

Mwanza, June 10th, 1916:

"Truly the Lord is loosening our grip of the things of earth, and preparing us for that glorious upward bound to meet the risen Christ in the clouds. I do praise God that He has given the Phillips' grace and backbone enough not to compromise in the matter of going to war. War, pestilence, famine, death, hell – these things had, a few years ago, seemed the spectres of a past age, and folks felt so secure behind British bulwarks that one might have considered that the Union Jack availed for the world to come as well as here. But now – God has certainly been shaking things, and we find no fault with Him. His purposes in judgement and grace are all of them perfect, glorious, and flawless. What have the people to say who believed that we were civilising ourselves into a millennium, now that 46 per cent of the world is involved in war? She is staggering through blood knee-deep, but she will be up to the chin in it before Christ extricates her, and begins His reign by shattering the nations like potters' vessels with His iron rod.

How blessed it is to feel that we are one with Him in all His designs and that we are ambassadors of the King of Kings, carrying His unparalleled proclamation of Sovereign grace to Lubaland. And how are we getting on? It's hard to say, but we're going right ahead, telling out the message and relying on God to work the results. The Husbandman has long patience for the seeds to come up and grow. Sometimes I'd like to scratch up the seed and see how it's sprouting but I know that if we sow bountifully we shall reap bountifully so we're sowing, sometimes with headache and touches of fever, sometimes with exuberance of spirits. Sowing among the men who work for us, and in the villages around. Sowing to Europeans and Africans, Jews and Gentiles. Sowing with paucity of expression and vocabulary. Sowing to big crowds gathered together to hear the Word, and often also in little words dropped to individuals. I don't know which will prosper, this or that, or whether both alike will be good, but will trust God for an abundant harvest.

During these last few weeks I've felt a great drawing to prayer. It seems to me as though the whole future of the Mission is in the balance. Either it will be an ordinary humdrum mission, or it will be a mighty deluge that will sweep from home to home, village to village, till billows of salvation and grace roll over this dark land. No one knows the great longings of my heart for God's very best to come to these dear Baluba. Let us pray right through until the blessing comes.

You ask if there's anything you can send. Thank you so much for your loving thoughtfulness and care. Among the most useful things are safety pins and needles (fairly large), cotton (cheap, small reels), brass-headed nails (the cheapest variety). Don't get small boxes and cards, but the cheaper assorted kinds in bulk. A safety-pin here will buy two eggs, and we can get a fowl for three needles."

Mwanza, 1st July, 1916:

"From time to time we are greatly encouraged by letters telling of prayer on our behalf, and indeed we realise that we are not independent units, but part of God's great Gospel army. Some do the praying, and it falls to our lot to do the preaching – and the tramping.

Since this is so, I feel that I am fully justified in laying before you all the burden of my heart. Rom. 1, 16 tells us that the Gospel which we carry is the power of God. For months we have struggled with language and other difficulties, in order to present the Gospel to the people. If we are equipped, as we believe, with the same dynamic as were the early Christian saints, then the same upheaval, the same conviction, and the same accompanying signs must be ours. We praise God for the one or two, who, we feel, are being stirred up to serve the Lord; but God is surely not satisfied with this little and so we cannot be satisfied. Now is the time for people to be shaken with a mighty conviction. Now is the time for these dark heathen to feel the burden of their sins, and flee to Christ, the sinner's only Refuge. No doubt the people are interested, but they are not aroused. They have 'not tasted the power of the world to come.' They have not shuddered at the awful gaping hell which awaits them.

Of course many are only now commencing to grasp the purport of our message, and again others start out with their bows and arrows to hunt when they know we are coming to preach. We cannot expect the harvest all in a moment. 'First the blade, then the ear, then the full corn in the ear' (Mark 4, 28). I have no fault to find, no disappointment to express. God has worked blessedly; but I feel that now is the time for us to unite in prayer, that God will do a mighty work of grace. He that sows bountifully shall reap also bountifully. So in the next few months we shall doubtless reap a harvest commensurate not only with our preaching but also with your praying. My whole being calls to God for precious souls. Oh for a Baluba Pentecost! Something which shall satisfy Christ Jesus, our blessed reigning Lord, for the travail of His soul.

Last week Brother Salter and I were out to the north preaching. We go from village to village, district to district, where there is not a saved soul. No one has ever heard the Name of Jesus. Truly 'darkness covers the face of the deep.' Oh, Spirit of God, third Person of the Trinity, move upon the face of the waters. Oh irresistible God, in the Name of the Lord Jesus, do Thou speak the word, 'Let there be light!' and there shall be light. Tonight, if you could sit with me at the table as I write, you would hear the sound of chanting, and the 'rub-a-tub' of the drums. A filthy devil dance is in full swing and, since it is Saturday night, the signal drum will presently go, inviting the people to the witch-doctor tomorrow morning, in order to prevent their coming to hear the Gospel. 'Sons of men, can these bones live? Prophesy upon these bones, and say unto them, O you dry bones, hear the Word of the Lord. So I prophesied as I was commanded. Come from the four winds, O Breath, and breathe upon these slain, that they may live. And the breath came into them, and they lived, and stood upon their feet, an exceeding great army' (Ezekiel 37).

Beloved, are we going to have a Baluba army when Jesus comes? It rests with me – and you! My Jesus, I don't want just a few for You. I want hundreds and thousands. I'm hungry, hungry for them to turn to God, so let us pray constantly and expectantly, as though our own souls were at stake."

The following are extracts from a personal letter written by Bro. Burton to a friend in Johannesburg:

"Brother, you can understand, I think, how I feel. We are now able to preach in Kiluba for half an hour at a stretch. The burden of souls is heavily upon us; the villages are in the hands of the devil. Never a Gospel shout to shake his hold has ever reached the people. I have not the strength or time for preaching and building too. This is the time when Christ may be theirs. I cannot put any time into bricks and mud. So we have all agreed to let the building stand over, and go in for quarrying living stones from all the surrounding villages, for God's eternal temple. I am keeping half a dozen labourers at work turning out 500 bricks per day until the rains set in, in September, and we are giving ourselves over to the language, prayer and the Gospel. I cannot tell you the inexpressible joy and satisfaction that floods my soul as I give out the message to the people as they sit around on the ground. Oh, Hallelujah! You understand. The power of God comes down, and the people are gripped. We want to preach Christ in every village within a day's march of here before the rains set in; there are many scores in all directions, some with just a few inhabitants, and others with hundreds.

Bro. Salter and I set out with the tent on Saturday or Sunday morning and preach around till Monday or Tuesday, and then we pay other visits during the week, or sometimes take more extended tours. Also we have long personal talks with our carriers en route. One or two men specially love to accompany us, and fire continual volleys of questions at us along the road. Then, as we lie in our camp beds at night, we can hear the people around the crackling logs, preparing their food, and at the same time detailing to an interested audience what we have been telling them along the forest paths during the day. Also, if we have preached in a village at mid-day, those who come in later, from the gardens or from hunting and fishing, wish to know what we have come for, and what we have said. Of course the villagers promptly go over the Gospel story again and again, discussing all the details.

This is excellent from three points of view. First, it carries the Gospel message to scores, and perhaps hundreds that we do not see personally. Second, it enables us to correct our expression, and couch the Gospel message in true Kiluba idiom. Third, it helps us, if we are still present, by showing how much of our message the people have intelligently grasped, and how correctly. We can thus counteract or guard against incorrect conceptions and impressions. At one time or another, some of our carriers and the men accompanying us have been healed by the laying on of hands in the Name of Jesus. Thus, when we proclaim Christ the great Physician, they readily and spontaneously testify, and also take us to others who are sick. I believe it will not be long now before we have a band of Christians equally ready to testify of this 'so great salvation.' Our Baluba suffer from many faults, but bashfulness and backwardness at speaking are not among them.

We are indeed mightily privileged in being able to carry Christ to this people. Mercy, love, reconciliation, grace, peace, are all quite strange to them, and even the words which we use to express these are only approximations. They have not a genuine expression for love, and the only way to say He has mercy is by terms that imply that it almost kills Him to stoop to such a soft and undignified thing. Their whole lives have been occupied with pillage, debauchery, murder, drunkenness, fighting, feasting, immorality, torture and the like. They still occasionally bury wives with a dead husband. The Government forbids it, but it is practised behind the officials' backs.

In one village near here an old man and wife listened earnestly to the Gospel, and we have some reason for thinking that the old man received the Lord Jesus. He died, and a few days later Bro. Salter went again to the village to preach and was told, on asking for the old woman, 'She died, and was buried with her husband.' We could read the remainder of the tragedy between the lines. The widow does not, as a rule, fear or resent being buried with her husband, but steps deliberately into the grave and, affectionately clasping the corpse, allows the earth to be shovelled in over the pair. Also poison trials are practised on the sly. The rite of circumcision – with every debasing accompaniment – is practised on boys from ten to twelve years of age. As soon as children's second teeth appear, the two front ones at the bottom are knocked out with a piece of wood, and the corresponding two top ones are filed to a point.

Many of the middle-aged men have half of one ear cut off: a sign that they were prisoners in the hands of the Batetela, who raided this district from the north some eight to ten years ago. This raid, and that of Mushidi from the south, are two useful chronological points, for many people do not know their own age, but if a fellow says that he became a man, that is, went through the circumcision ceremony before the Batetela came, we know that he is about 20 years of age.

We come upon many signs of old villages in the forests and along the watercourses, but sleeping sickness, smallpox, and the small value set upon human life have evidently thinned out the population. Moreover, in order to terrorise these people, the Batetela raiders impaled vast numbers on sharp-pointed stakes and left them to struggle until death intervened.

It is just exactly a year ago since I left Johannesburg Station amid the tears and cheers and prayers of a big crowd, and this morning (July 2nd) at the meeting, as though to commemorate that notable event, God gave us two souls. They cried aloud for salvation. My great longing is for a real harvest among these people. I have watched one of these for some time with real interest, for he has been another Nathaniel: absolutely guileless, and true to his convictions from the first time we presented the Gospel message to him. I see that it may not be long now before we shall have Congolese ready to preach and teach their own people. But, oh what problems we are up against! These people know no self-restraint. They have no home government. The children are never punished in the home or taught to obey. They are outrageous liars. Truly it will manifest the grace of God in all its grandeur and power when these dear folk are turned into saints and made fit to preach the Gospel.

One lad seems to be heart and soul in winning others. He accompanies us from village to village, helps in the singing, and acts as exhorter after we have done preaching. He is at present cooking for us. We go very slowly as these people are apt to get 'swelled heads' if one takes undue notice of any special one. But I think that he may later drop cooking and continue to help us entirely in the preaching. He has not yet received the Holy Spirit."

Mwanza, July 4th, 1916:

"We had felt that we might move on now that the dry weather has come. I know therefore that you will be interested in hearing of our final decision. My health has not been good, and therefore I believe it would involve too much strain to start a second station this year. Hence we are staying right on here. We have got a run of the local paths now, and the direction of the villages, and are by degrees getting into a sort of circuit plan, by which we can go out for four or five days' trips, preaching at a round of villages. In this way, I believe that by degrees, as the work of clearing, building, etc. lessens, we may be able thoroughly to evangelise a very large area without much difficulty or fatigue.

I started in on a big building, to be used as a chapel and school but, as I cannot get the necessary speed out of the villagers for turning out bricks, I am contenting myself this season with the brick making and timber hewing. In this way we should be able to put up the building next season with little trouble or delay. But beyond the chapel I'm taking no responsibility, and making no promises, as I feel that I have all too little strength and reserve force (this climate takes it out of one terribly), and I want to use what I have in winning souls for Christ.

The things that are seen (bricks and roofs) are temporal, but the things which are unseen (souls won for Jesus) are eternal."

7

New recruits

Dear Brother,

"In reply to your suggestion that I have not sufficiently introduced my wife to the friends who are interested in the Congo work – I would give the following account of her and of our meeting.

Soon after my arrival in South Africa in 1914 I spent three months in Basutoland (Lesotho today) with a Brother and Sister Saunders. Mrs Saunders was my future wife's elder sister. Later I was ministering for some weeks around Bloemfontein, where I was the guest of a Bro. and Sister Raine. Mrs Raine was my future wife's younger sister. Then at a Convention in Johannesburg we – Miss Helen Trollip and I – were guests in the same home. Naturally, having met her sisters, a bond of interest was formed, and at that time we had blessed seasons of fellowship together over God's word.

Miss Trollip had been saved and filled with the Spirit some time before, and, like myself, she had the unspeakable privilege of a godly home and parentage. In addition to this, many qualifications made her eminently suitable as a missionary. Born among the Africans (her grandparents having gone out to settle in South Africa from England), she understood them thoroughly, and already knew something of the Xosa language.

Having taken a fair share with her parents, brothers, and sisters in the managing of the farm, and putting together of the home, she was already trained as a pioneer – and having been instrumental in leading those around her into deeper blessing, she had for years in a quiet and steady way been prepared by God for future service. But for myself, I had been called to Central Africa and, believing that it was too unhealthy a place for me to consider taking a wife there, I had resolutely put from my mind all thoughts of matrimony. Hence, when I left South Africa for the Congo, Miss Trollip and I were only warm friends, and as such used to occasionally correspond.

In 1917 I cleared much of the undergrowth from around our Mission home and, realising that the anopheline mosquito (which carries malaria) breeds out in pools, puddles and damp hollows, I drained or filled in all these within 300 yards of the house. Then as the rainy season started we were delighted to find that the anopheline mosquitoes did not return, and that our mission site remained comparatively healthy. Thus I realised that my former conclusions, as to the Congo being too unhealthy to allow of my taking a wife there, were groundless.

Another matter which was of importance in turning the scale of my opinion was the fact that women in the Congo have so often and so shockingly been treated by white men, that we male missionaries could not properly reach them. If won they must be won, for the greater part, by women (It was about this time that God, unknown to me, gave Miss Trollip a very clear call to just such work, so that the elders of her assembly in South Africa laid hands upon her, separating her to the ministry of the Gospel).

Now what follows is more easily felt than told. The married people will say 'Why, we felt that way too,' and as for the single ones, well, I hope that they will also enjoy the same. The fact of the matter is, as soon as I permitted myself to acknowledge that it was feasible to have a wife in the Congo, I found that I was head over heels in love. Now Brother don't expect me to tell you all about that part! I can't! But anyhow the end of the whole matter is that I went to South Africa alone and returned to the Congo with a wife. And how can I sufficiently praise God for His gift. One prepared for me long before we met, and just suited in every sense to be my help-mate and life companion in the work of carrying Christ to the Congo – 'The woman whom the Lord has chosen' (Gen. 24, 44)."

Having completed the construction of a fine big church and school building, whose seating capacity is 400 or 500, Brother Burton became so weak with fever that he felt it advisable to get right away from Mwanza and the work, and to have a complete change. In September, 1917, he accepted an invitation to visit his next door neighbour, Mr Dan Crawford at Lake Mweru, a distance of 21 days' journey. He was away from home altogether two months – spending a happy time in roaming the forests, splashing in the streams, preaching in outlandish villages, far away in almost unknown corners of the north end of the great Kibara plateau.

The letters dated January 18th, July 15th, and November 15th, 1918, were written to Mr Thomas Myerscough, Preston; and the letter also contained in this chapter dated Bukama, July 21st, 1918, was a printed circular letter to friends in South Africa.

"Despite the efforts of the Catholic priests to forestall us and prevent our preaching in the villages, our work is spreading gloriously. We have a nice band of Christians out preaching and living in the villages. It is hard for those at home to understand what these dear fellows have to endure for Christ. On several occasions we have found that there was famine in the places where they were preaching and, being unable to obtain food, they went without for two or three days at a stretch in order to bear the news of Christ to their heathen neighbours. They are open to insults and abuses from enemies of the Gospel such as our white skins save us from. They are exposed to the dangers and discomforts of the rains and floods. On more than one occasion they have very narrowly escaped the troops of vicious elephants which roam the country at this time of the year.

Today, news comes of one dear fellow who is lying ill in a village 19 miles from here – an inhospitable place – where people seem to divide their time between beer drinks and inter-village quarrels. I was with him last week, and he told me how in one village, which he regularly visits, 26 are born again and awaiting baptism.

Here is a little piece of multiplication. Our evangelists are now usually about six in number (though sometimes as many as ten or a dozen Christian preachers are out). Each one of these holds from two to six meetings per day – say an average of three. They frequently visit six or eight villages a week. The services are not always well attended, though occasionally very large crowds gather. Usually the number present will be between 20 and 50. Average 50 people per service, three services a day and six evangelists at work, and you will thus see that in the 30 or 40 villages evangelised, there is a weekly attendance over all of 6,300 hearers. Here is a land which, when we entered it two and a half years ago, knew not even the Name of Jesus, excepting where the Open Brethren are at work, and where now 6,300 are being regularly preached to each week. Of course, our hearers change, and I suppose that over twenty times that number altogether have now well heard and grasped the purport of our message. Surely 'He that sows bountifully shall also reap bountifully.' One of these days you will meet many of them in glory, and see their happy faces, and hear their testimonies as to the grace and love which they found in the Lord Jesus.

And our converts have to stand some hard knocks too. One village – Kabango – has been blessedly stirred. The people have been visiting us fairly regularly, and some have confessed Christ. But between them and us is a vindictive, ambitious young Chief. The Chief and people have remained steadfast at Kabango despite this young fellow's threats and insolence, so he raided Kabango village, carried off all the goats, ducks, and chickens, stabbed an old woman to death, broke their cooking pots, and generally destroyed or abused all that he could lay hands upon.

I visited Kabango a week ago and, amid the ruins of the cooking pots and the piles of destroyed food, I preached the Gospel to a big gathering, and was delighted to find that there was no vindictive revengeful spirit, and that the young converts had no desire for retaliation, but had humbly committed their loss into God's hands, saying, 'He is our Father, let Him do unto us as He sees fit.'

We have another white worker with us, Brother Gatzke, a South African. He is already a great help, and is quickly picking up the language. He is not altogether a stranger to us as I baptised him in the Pretoria Swimming Baths about three years ago. Brother Salter is just now away at the camp of a friendly trader on the Congo River. In my absence he had all the mission work on his shoulders. He was taking two sessions of school per day, and was busy with translation work besides, so that overwork brought on a bad dose of fever. I believe, however, that, by going away for a complete change of air and surroundings, he will soon be fit again.

Many of the local people have been used as carriers for the German East African campaign, and have returned home with a brutal, swaggering, murderous spirit. The Administrators collect the poll tax with difficulty, the lives of the white population are often in danger, and scarcely a week goes by without our hearing of half a dozen Africans being shot down by some white man in self-defence. We of all white people are the safest. We only carry a rifle when we want to shoot meat. We greet the people in their own familiar way, tie up their wounds, pray for their sick, ask God's blessing on their villages, and are well known as their friends.

A few days ago I was crossing a river on a rickety old bridge when I saw armed men lurking in the grass on the farther bank. They were manifestly evil intentioned, but to disarm suspicion and show a friendly spirit I shouted a kind greeting, and asked them how many baboons they had killed, and passed by quite unmolested, though my carriers said that they had remarked: 'We're after the baboons that wear clothes and have no tails.' I later learned that a Government soldier was shot through the neck and thigh with poisoned arrows near the same spot only about an hour before. A week before I was cycling along the path, enjoying the trees and flowers and the cool morning air, when I ran into a group of armed men lurking in the bush with arrows on their bow strings ready to shoot. One chap was very impudent, but another said 'Bwana, I know you are a missionary. It's a good thing that you are our friend or you would now be food for jackals.'

At present we are overworked and under-staffed. Last week the father of a very powerful chief, who rules over many thousands of people, came to me with a present, to beg me to go and teach them. I have too much work as it is and cannot possibly go, though it is heart breaking to refuse. Where, beloved, is the man who will say: 'Lord, here am I, send me'? I suppose that within a few months the Catholics will visit those villages, and despite the objections of the people (who hate them) they will place a youngster there with a Catholic catechism, and then having formally claimed the district we will be forbidden to enter. The same thing happened last year when three men tramped a day's journey to ask me to visit their villages. I could not go but sent another Christian. Today the Catholics have stepped in. The people were so eager for the Gospel that they accepted false for true, and we are shut out.

The last dry season five or six deputations came. Some of them tramped three and four days' journey to beg us to go and establish a Mission among them. These three or six (or whatever number the deputation consists of) often speak for thousands. Those thousands have vaguely heard of white missionaries, with a message of salvation and life. They have sent to ask us (you and me) to give them the message. I am doing what I can. Day and night we are busy. Will not some one who reads this page, some one who is strong in body, and knows how to lead souls to Christ, somebody filled with the Spirit, and with a concern for Africa's perishing thousands, come and 'put a shoulder to the wheel' with us?

An old man tightly holding a charm made of antelope horn, yesterday violently refused to come near our meeting. He cursed me roundly. A few months ago he was an eager listener. His excuse is: 'You say that you are pointing to the forgiver of sins, Jesus Christ. The priest followed close on your heels and declared that he alone had the right to forgive sins. Where then is the real Saviour? I want none of your words. This is my saviour,' he said, flourishing his charm in my face.

That old man is one of hundreds who are being thus befogged. Surely we are not going to forsake Jesus and these Baluba. He asked us to 'go into all the world and preach the Gospel to every creature.' Is it not worse than criminal to let these heathen ask for the Gospel in vain, while people are in South Africa, America, or elsewhere, who might be, who ought to be, here?

We have a fine lot of young fellows learning rapidly, and eager to be off and preach. But we feel that, while not restraining them, we must urge that they be filled with the Spirit. We praise God for all He has done since we first set foot in this land, but our great cry is 'God send us a Luban Pentecost.' Will you see this matter through with us in prayer?"

Bukama, July 15th, 1918:

"I think that you heard of my marriage on May 23rd with Miss Hetty Trollip. Two days later I left the Karoo with my wife for Johannesburg to complete our Congo outfit. Your kind gifts have been a real Godsend. On the day of my marriage I only just had enough to pay for the rings and certificate. Next day a long standing debt due to me of £2 came to hand which enabled me to bring my wife to Johannesburg. Then money came to hand for outfit, and so we've gone on. On the day that I sent off my luggage by train to Elisabethville (Lubumbashi today) I hadn't the cash for my fare. Then two of our party of five arrived in Elisabethville short of funds, and so we had to come on without the provisions needed for the journey. But God has been so tender and faithful.

On the day after our arrival at Bukama our American Sister remarked: 'Oh, how I would love a nice apple.' There were no strangers within hearing, but next morning a Greek, a perfect stranger, and for no apparent reason, sent a lovely case of Cape Colony apples. Next day as we were wondering what to do for breakfast, there came a man with a present from a Government official, of paw-paws and pineapple.

On Sunday we had no bread, and didn't know what to do for dinner, when a little Belgian trader came down and invited us all to dinner, giving us eight or ten courses. If any one were to ask us 'Lacked ye anything?' we can honestly answer 'absolutely nothing.' We have fed and lived sumptuously, and El Shaddai is paving all the way before us. Ever since reaching Elisabethville I've been joyfully greeted with a cheery 'Wakamapo Bwana' (Greetings Sir!) by people on the street, at the passing railway stations, and along the river side. Numbers are believers.

One big sturdy fellow came smiling to me at Kambove, where I was changing trains, and told me that he had heard me preach the Gospel, and had believed. Here at Bukama, about 20 people came along on Sunday morning, unasked, and said that they had heard me preach last year at Bunda (25 miles away from Mwanza) and that they wished to hear more of God's word.

The news has reached this part of the country already that I am married and returning with my wife. Hence at several places we have had somewhat of an ovation. I do thank God for a wife who is one with me in my love for the Congolese and my desire for their salvation. By the wayside and among the great throngs at Elisabethville it has been a deep joy to me to have her stand alongside me as I gave out the word.

All the new recruits are already making big strides with the language, and are able to say a number of simple sentences as well as to understand a little of the underlying grammatical structure; and I believe that if I can give them an hour or two daily they will very soon be most useful.

It becomes increasingly hard to get provisions at a reasonable rate. But we praise God for a fine harvest of groundnuts and millet last rainy season. I've made arrangements for a good billy goat from a herd of good milkers to be sent to me at Mwanza in order to improve the strain of our goat herd there.

Also we have a good selection of garden seeds, so that all that we reasonably could do, we are doing. On the other hand it is hard to balance things. We must not spend too much time in attending to these matters or we shan't have strength and time for preaching. All the time new out-schools are going up, Congolese preachers need support, and fresh developments have to be met. But God is faithful. I needed six new blackboards for the school and had not time to make them; but when I reached Elisabethville a fortnight ago, our import agent remarked: 'Mr Burton, there are six black boards for you at the station.' Our Father knew I couldn't make them, and couldn't buy them, and so He sent them. All along the way, similar instances have occurred. Our translations cannot be accepted for publishing unless typewritten, and so a brother in Johannesburg presented me with a wee typewriter.

Naturally in these times our outlook is more or less circumscribed, but I think that in the minds of all of us is the determination to push forward in the Gospel fearlessly, deliberately, sanely, with all the powers at our disposal. You know a little of the difficulties that have beset our baby Congo Mission: of the dissension through our not having a thorough understanding from the start. We have so arranged matters that, I think, in future we shall all be able to work with a better understanding. I am afraid of over-organising. It almost invariably ends in 'too much boss.' But, while desiring that each individual should enjoy to the full the Lordship of Christ Jesus, I think that we have so dealt with the difficulty of admitting fresh missionaries and equipping them that we shall have some degree of order and mutual responsibility.

I know more and more of the way that prayer opens every door, overturns every barrier, and subdues every contrary spirit. The Name of Jesus is unconquerable, and I believe that in heaven, if disappointment could enter, one of our keenest disappointments would be that we had not achieved more in that Name, and resorted more to prayer in that Name."

Bukama, July 21st, 1918:

Bukama on the highest navigable waters of the Congo, where we are encamped, while waiting for the river steamer.

"In South Africa, we hear of a brother working a 'needy field,' when perhaps he ministers to 2,000 or 3,000 people, and other missionaries are only ten to fifteen miles away. We hear of Salvation Army, Methodists, Pentecostal people, and two or three other denominations, all working among 3,000 people, and yet this is described as a 'needy field.' We hear of people labouring for years among a tribe indifferent to their message, yet this is described as an 'open door.' Hence when I have written telling of open doors and needy fields, earnest well-meaning people have said: 'Oh, but we must not turn too much attention to the Congo.'

Therefore to clear misgivings let me give a concrete example of this 'needy field' and the 'open doors.' I will take the spot where I now sit, Bukama. The country around is well populated in parts and the language is so similar to that at Mwanza that the inhabitants understand every word. Yesterday I went to the nearest village. The Chief had once before (over 20 years ago) heard of Christ, but of the crowd of 300 villagers who sat around, not one knew Jesus. They listened eagerly, almost enthusiastically, while I preached for some three quarters of an hour, and afterwards the Chief said: 'Twenty years ago I told these people that God would send a preacher. But now you come, you preach once, and you go.' Then pointing to a crowd of children he said: 'Are these to grow up without the light, without a book, and without Jesus? Why don't you stop?' This is only one of a hundred villages just waiting, yet our own mission station, nine days tramp to the north, is the nearest centre of Gospel Light. Away in these forests are great populations that have never heard of Jesus' Name. One may journey for days south, past village after village, including the Funda-Biabo district, rich in tin and other minerals, but there is not a single Gospel preacher. Due west, again, one may journey for weeks in wild untouched country, including many big stockaded towns such as Kinda. An occasional trader has penetrated with his goods, the recruiter goes to obtain labour for the mines, and the Government Official sometimes collects tax, but the tardy steps of the messenger of Christ's Gospel do not echo in one square foot of all that great dark waiting region.

Big areas as big as Zululand, as big as Swaziland, as big as Basutoland (today's Lesotho), as big as Pondoland, with waiting thousands upon thousands, are at present without one single missionary. God bless all the noble, faithful missionaries who are laying down their lives for Christ and the Gospel in these lands of South Africa. I know something of their work, and it is splendid. But this I do say: There is no comparison whatever between the needs of those lands and the needs of the Congo. For the scores of white and scores upon scores of African gospellers in South Africa, the Congo has so painfully few, that there is absolutely no comparison.

Supposing you were to start from here, you could go by steamer for eight days, or 17 days on foot, then 270 miles by rail, and again 40 miles by boat, past great kingdoms, and large villages, without a preacher who knows the language, excepting Brothers Salter, Gatzke and myself, and a handful of poorly instructed Congolese preachers. Again and again we have received requests from large regions and small hamlets, powerful chiefs and petty headmen, just pleading for the Gospel message to be carried to them. People have come and worked for us for several months in order to hear sufficient of the Gospel message to carry it back to their own villages.

The other day we had just finished preaching in a place, and before leaving three or four big men came to me begging me to go to their village, two days' journey away. I could not go, but talked with them and found that they were earnest believers and, although unaided by any white missionary, one African who has learned the word from Mr Crawford – twelve days' journey away – believed, learned to read, and so successfully evangelised his own home district that scores had believed – young and old. I told them that they should put up a meeting house. They said that they had already built one and that they had prayed for nine years for missionaries but, excepting for one day when Mr Crawford passed through and baptised 50 or 60, they had never had a missionary.

How does this compare with South Africa where you have an average of one missionary to 7,000 Africans, and in some places the people are better evangelised than in our own English towns and villages? Around Mwanza, within a radius of 37 miles, we have, roughly speaking, a quarter of a million souls – about the same number as the people on the Rand (today's Gauteng). Yet on the Rand Compounds you have over 50 white and 300 African Christian workers. I once went to preach on a Rand Compound, and as soon as we had finished a Presbyterian African preacher took our place, to be followed by a Methodist. I understand that in the course of a single Sunday, five different Protestant denominations preach there. In the meanwhile our villages can sometimes get the Gospel once a week. Some hear it once a month, some once in six months, and some (Oh! that the unfairness and disproportion of it all might grip my readers) only once altogether in a lifetime, and some have never heard it even once. Against all your white and black preachers on the Rand please balance Bro. Salter, already weakened with fever and needing a rest, Brother Gatzke, still new in language and experience, and myself, limited and encumbered with building, furniture making, Government correspondence and general mission business, and four new recruits to train and teach. Friends, is the remark fair, I've so often heard that, 'We must not neglect South Africa for the Congo!' Is it fair?

I do not want to slight another to deflect attention to our work. I know that there are compounds on the Rand that are sadly neglected, but not by comparison with the Congo. When our company of seven missionaries has grown to 50, and our Congolese preachers have swelled to 300, then, and only then, will it be right to talk of devoting attention to Lubaland which should have been devoted to South Africa.

Now, as the above need pressed in upon us, and at the same time a Government request arrived that I should go to Elisabethville to make some agreements with regard to the land on which our mission is established, I determined to continue the journey to South Africa, and present the needs of the Congo at the Easter Conferences of the various Christian Assemblies. I bless God for all the encouragement given me by Pentecostal leaders. On several occasions I was able, before large assemblies to voice the Macedonian cry: 'Come over and help us.' There is a splendid missionary spirit stirring in many South African hearts, a desire to sacrifice all for Christ and perishing souls. Over 40 volunteered for the Congo, but as there were only sufficient funds for three, a choice had to be made. Here let me say that with the most careful selection possible, the obtaining of the very cheapest prices, and a free pass for ourselves and goods over part of the line, it has cost a little over £100 ($500) each to outfit our missionaries, and land them and their goods in the Congo from South Africa. I am sure that if any blame attaches to me it is that I have advised an outfit too restricted rather than too ample. Many people are surprised at this cost, as they do not realise the size of Africa. It is just a month since I left Johannesburg, and we have not yet reached our destination. There we were shivering with cold in underclothes and a great coat, but here we pour with perspiration in a cotton shirt.

Since our mission is 400 miles from the nearest shopping centre, we have to carry with us clothes, tents, baths, lamps, camp furniture, food supplies, cooking utensils, bedding, etc., etc. Moreover, we have to pay customs on the Congo border, and hotel expenses while awaiting train connections, so that I say it costs a little over a hundred pounds per head from South Africa.

To return to the recruiting. The missionaries who are accompanying me are Brother Bakker, a young compositor from the Pretoria Assembly; Sister Rickow, a fresh arrival from America, and Sister Toerien, an experienced worker of tried and proved calibre, who has done good service for a number of years in Swaziland, Cape Colony, and the Transvaal.

On Sunday evening, June 23rd, we left Johannesburg amid the loving 'God speeds' of many friends who crowded the station platform, singing hymns. I cannot help contrasting this journey north with that which I took three years ago. Then we ventured forth as strangers, without a word of the language, and in an unknown land. Today, I am privileged to preach the Gospel to the Baluba at practically every halt, and at Elisabethville, Kambove, and Bukama one person after another has recognised me and runs forward to joyously greet me. It is indeed blessed to find these people, as much as 600 miles away, who had trusted in the Lord Jesus through the word spoken at Mwanza.

While we rejoice in the fact that we are now seven missionaries in the Congo, I feel that we must seriously face a thorough evangelisation of these untouched people, and for this it is manifest that we are bound to have further new recruits with as little delay as possible, as it is nine months after their arrival that our fresh missionaries begin good preaching. Let me tell you all the kind of recruit we want and then you will pray. Naturally, we want those who are physically strong, mentally clear thinking, spiritually consecrated, and doctrinally sound. But at present, a lion's share of building, carpentry and business comes upon me, not because the others are not willing – I bear them record that even beyond their strength they have thrown themselves into the work.

But as missions and out-stations multiply, it is clear that we must have a man who can build and carpenter as well as preach. For weeks together I have had to neglect important business correspondence as all my strength was given to building, etc. Hence, I want someone who will take a share of this from my shoulders. Then again we want young sturdy fellows who can spend a considerable part of their time off among the out-stations, and opening up fresh villages for the Gospel.

This is a work which to a considerable extent has fallen on Brother Salter's shoulders, and his insight into Congolese character and unflagging zeal in the Gospel have particularly fitted him for it. But it is heavy work, and saps one's energy. Hence others are needed – men of resource and initiative, who can spot an opportunity when it is presented, and who will not lose a chance or lapse into self-centred complacency. Naturally every one of us will have a good share of itinerating, but chiefly in superintending our evangelists, and in preaching within a radius of two or three days' journey from our missions. To go further would often mean to neglect places nearer at hand. Hence the necessity of those who are free to move farther afield.

Now so many letters and enquiries have been addressed to us on the subject of missionary support that I think it will be well to explain the matter thoroughly, for I feel that the work sometimes suffers owing to the fact that the position of our missionaries is not well understood. I am sometimes asked: 'What is the least sum necessary annually for the support of a missionary in Central Africa?' The question as put is in itself an injustice to the missionary. Surely a fairer question would be: 'What is the sum required annually to enable a missionary to do the most efficient, unhampered, whole-hearted work for Christ in the Congo?'

Two can live more cheaply together than two separately. A man can exist in Lubaland on £60 a year, but as he would have to do his own washing, cook his own food, tend his own chickens, dig his own garden and would not be able to pay for the carriers necessary for itinerating evangelisation, he would have no time for preaching at home, or money for preaching afield (Under conditions existing in 1921 we reckon an adequate sum for which a person can do good work for God in the Congo is £85 to £100 per year. The latest estimates lead us to select £350 to £400 as an adequate sum for complete outfit and journey from England to the Congo. This estimate includes customs, fees, licences, etc.)

A worker costs sixpence (6d = 12c.) per day and hence for this cost – an extra, say, £7 ($35) per year – the Congolese can cook, and the missionary has so much more time for preaching. Another worker to garden, wash, and feed chickens will free the missionary for still further time and strength in the Gospel. Since in this country an ordinary labouring white man is worth £1 ($5) a day, surely it is sound economy to give any missionary worth his salt this few extra shillings which will free him to devote his whole time to the spiritual interests of the people. Thus given good, sound, keen, Spirit-filled missionaries (and as a purely business proposition it does not pay to send any but first rate men and women to this land where itineration and living expenses are so high), and a proper support, we can do business for God. I would rather have two people sufficiently equipped to do God's work without limitation and distraction, than six missionaries who are always tied up for lack of funds and have to spend time and thought and strength in household duties, which should be devoted to the Gospel. The missionary who is whole-hearted for the Gospel will put every spare penny to sending out local people to preach in villages to which he himself cannot go. This is the policy which Brother Salter and I have consistently followed.

As God has blessed us with money which was not needed for our own simple and immediate needs, it has gone to establishing our schools and sending forth Congolese. We need an outpouring of the Spirit. Our believers are fine, but they need the touch of fire. Will you not join us in prayer that this mission may not only be Pentecostal in name but in deepest truth, and that it may be said of our little band – not for our sakes, but for Christ's – 'They that have turned the world upside down have come hither.' "

The following communication was written by Mrs Burton to the 'Beloved Saints in the Homeland.'

Bukama, Belgian Congo, July 22nd, 1918:

"I feel I know you all through my husband, and so would like to greet you in the Name of Jesus our risen Lord. We may never have the joy of meeting in the flesh, but as children of our Heavenly Father with one mutual aim and desire in life – that of winning souls – I feel assured that we have already met in spirit around the Throne of Grace, worshipping, praising and communing with Him we love and adore and delight to serve. I feel you will be interested to know something of our visit to a village some days ago.

We had made arrangements for a service with the chief of the village on the previous day, and had planned to arrive there about 5 p.m. When we were still half a mile from the village we were met by scores of children and young folks who gave us a hearty welcome and escorted us to the centre of the village square, where we were met by the chief, who had already, in a loud voice, commanded his subjects to assemble for the service. In less than ten minutes there were about 300 seated round us scanning our faces and waiting eagerly for the Words of Life.

Only one, the chief, had ever heard the precious words before. Some 20 years ago he had heard the Gospel message from a certain Mr Campbell and although he did not feel himself competent to 'pass the word along,' he had often told his people that God would surely some day send someone to tell them of a Saviour who died for them. It was blessed to witness his joy as he realised that the prophesied time had at last arrived. The people listened eagerly, and in true Congolese style – punctuating the discourse every few minutes with questions and expressions of appreciation – as my husband told them in simple language the old, old story of Jesus and his grace. How my heart did go out to them in Christian love, as I silently prayed that God would bless the words spoken and make them to sink deep into their hearts and bear fruit to His glory. It is such a joy to me to be present at these services, though as yet I can only take a small part in them, as I know so little of the language. We four new missionaries are studying hard at Kiluba, and trust in a few months' time to do our share towards ministering to these poor heathen in darkest Africa. The majority of them manifest a real hunger for the Word of God, and when we realise how few there are labouring among these thousands, we are burdened in our souls, and cry again and again to God to send forth more labourers into this large corner of His vineyard.

And does He answer prayer? Surely, surely, when we pray the prayer of faith and according to His will. I praise Him I am here today in the Congo in answer to prayer. For years I had prayed 'Lord, send forth labourers into the harvest,' but a few months ago, He led me to add, 'and if you want me, make me willing to go where You send.' Not long after offering this prayer He called me, and immediately opened the door and made me willing to go where He was leading. My heart is full of rejoicing for I know that I am in His will. Pray much that our little missionary band will be a mighty force for God in the Congo."

Mr Burton wrote on November 15th, 1918:

"Sister Toerien had a bad dose of 'blackwater' fever, and now I'm down with a mild attack of malaria. About the middle of August we received £48 from you through Brother Bowie. How could we carry on this work without your help? My wife and I have just been out for a fortnight's tour of inspection to our out-stations. It was a time of rich blessing. We had a number of fine crowds at the various villages. At Bunda – a day's journey south from here – I baptised 19 – including the brother of the chief. We had a holy happy time together round the Lord's Table, and a few days of mutual counsel and instruction. The subject of 'foods offered to idols' presents a particularly difficult obstacle to the Gospel in that district.

A man came to me the other day with the following story: 'I have had three wives, and have lived in darkness. When I heard the Gospel, I called my three wives together and said, you cannot all live with me, for I am going to trust in Jesus. I want you all to believe, but whether you are converted or no, two of you have got to go. If only one believes, that's the one to stay with me. Two preferred to worship the dead, but one joined hands with me, and now we two want to be baptised.'

So I baptised him and his wife on confession of their faith, and now they are apparently going on well. I have had two faithful workers in my carpenter's shop: men trained by myself. For some time they have loved the meetings, and delight to shut up the carpenter's shop and have an afternoon out in the villages with me. I was pleased this morning when the two told me that they desired to follow Christ in baptism.

Two months later – Sisters Toerien and Rickow are now preaching, evening by evening, with Luba Christian women, in all our local villages, and this relieves me somewhat to train our evangelists, which I hope to get down to in earnest with as little delay as possible."

8
What God has done

An account of the work of the first two years and nine months in the Congo – given by Mr Burton in South Africa in April, 1918.

"How much we have to praise God for; His faithfulness and love to us in the Congo, and His confirmation of the Gospel message have been beyond all that we could express. I am once more in Johannesburg after an absence of two years and nine months in Baluba country – the very centre of Central Africa – having come south on a recruiting campaign to get more missionaries for the Congo regiment of the King of Kings, and I believe I can gain at a distance and give a clearer retrospective view than on the spot.

What has God done?
Work has sometimes seemed to go very slowly, and we have longed to see some mighty impetus, some tremendous outpouring of salvation and blessing. But rather God has seen fit, on the whole to build up line upon line, precept upon precept, here a little and there a little, so that only after a long look back can we appreciate the distance travelled and grip the true perspective of the work accomplished and blessings received. Today, however, I can sit quietly and compare the first days after our arrival at Mwanza Kajingu with the last days before I temporarily bade my Congolese friends farewell to journey southward.

Improved conditions of living
Think of the Mission station as we first found it and surveyed it. A trackless, forest-clad hill, covered with dense vegetation, long grass, tangled creepers, gnarled and twisted trees and mosquito-infested bush. Now compare this with the trim little mission house, the fine airy chapel, the splendid sweep of well-cleared land, the neat garden, the healthy fruit trees, and the straight wide paths, upon which I took my last look.

Then I think of the contrast between the flimsy camp furniture with which we first entered the Congo and the substantial tables and cupboards, beds and chairs of today. Moreover, we have a good stock of well-sawn planks cut by workers trained on the mission, seasoning for future work. During the first nights of our Congo experience we had to get under the netting soon after dark to escape the hordes of mosquitoes bearing deadly malarial poison, and eager to inject it into one's veins, but now, as the result of many months' hard work at clearing away the bush, damming, draining, felling trees, and digging out roots, we see and hear so few mosquitoes that we are able to sit reading and writing on our veranda far into the night without inconvenience and danger. Moreover, I believe that after a few months of further clearing and the careful prevention of any standing water about our kitchen and bedrooms, we shall be completely rid of even the few remaining mosquitoes.

The above features have turned our mission hill, until recently a pestiferous hotbed of disease, into a healthy, wholesome mission headquarters. Then we used expensive and often unpalatable tinned milk, but today our fine herd of goats give us a beautiful jug full of fresh milk each morning as well as an occasional kid for meat. At first we had not even a garden to fall back upon, but today in addition to a vegetable garden, and a knowledge of several edible leaves and roots which grow wild, we already have fruit from paw-paws, mulberries and Cape gooseberries, while orange trees, lemons, limes, mangoes and custard apples should also give us fruit within another two years. So much for our physical surroundings!

Language
I would next mention how God has helped us in studying the Kiluba language. Various neighbouring dialects have already been reduced to writing, and of course these were a great help to us, chiefly the Luba-Sanga, of Mr Dan Crawford, a fortnight's journey east of us. We have found that about one word in three of the Luba-Sanga is the same in general form as at Mwanza. Approximately, therefore, the relationship between the languages is similar to that existing between the English and Afrikaans in the Union of South Africa. Thus on the whole we were practically dealing with a new language and had no experience of Bantu formation on which to work. We reached Mwanza knowing nothing of the tongue of the people and having a Nyasaland (today Malawi) man to interpret who only had a smattering of English and less of Kiluba. Within a month after our arrival this fellow left and we were absolutely cast upon the language of the Baluba for every intercommunication

between ourselves and them. Realising that the Luba tongue was to be the tool with which, by the Spirit's power, we were to hew living stones for God's temple from Central African quarries, we always carried a notebook and pencil jotting down every expression, until today we have about 15,000 words and phrases, and can converse with our local people with perfect freedom, while Luke and Acts in Kiluba-Badia are just about ready for the press.

Evangelisation

But above all the foregoing results I am sure that the question that will be rising in many minds is – what about souls? What about the Gospel, and the all-important work of winning men to Christ, and turning heathen, steeped in darkness and superstition, into saints of the Most High God?

To gain a right conception of what has happened in this realm please grip the fact that as a rule we have been presenting the Gospel to this people for the first time in their lives. Of the many thousands who are continually hearing the Gospel, I suppose that scarcely one in a thousand had heard it before we came. The Name of Jesus Christ was unknown and, though eternal life was often spoken of, yet none knew how to obtain it. The people were simply living in the grossest immorality and worshipping the spirits of the dead, spending their spare time in witchcraft, fighting, beer drinking, and similar things. Today, however, from our two mission stations, and out-stations, with our faithful band of Congolese helpers, we are constantly sounding out the glad tidings and are surrounded by a vigorous and growing young church.

Our Christians love to help us to win others, and will willingly and ably join us in preaching and teaching. Our prayer meetings are real revival centres, and the people don't come to hear their own voices but to do business with God, and to get answers. We prayed God to settle missionaries at Kabongo, seven days' journey west of us. At that time Mr Dan Crawford, a fortnight's tramp to the east, was our nearest mission-neighbour but, praise God, He has heard and the American Methodist Episcopal Mission has put a young couple at Kabongo. Then we asked God for missionaries for Kabumbulu and Nkomeshia to the east, and two young 'Open Brethren' missionaries have taken over those spots. After that we prayed for the great town of Mutombo-Mukulu, with its 35,000 inhabitants, 16 days' journey south west from us, and I heard from a missionary in Elisabethville that he has missionaries for that place.

When the Catholics endeavoured to oust us from Ngoimani, you should have heard the battle of prayer. And in Jesus' name it prevailed. Today they have resigned all claims on Ngoimani. Our converts were almost all among the young men, and so our Christians made the young women a matter of prayer, for questions with regard to the overturning the heathen marriage customs were becoming acute. Today we rejoice to see that the young women are also on the move and a number are asking for baptism.

I would also record a number of blessed healings in answer to the prayers and laying on of hands of our Christians. They are beginning to find the power which is in the Name of Jesus. They are also crying earnestly to God for the baptism in the Holy Spirit.

So much for our brief retrospect. Now let us take...

A look ahead

'This Gospel of the Kingdom shall be preached in all the world for a witness unto all nations, and then shall the end come'(Matt. 24,14). We used carefully to discriminate between the Gospels of (1) – Kingdom, (2) – Grace, and (3) – Glory. But a phrase in Heb. 4, 16 'Throne of Grace' has caused me to be somewhat dubious as to the accuracy of this division. 'Throne' certainly denotes kingdom, yet grace is as clearly linked with it as e.g. Ps. 45, 1-2, where grace is poured into the King's lips. I believe in one Gospel expressed in one word – Jesus. Paul in Gal. 1, 8 pronounces a curse on the man who would introduce any other Gospel. It is Jesus by whose grace we are saved, to whose sovereign sway we gladly bow, and whose glory we joyously anticipate, and when He is proclaimed as at His own request, 'in all the world', then shall the end come. The sand in the hourglass of the 'Times of the Gentiles' has nearly run out. Where four or five years ago, Lubaland stretched 600 miles from East to West in vast darkness, and 500 miles from North to South, without a Gospeller, today little beacons of Gospel light are ablaze here and there. Now, Oh God, for Your rushing mighty wind of Pentecost, to fan the flame into a roaring, irresistible, all-devouring prairie fire. Let it come, Father, in Jesus' Name! (We would not overlook the splendid work done by the Garenganze Mission among the Luba-Sanga, or by the American Presbyterians among the Luba-Lulua villages).

From as much as five days' journey, chiefs and deputations come, asking us to send them the Gospel. We are over-worked, and undermanned. So I have come to get missionaries in South Africa for Central Africa, while Brothers Salter and Gatzke hold the fort. The missionary spirit in South Africa has made splendid strides. I believe that we shall soon see assemblies of Spirit-filled people right up through Rhodesia (today's Zimbabwe), while Portuguese East Africa and West Africa (Mozambique and Angola today) are also being occupied. In response to my call for Congo reapers, over 40 have stepped out. Some are too old, others too young and inexperienced. Some are physically unfit. But, had I the money, I believe at least six might return with me. We do not, however, feel that it is right to send missionaries to the fever stricken parts of Central Africa without a simple and efficient outfit of clothes and supplies. Hence only three are now stepping out for the Congo, though I trust, if Jesus tarry, that we may see others there before the end of the dry season.

We propose to open up a new station immediately on my return north, and are looking to God for a big crowd of Baluba, saved by grace, to meet Jesus in the clouds of glory."

Mrs Burton writes in the Missionary Herald of a visit to the out-stations of the Mwanza Mission: Brother Burton was married on May 23rd at Cape Colony while on a tour to South Africa for recruits. An account will be found in Chapter 7.

"For reasons many and various we were compelled again and again to postpone a much-needed itinerary visit to the Mwanza Mission out-posts. But eventually, early on the morning of October, we set out accompanied by our carriers and six Congolese evangelists, the latter to travel out and preach at wayside places, while we visited the villages along the main route. The early morning tramp through forests – the trees sparkling with raindrops and the fragrant tropical flowers flooding the air with rare perfume – was delightful. Our first halt was at a place called Sanga where we held two meetings and spent the night. We proceeded on our journey before sunrise next morning for Bunda, a distance of twelve miles from Sanga. After travelling a few miles the weather became so threatening that we had to take shelter in a hostile village where just a year ago a soldier, collecting taxes, had been shot. But God inclined their hearts towards us and they very kindly placed a hut at our disposal where we sheltered till the storm had spent its force and we could again resume our journey.

Arriving at Bunda at 2 p.m. we received a royal welcome from men, women and children who ran some distance to meet us, so delighted were they at our arrival. All seemed to be shouting and chatting, but none were listening except ourselves. After the many greetings were over and we had satisfied them with answers to their various questions they gave us an opportunity to partake of the delicious warm lunch so kindly provided by our Bunda evangelist. We did full justice to it, as this was the first food we had tasted that day. During the afternoon we had a good service in our little chapel, having an attendance of over 100 including 19 young converts who were very desirous of being baptised. One of these was the Bunda chief's young brother, a fine earnest Christian. After fully discussing doctrinal points with them and being assured in our minds, as far as human judgement could decide, that they were wholly aware of the seriousness of the step about to be taken, we decided to hold the baptismal service on Sunday afternoon, to be followed by the partaking of the Lord's Supper. Next morning, on account of our carriers' and evangelists' woeful complaints that they were 'meat hungry,' Mr Burton walked a distance of 15 miles and, much to the satisfaction of all concerned, succeeded in bringing in two fine buck. The Congo is teeming with many kinds of wild game, but owing to the inhabitants having only crudely made bows and arrows and primitive guns, very little success comes their way. Saturday afternoon and evening were spent in holding services in Bunda and adjoining villages.

At 9 a.m. next morning we congregated at the river and there, in the sight of God and about 150 spectators, including the chief and witch doctor, 19 dear souls – 14 men, four lads and one woman – followed Christ in baptism. It was a touching sight to witness such a scene, and we realised at least in part what it was costing them to take such a step. For instance the chief's young brother came to us the previous evening rather perturbed in mind and informed us that some of the villagers were threatening to bewitch him. We prayed for him and encouraged him to put his trust in God, and, praise His Name, He dispelled all his fears and gave him faith to be baptised with the others. Then another of the men had three wives, but he gladly parted with two of them so as to follow Christ's teaching in this respect. The wife he kept was the woman who was baptised. Oh, beloved brothers and sisters! When we see precious souls being saved from darkest heathenism with all its hideousness and made to be sons and daughters of God, our hearts cannot help leaping up with joy and praise.

Some white folks do not believe there are any genuine cases of conversion among these Central Africans, asserting that their professions are only for mercenary motives. But thank God! It is our privilege to be personally acquainted with many bright Christians in this country who have sacrificed all in earthly position and possessions and, with Paul, have counted all things but dross that they may gain Christ. Praise God! He can make the blackest heart white and pure. During the baptismal service, and after, my thoughts dwelt much upon that universally favourite missionary hymn, 'Send the Light', and my memory went back to the time when a few months ago the Lord led me to pray more earnestly for the door to open for me to take the light. And He did, praise Him; not only did the Master send me, but three other missionaries as well to swell the Congo band. But what is our little company among so many millions? Because we see the great need of more workers we feel like calling out across ocean, mountain, and plain, 'Bring the light' and praying, 'Lord, send many over to Macedonia to help us.'

After the communion service some of the newly baptised lads came forward to inquire of Mr Burton what course they should now pursue regarding the custom of eating food which had been enchanted and possibly coming under the Scriptural heading of meats offered to idols. Strange to say, he had never been confronted with this problem before. One is constantly coming face to face with some strange new custom or superstition. We realised now, because of the inquiring young converts, the matter needed to be investigated and dealt with immediately. So about 4 p.m., accompanied by the Bunda evangelist and two other tried and trusted men, we climbed to the top of the beautiful hill at the back of the village, far away from the crowds, and there with the assistance of the three evangelists Mr Burton thoroughly went into the different laws and customs relating to the partaking of food. I cannot deal with the subject here, as many of the customs connected with it are not fit for publication.

The Bunda hill, in height 500 feet, afforded a splendid point of vantage from which to take triangulations and my husband spent a profitable half hour with his prismatic compass taking much-needed observations for the filling in of his local map. From the hilltop one has a grand view of stretches of the great Congo River and of the Lovoi, one of its numerous tributaries, Lakes Kisale and Niange, and many important hills and mountain ranges. The combination of all is a most imposing sight. Bunda is one of our most strategic points, situated as it is just inland from several big riverside and lakeside villages and at the door of Lake Kisale.

We intended making an early start Monday morning but, owing to Mr Burton having a sudden attack of fever and dysentery, our plans had to be altered. God graciously answered prayer and next morning he was so much better that we were able to start off before sunrise for the Kisale villages. After travelling five miles through beautiful woodlands along a well-kept path upon which we saw the spoor of many kinds of game, we arrived at the beautiful swift-flowing Lovoi, before mentioned as a tributary of the Congo River. We crossed over in a canoe of typical local construction – the trunk of a large tree hollowed out. I keenly enjoyed the novel experience, notwithstanding the fact that a capsize would possibly mean the amputation of some limbs by crocodiles which frequent this river during the dry seasons!

After crossing the Lovoi we marched some six miles farther till we came in sight of Mangi, the first of the many lake villages, where we pitched our camp for the rest of the day and night. Where the road led over the brow of the hill the vast Kisale Lake came in sight and the panorama was so imposing that we sent our carriers ahead while we sat down on a log to enjoy the glorious scene. On the foreshore, thickly populated fishing villages bordered the Lake and thence, as far as the eye could reach from the eastern horizon to the west, lay vast stretches of papyrus with occasional open waters gleaming in the morning sun, while to the south east one could dimly descry the towering fastness of the Kibara mountains.

The drunkenness, villainy, and filthiness of Mangi made our hearts sad; but, as we prayed, God gave us faith to believe He was able to 'save to the uttermost all who called upon Him' in this Satan-bound village, as He had in others.

While working at Mangi and visiting among the adjoining villages, we were sometimes tempted to feel discouraged at not seeing greater results but, when travelling about and coming upon these wild unevangelised places, and comparing their inhabitants with our own people around Mwanza, we again take courage and praise our God for the mighty change He has wrought. During the afternoon no service was held, owing to the fact that the people of this and several other villages were indulging in a great beer-drink. Some hundreds were present and, after being spectators for a while, we came to the conclusion that some 2,000 gallons were being consumed! It was a saddening sight! Towards evening during a short interval an opportunity offered itself to hold a Gospel service. Considering existing conditions it was fairly well attended, though rather disturbed. God grant that His truth spoken may sink into hearts and convict of sin many of the listeners who sat or stood around that ring! (There is now [1921] a company of believers in this village).

Wednesday – off to Kikondja where we spent part of the day visiting among the few Europeans who comprise the white population of this small but rather important lake town. It is through the medium of the wireless station here that we are linked up with the outside world. We were requested to read an official radio-gram to the effect that the whole of the Kikondja district was placed under quarantine, so as to prevent anyone from entering the district on account of a most serious and contagious epidemic – Spanish influenza – which was spreading up from the south and had already reached Elisabethville (today's Lubumbashi). On account of these restrictions we were not allowed to visit our farthest out-post which lies beyond the protected area, so had to return by another route via Ngoimani, our second newly established Mission Station. En route we called on a Belgian couple who were pleased to have us spend part of a day with them. I was the first white woman this Belgian lady had seen for two years, so you may imagine her delight at having us. I was glad to embrace the opportunity of speaking a word for the Lord Jesus.

The country between Kikondja and the home of these Belgians is infested with elephants, and I must confess to having cast many an anxious glance through the trees on both sides of the path as I was being carried along in my machilla (carrying hammock) especially after we had passed by the path side a monument under which the mutilated body of a white man, killed and dashed to pieces by an elephant, had been buried just a year before! Two days following this, we travelled through forest country inhabited by elephants and many other wild animals. We constantly came upon their tracks as they crossed and recrossed our path, but God protected and brought us safely through. We called in at several villages so we and our Congolese evangelists had many opportunities of telling 'the old, old Story.'

On Saturday morning we entered the valley of Ngoimani with its picturesque palm groves and winding streams and paths, and another ten miles' travel brought us to the whitewashed Mission Home nestling so snugly against the side of the mountain. Brother Gatzke, one of our young co-workers, assisted by a Congolese evangelist, is faithfully labouring here for the Master. There is a large scope for work, and these two are kept busy visiting among 20 villages situated within a radius of 20 miles of the Mission Station. This district has been very wild. Five months before the Mwanza Station was opened, the Administrator who first attempted to collect the tax was attacked by an overwhelming force of Baluba. Forty men had to be shot down by him and the soldiers with him, before they could make their escape. The people are now quieter and the whole district lies open to the Gospel. The station was opened two years ago and, soon after, the Roman Catholics endeavoured to dispute our rights to it. They set up an opposition chapel, and it is only by the marvellous intervention of God that they have now withdrawn. The buildings already established are a large temporary mud chapel and a cosy little cottage – which is a great credit to Brother Salter, the builder. Since the first days of uphill work there has been slow but real progress, so that today considerable crowds are listening to the Gospel from end to end of this beautiful valley. While at Ngoimani, I was laid up with fever for two days and was still somewhat shaky when my hammock carriers picked me up for the last stage of our journey back to Mwanza.

Five miles from Brother Gatzke's, we climbed the range of hills which bounds Ngoimani valley on the south. From here we were able to trace practically the whole course of our 95-mile journey and Mr Burton was again able to take observations for his survey. On nearing home our way lay through the village of Shimbi where the Gospel is regularly preached, and being tired we had intended just to skirt the village. The people, however, would not allow us to pass by, but crowded round in large numbers. We therefore gathered them together in the roughly erected chapel and held a good service. Though weary with the long journey and hot sun, we were amply rewarded for our halt by the opportunity of preaching the Gospel to 80 or 100 people, young and old. An hour later we were back in our dear little mission home at Mwanza, after an absence of about a fortnight.

Let me emphasise a few important facts in connection with the life and work in Lubaland. The need is great; the darkness dense; and the pleading call of many most impressively pathetic! Is it worthwhile sacrificing home, friends, comforts, all, in response to the call? Yes! A thousand times, Yes! Happy is the man or woman who hears this call and responds. But all are not called to this service; many who are unable to go to the mission field can through prayer touch hearts for God in China, in India, in Africa, and other heathen lands where missionaries are giving their lives in proclaiming the truth, so that souls for whom Christ died may learn to know and receive Him as their Saviour and Redeemer. Beloved! the Master's command sings out, 'Go ye into all the world.' Shall we be guilty of hearing and not responding? Our blessed Lord sacrificed all, even to His life, for us. Shall we not, by His grace, be willing to give up all He asks of us for the sake of the millions of sin-bound but precious souls for whom He gave up His life? Beloved! pray, and if He sends, come !"

Miss Toerien in a communication to 'The Missionary Herald' for July, 1919, describes the surroundings of the Mwanza Mission.

"My precious Jesus and my Lord,
Thou purest source of joy to me;
Earth has no joys which can afford
This bliss which I have found in Thee.

Dearer than life, O Christ, Thy love,
Sweeter than all beside to me;
Nothing have I in heaven above,
Nothing on earth compared with Thee.

I praise my Heavenly Father for His wonderful love and goodness to us all, especially in the last two weeks. Sometimes when I am busy, or when I walk out after sunset to pray, such a sense of God's overwhelming love seems to take possession of me that I cannot help but get down and weep for joy. Oh! the Son of God is real to me, and He is so very near to us all, praise His wonderful Name. There is sweet rest in these everlasting arms of love. As you have all heard about our trip from Johannesburg to Mwanza, I will try to describe Mwanza Mission Station.

The mission home

The house in which Mr and Mrs Burton live is built of brick with a grass roof. It consists of five rooms, three large and two small ones, with a fine large veranda. The building nestles among some grand old trees; the grounds are well cleared of brush and weeds in order to keep off mosquitoes, and there are many great, grey granite rocks about the place. A few yards back of the dwelling house is the kitchen which must be a distance from it in case of fire.

As it happened, one afternoon while we sat on the veranda having our tea, we heard the men shouting and the drums beating. We rushed up to Mr and Mrs Burton's house. When we got as far as the new chapel we saw flames leaping up in the air, but were relieved to find that it was only the roof of the kitchen which was afire, and not the dwelling house. The men did everything they could to clear everything out of the burning kitchen, so that not much damage was done. After the rush and excitement were over, Mr Burton offered up thanks to God, right there in the open where we were gathered together, that nothing worse had happened.

Still farther back, we find the workers' quarters, which are kept in good condition. There are some fruit trees which will soon be bearing, and a garden space all enclosed. In front of the house there are flowerbeds being made, and grass is being planted to beautify the grounds. Around all is a fence to prevent people from coming and going all the time. Outside this fence to the left is the carpenter's shop, where carpenters are constantly employed.

The chapel

Leading directly down from the main house is a well-made path to the other buildings. The first of these is the new chapel which, when filled, holds 400 people. There is a platform, and below, on both sides, there are pieces of plank cut from trees and placed in rows to serve as seats for the worshippers, the men sitting on one side and the women on the other. A meeting is held in the chapel every Sunday morning at 8:30 which may last for two hours. During the first part of this service the Christians gather round the Lord's Table to partake of the emblems of the broken body and shed blood. In the last part of the meeting the sinners are faithfully dealt with, and it has been my privilege since I have been here to see some stepping out of darkness into light. Praise the wonderful Name of Jesus! It means much for the Baluba to leave their heathen customs and superstitions.

One Sunday morning during the service, a young man testified to the fact that he had been saved through the precious blood of Jesus Christ, God's dear Son. After the meeting, we gathered around a fire, to which the heathen charms were committed. I can only remember two of them – one was against sickness and the other to make him successful in hunting. Let us pray that he may learn the healing power of Jesus' Blood, and that he may be successful in hunting precious souls for the Kingdom of God. We have had two baptismal services since I came, and it was a joy to see precious souls buried with Him in death and rise to newness of life. There was also a burial service in the little graveyard at the back of the Chapel, when a little baby of Christian parents answered the call of the Good Shepherd, Who said, 'Let the little children come to Me and do not stop them because the Kingdom of Heaven consists of such as these.'

Temporary houses
The old school building is still standing, and has been made into a two-roomed house since we arrived, Mr Gatzke and Mr Bakker staying in it for a time until they went to Ngoimani. Miss Rickhow and myself were living in another two-roomed house further down the hill. One day just as Mr and Mrs Burton had returned from a trip to different points in the work, we were about to sit down to tea when a terrific wind-storm came up. We were trying to prevent things from blowing about too much in the house when Mr Burton shouted to us from the door to get out as quickly as we could, as the roof was falling. The front of the house collapsed entirely and we thought the whole house was going to tumble down, so we got our things out as fast as possible, handing them to the workers through windows and doors. In a short time we had everything moved up to the old school, it being unoccupied at the time. There have been some repairs on this, and we have found it a comfortable little 'Home, sweet home' ever since.

Village work
Congolese evangelists are always in the villages telling the Story of the Cross. Certain days in the week they are kept on the station, and every morning they gather for a little Bible study given by Brother Burton, and are then sent out on tours for the rest of the week. One of these men has charge of the school which is held four days a week, the men and boys coming in the morning and the women and girls in the afternoon. On weekdays when there is moonlight we often hold meetings in the villages, and on Sunday afternoons when it does not rain. There are many villages close by, nestling among the great wild forests. Here we find vast and wonderful opportunities to proclaim the Gospel of Christ our Lord.

Last September Miss Rickhow and I went for our first trip to some of the more distant villages. Some of the Christian men and women accompanied us and preached. We left Mwanza on Saturday afternoon and walked until we reached a village called Shimbi. The old chief came out to greet us. A shelter had been built there, with a grass roof fixed on poles, where we were to stay for the night. After our camp beds and folding table had been arranged, we sat down to tea. After that, the people gathered round a big bonfire and we had a service there under the starry heavens. We prayed and sang, and the local helpers gave out God's Word. We trust that in the days to come we may see results which will stand for eternity. After the service we silently committed ourselves to our heavenly Father's care and keeping, and went to rest, to awake in the morning refreshed and with thankful hearts for the many blessings that God had bestowed upon His children. We had breakfast, and then our carriers started off with their loads. We followed with the Christians to the next village, Mwana Mununu, where under a large spreading tree we held a service. Here the villagers seemed eager to hear the Story of the Cross, and there was an attendance of 50 – a good number for a small village.

From here we went on to Chigala. We had a body-guard – a number of children – coming out to meet us. Oh, the shouting and the noise they made in welcoming us! As we arrived at this place we were welcomed by the old chief who came, unannounced and without ceremony, right into the house where we were staying. Late in the afternoon of that day we went over to another village some distance away, where we were called 'Fathers.' The Roman Catholics had been there and, as they also wear loose clothes, the people no doubt thought we were the same, as they are unaccustomed to white women, very few having ever been there. There was a good attendance and they listened to all that was said. I noticed one very old woman, with one foot in the grave, so to speak, and I thought how sad to be in utter darkness without Christ and without hope. Pray for this poor soul, that she may accept Christ before it is too late. Returned to Chigala; we had our tea, then went down a little distance in the village where they were making a fire for the meeting. While the service was in progress the old chief came. He sat down in an old steamer chair, trying to undo the little greasy strings of hair at the back of his head. Suddenly a girl jumped up, crying 'Snake, snake.' This caused quite a disturbance, and for a time the attention was divided, until everyone was convinced that the snake had gone. At the close of the service we went back to the little schoolhouse for the night. The tsetse fly, which causes sleeping sickness, is found in this locality; but we were in our Father's keeping, so nothing harmed us.

Monday morning we were off very early for Twite. This is a place which hunters like to frequent, for there is wild game in the neighbourhood – elephants, lions, leopards, buffalo, etc. – but during our short stay we did not come across any of them. Passing through the forest on our way there we saw old tracks of buffalo, but that was all. In the evening we had our usual service round the camp-fire. Two poisonous red spiders caused a little disturbance with their wild running about, but the attention otherwise was good.

On our way back to Mwanza, the Christians had the opportunity of delivering messages at villages along the way – Sanga, Kalwenia, and Kisungu. While we were having our service at Kalwenia, we heard wailing in the distance and soon some women passed us, holding their left hands on their heads and crying – because a person had died. They always make a great show of their grief. Very often after we have retired for the night we can hear them down in the villages wailing because of some departed one. At first it was hard to get accustomed to. At the last village, Kisungu, we had a good attendance in spite of a beer-drink that was on.

Do not think for one moment that we are looking for great numbers to attend our gatherings, and that we are satisfied with only that. No, God forbid! We earnestly pray and trust that you will hold those who sit in utter darkness here in Congoland before the Throne of God, and that there may be those who, although their faces are black, may have their hearts washed whiter than the driven snow. May God keep us all faithful to the very end, so that His Kingdom may be extended and that wonderful Name, the name 'Jesus', be glorified."

9

Cords lengthened and stakes strengthened

In April, 1919, the work of the Congo Evangelistic Mission had extended over a very large tract of country. With a staff of thirteen evangelists on an average, an endeavour was made to preach the Gospel in every village at least once a month, and frequently the Gospel message was preached weekly in many villages. A considerable portion of Brother Burton's time at this period was occupied in training young fellows who eventually took charge of out-schools established in important centres.

Letters dated April 13th, August 10th and November 26th, are Reports; and the letter dated May 28th, 1919, also contained in this chapter is addressed to Mr Thomas Myerscough.

Mwanza, 13th April, 1919:

"Week by week the correspondence pile has increased, until now it numbers some 150 letters. Requests for news of our work, loving prayerful messages of interest and sympathy, leaders of meetings asking for a word to stimulate missionary zeal, applications from would be missionaries, gifts for the maintenance of our work, letters of enquiry on spiritual difficulties or Scriptural themes, enquiries from Government officials about the language and disposition of the local people, tax papers, correspondence about our proposed new translation of the Scriptures, and so on – the pile increasing week by week. I have manfully done my best to deal fairly with each letter. Night after night I have sat late into the night surrounded by buzzing mosquitoes, writing away till my brain and eyes could work no more. Day after day, amid the scores of interruptions which continually dog the steps of one who has the direction of a work like this, I have snatched a few moments here and there to try and overtake my letters. Frequently, just as I have settled down to a few quiet days of writing, a fellow missionary or evangelist has needed my attention or assistance, and my wife and I have had to leave letters, etc. to go off for a week or two into the forest with the tent, to visit distant villages. Then the Spanish influenza swept down upon us. Considerable portions of each day have been occupied in visiting the sick, while the buildings, usually occupied by our workers on the Mission hill, have been turned into a sort of little hospital where we receive, care for, and feed up our believers and preachers. Two days ago came the message from a distant under-chief, saying, 'Bwana, it is now three weeks since you sent us the word of life, and you yourself have not been for months. Our eyes are continually on the path. When are you coming?'

Now, what am I to do? Shall I write an answer to your letter, an acknowledgement, perhaps, to your gift – leaving old Kabango to look in vain along the path for my coming or shall I put off your letter, and take Kabango and his people the Word of Life for which they wait? One of our evangelists has just come in from a five days' journey southward with a list of 15 names. Fifteen precious souls won by and for the Lord Jesus. They are waiting for me to baptise them and to help their leader to put the assembly into scriptural order. They also wait for the gift of the Holy Spirit. I cannot neglect such a precious charge. Hence, I must leave the Sisters in charge of affairs at Mwanza, and start off, leaving my letters to accumulate for another fortnight.

My wife and I are still very weak, and just recovering from Spanish influenza. This week I am holding a conference with the Congolese Christians, and several of our evangelists from a distance have come in to discuss difficulties, and for encouragement and building up. Last Saturday two believers (who received Christ months ago in a village a long day's tramp from here) sent a pathetic request asking when would I come and baptise them. I praise God that now all the three ladies are able to preach a little in Kiluba, and of course the present press of work cannot continue.

When some months back we were grieved and praying much, because we were not seeing souls yielding to Christ, God gave us a blessed trophy. Our evangelist, Shalumbo, went to the village of Lubembei, 16 miles from here, and found there a man, Sani by name, taken by an evil spirit. This man, in paroxysms of frenzy, had clawed and dug with his fingernails a deep pit and cave right beside our little chapel. In this he would sit, trembling under the power of the demon that possessed him, while people came from long distances to consult him and seek his aid in the dispelling of disease. Our evangelist, seeing that the cave was likely to endanger our chapel walls, took a hoe and with the help of a fellow Christian, filled in the hole. The people stood awe struck, and the chief begged him to desist, declaring that by so exciting the demon the village would incur his wrath in all sorts of misfortune and calamity.

Presently poor Sani himself appeared, and looked the picture of misery. His hair matted, his nails like birds' talons, and his body caked in mud and filth. Shalumbo told him of God's love and the delivering power of the Name of Jesus. Then, upon Sani's request, he commanded the demons to depart into the beasts of the forest. Sani went off and washed at the river, and then returned to accept Christ. Later, when our chapel was demolished by a tornado, he was one of the first to offer to repair it, and since then he has visited us with six others from the same village seeking salvation.

Another token of God's blessing may have far-reaching results. One of the freed slaves, who came to us from Angola three years ago, desired to visit his home twelve days' journey to the north of us. We gave him provision for his journey, and he disappeared for nine months. Then one day he reappeared with a train of 34 of his fellow villagers. His Gospel message had received a great hearing among the big villages to the north where Christ's name has never before been heard. Of those who returned with him five have definitely accepted Christ, and the others were enquirers. Some of them were village headmen and people of considerable importance in their own sphere of influence. They have settled down to spend the rainy season with us, and to hear more of the Gospel, building a temporary village near the Mission, and supporting themselves by iron-work and grass cloth weaving, at which they are very skilful. They have begged us to return with them, or to send someone to carry the Gospel to their people. Oh, my God, send a messenger to reap those great unharvested fields (It is in these villages that Brother and Sister Johnstone have begun work, commencing in July, 1921).

Another step forward has been taken in the selection of a third mission site, at Kisanga. It is a big village two days' journey from Mwanza, and two days from our Ngoimani station. Brother Gatzke hopes to take charge of this work, and from this centre, by aid of Congolese evangelists, he should be able to reach five or six centres of village life. We have rarely received a warmer reception or a more hearty response to our Gospel message than we received from the big crowds who sat eagerly around us at Kisanga, and there is no doubt that God has opened to us a great and effectual door in that place.

At Mwanza we are already making busy preparations for the dry season's building programme, which will (D.V.) include a new brick house for the Sisters, and other small buildings. Sawpits are turning out planks in the forest for doors and windows, and labourers have now been at work for some weeks making bricks and piling firewood for burning the brick kilns. In about six weeks' time when the last rain has fallen, the mission hill will be a hive of activity. Here, again, a blessed door is open to us for the presentation of the Gospel. We have commenced a short, bright early morning Gospel meeting with our workmen, and if you could pop into the chapel at 6:15 a.m. each morning you would see a quiet and attentive company listening respectfully to the Gospel. We trust that many who come from distant villages seeking work may return home with God's message of eternal life in Christ Jesus, and I trust you will pray:

(1) For us that we may have wisdom in winning and teaching those people for Jesus;
(2) That others may be thrust forth of God to assist in the work;
(3) That our white mission staff may speedily become more efficient in the language;
(4) That the New Testament now in the course of preparation may speedily be placed in our believers' hands;
(5) That God's Holy Spirit may speedily and mightily be outpoured upon this land."

Mwanza, May 28th, 1919:

"Less than four years ago we were stranded here, almost penniless, and with meagre outfit, to face an unknown land, but in Jesus' Name. Today, we praise God for the happy bands of believers, for the freedom in the language, for the earnest attention at the Gospel meeting which I hold each 6:15 a.m., for the band of faithful prayers and supporters in the homeland, and for a loyal whole-hearted wife.

If the Philistines fill this well, praise God we have still that precious Name, and the Congo is large. He will lead us to 'Rehoboth.' They cannot undo what God has done.

We are not chaff to be driven away by every wind that blows. I learnt a beautiful lesson from a massive and graceful tree which was blown over by a recent gale in front of our little Congo home. Today the roots stick ten or twelve feet into the air. The roots were massive and many. The limbs were sturdy and straight, and to all appearances the tree was absolutely solid. But the ground was shallow. Then I thought of Paul's prayer that (Eph. 3, 17-19) the Ephesians, being 'rooted and grounded' in love, may comprehend the breadth and length and depth and height of that love. The roots of my life may be feeble, but oh what a depth of soil, oh what an expanse of virgin-land. I am grounded in God's eternal limitless love. It's finest heavenly loam. It supplies nourishment and vigour. No shifting sand this. Some feeble 'heath in the desert' (Jer. 17, 5-6) may blow to and fro anchored to sand – but God promises His children that they shall be as a watered garden, and as Mount Zion that cannot be moved. It's not a theory, or a college education that we are planted in. It's God!"

Mwanza, 10th August, 1919:

"In this happy busy Congo life of ours the details are not sketched in sombre greys and browns, but in the most vivid contrasts of light and shade, depths of sorrows and perplexity being beautifully blended by the Master's hand with joyous triumphs and blessed heavenly grace, and meanwhile the continually changing conditions are used of God for the fresh manifestations of His love and saving power.

Just now there is a great shortage of labour for the vast copper fields of the Southern Congo, and white labour recruiters, some of whom are none too scrupulous in their methods, are drawing our people from their villages and homes to the great centres of mining where many of the poor simple folk fall an easy prey to the vice and sin that are so rife around such places.

And yet among these, who being unable to obtain their tax money locally have left for copper fields, there are some fine examples of God's mighty keeping power, as letters, etc. testify.

A few weeks ago I was sitting in the tent in a village a long day's journey from home when a great shout of welcome went up. Some men had returned after completing a year's contract on the mines. As the local Baluba keep in touch with each other down on the mines, I began to enquire after many absent friends. How's Shindana and Moleso, Beleji and Mukumadi? At last I asked about the sturdy little dwarf, Matokembadi, who had left home about two and a half years ago after receiving life eternal in Christ Jesus. Messengers had, from time to time, brought news of his true testimony for God among those sinful places where our boasted 'civilisation' has begun to make itself felt. The returned workers told the following story: 'The Spanish influenza seized us on the mines, and many died. Some invoked the aid of the departed spirits. Others put on charms. Matokembadi was very bad, and we often asked him to let us awake the spirits of his dead relations, but he always refused saying, 'Don't I tell you that I belong to God? If He wants me why should I refuse to go?' And so he died maintaining his testimony, rejoicing to meet his Lord and refusing heathen tradition absolutely. Thus, while grieving to part with our black friends, we rejoice to know that some are carrying the Gospel message far beyond the limits of our little ministry, and sealing it with faithfulness even unto death.

Nearer at hand also deep gloom was cast upon us by the fact that the chief of a large village was bribed by Catholic priests with presents of whisky to allow Roman Catholic Catechists in his village where a blessed work has been going on for God for over two years. But now for the bright sunshine of God's overruling power. The village counsellors are attending our little chapel, and upholding our evangelists as never before, and only the week before last I had a note saying that a man with three wives had stood up in the meeting, and, publicly renouncing two of them, had received the Lord Jesus Christ.

Another example of how our Lord has turned our mourning into songs. Mushyala – his name means the 'waiting one' – is to all appearances a very weak and irresponsible man. But he heard of God's grace, and received salvation soon after his wedding. His father-in-law was furious and said: 'If you don't give up this doctrine, I will give my daughter to your rival.' Mushyala came in great distress to our believers saying 'I would rather give up my wife than give up my Jesus.' We prayed over the matter. The irate father-in-law called Mushyala and the other suitor for his daughter's hand. He then said, 'Since Mushyala refuses to be done with these words, you (the other man) may take my daughter.' Poor Mushyala prayed still, though he saw his wife apparently being given to another. But at the crucial moment, the girl said, 'But have I no choice in the matter? I don't want the other fellow. Come on, Mushyala, let us go!' And go they did, despite the raging father-in-law. Sequel: The last time that our evangelists visited the village Mushyala's elder brother also professed faith in Christ.

Some four or five weeks ago I was feeling very depressed, as we had not seen conversions in our Sunday morning Gospel meetings for some weeks, and numbers were going down. I mentioned it in a letter to the two young 'Brethren' missionaries who are now working just a day's journey from us, and I am sure they joined with us in prayer. On the next Sunday three or four came from a village away to the east, and after accepting God's free gift, they returned with our Christians to an idol burning. Next Sunday seven came with our evangelist from a village to the south, to tell how they have found Christ. Last Sunday two men and two women came in from a village a day's journey westward 'seeking for Jesus.'

And this morning a middle-aged man, who had listened to the Gospel for the last four years, living at the foot of the Mission hill, listened earnestly to a talk on 'Behold, I stand at the door and knock,' and later when the invitation was given he solemnly and definitely invited Jesus into his heart. So, praise God, He continues to give us the garments of praise for the spirit of heaviness, and the oil of joy for mourning. And now, as if to crown joy with added joy, three lads arrived as I sat writing, with a very dirty hymn book in the hand of one. They have come from Ngoimani. I called one to me and enquired if he could read. They all read well. Where had they learnt? At the Catholic priest's school. But now they have learnt the folly of that false religion, have found Christ through the testimony of a Christian at Ngoimani, and have come to confess Him.

Hallelujah!

When the clouds begin to gather, and the sun, which for months past has poured down heat with uninterrupted and relentless fury, is veiled by occasional fleecy films, the people smile to each other in happy anticipation, and remark, 'Mukutukutwi' – the harbinger of approaching rains. The morning and evening sun is like a ball of fire in a bank of black smoky mist, and if the rain is up to time we should have the first showers in about three weeks' time. Hence the local smithy is a hive of activity as the villagers bring their primitive axes and hoes to be repaired in preparation for the seed sowing.

We, too, have been preparing to sow God's good seed. Last week I called together our Christians and prayerfully read over to them a list of the local districts, out-chapels, and chieftainships, asking the old Isaiah question: 'Who shall I send, and who will go for us?' One by one they filled in the list, and by careful arrangement, putting a weak Christian with a strong one, one who cannot read by another who can, a hasty one with another of more cautious temperament, we have managed to plan not only for the occupation of all our present territory, but also for the evangelisation of two big new districts. Thus this rainy season should see a seed sowing of the word of life, and watered by your prayers we look forward to an abundant harvest."

Mwanza, 31st October, 1919:

"I feel the call of those great over-ripe harvest fields intensely. I would gladly lay down my life today to see them well occupied for Jesus. But from morning till night I have written telling of open doors, and yet I have made known so little. We do not want a little station here and there amid the darkness. We want to see main stations so placed that, with the assistance of Congolese evangelists, every village and hamlet shall regularly hear the Gospel. I believe that nine main stations (or even less, if God gives us really reliable workers) can thoroughly tackle the whole section. Within the last twelve years nearly the whole of Nyasaland (Malawi today) and North East Rhodesia (today's Zambia) has been thoroughly occupied for Christ. Now here is the great Central Katanga. 'We can do it if we will.'

> *By the grace of God that sought us,*
> *By the Spirit here to dwell;*
> *By the precious Blood that bought us;*
> *We can do it if we will.*

Spirit-filled assemblies of baptised believers in every village honouring and showing forth the Lord's death and winning their brethren for Jesus – with Bibles as common in the land as the fetishes are now – that is my prayer and expectation.

Both your gifts have come safely to hand. The one came just as we were starting off on our journey, and the other just as we returned. The interest and work which you put into collecting and sending these sums of money is much appreciated; and the Congolese Christians, as well as we whites, know vaguely that away there in Bulaya, the land of the white man, there are warm loving hearts, intent on bringing the Gospel message to darkest Africa. Also we feel that a letter from 'the Scribe' is sure to contain a breezy, sunshiny contagion and life, so that we look forward to your letters with joy.

Hettie often talks of the possibility of our one day popping in at 134 (The home of Mr Myerscough, the Hon. Treasurer of the Congo Evangelistic Mission, was then at 134 St Thomas' Road, Preston, England) – familiarly known to those who have enjoyed its hospitality as 134.

Personally I don't like the idea of leaving the Congo, even for a furlough, but I must confess that it will be one of the happiest days of such a furlough when I can introduce my wee South African wifie to the friends at Preston."

Elisabethville, Nov. 26th, 1919:

"I have received most encouraging news from Brother Salter, in England, to the effect that more missionaries are on their way to join us, and that we may expect Brother Salter himself towards the middle of next year. This is in answer to many, many prayers. How can we praise God sufficiently? When one thinks what this will mean in many precious souls hearing the Gospel of their salvation, who today are sitting in darkness, how the heart wells up in gratitude to the 'Lord of the Harvest' for thus answering our cry for labourers.

Naturally, the prospect of others coming set us considering which is the best direction for a forward movement. Of course Christless villages abound all around, and one could start in anywhere. But in the Scriptures we find that Paul, for example, by selecting a central spot at Ephesus, so preached and taught that (Acts 19: 10) all Asia heard the Word. Being a place to which many people gathered for the worship of the false goddess Diana, the crowds coming and going carried the news.

Our Baluba catch fish by throwing poison into the stream. As it drifts down the poison sickens the fish and they rise to the surface and are caught. The fishermen do not put the poison at the mouth of the stream, for it would not go up against the current. They select spots where the stream carries the poison to the fish. In the same way we like to select spots where the Gospel will radiate. For example, if a chief rules over a large district, the outlying districts send their tribute to him or come to pay homage. Where there is a Government post, the people come and go to pay taxes. From amongst these a wide selection may be made by selecting a site with a big population close at hand on which to work; for then the Gospel would radiate and work into all the little out-of-the-way corners of the land. Thus my wife and I set out for a month's journey to map the country, find where the heaviest populations are, and of course to preach.

As a matter of fact, we were altogether 43 days in the bush. We travelled about 550 miles, and mapped about 770 villages, considerably over 600 of which have never heard the Gospel of the Lord Jesus before. How I wish that I could tell you of the scenes, so vividly impressed upon my mind that death alone will erase them. In many villages they just flocked around us, hemming us in with a solid wall of faces staring, wondering, listening. What wonderful meetings we had! The very first time in all their lives when they had heard the name of Jesus. They passed that Name from mouth to mouth, as we told them of the power of it, the love that was at the back of it. How, that this Name means 'Saviour' with all its setting of agony, bloodshed, ignominy, and death, but that the name now has a resurrection side to it. God hath made that same Jesus – whom ye crucified – both Lord and Christ. That there's healing, liberty, fellowship, and assurance of answered prayer, all in the Name.

How often young and old, in villages many days apart, would say 'Bwana, please repeat it. We have only heard it today, and don't wish to forget it: Jesus, Jesus.' One old chief came out of his hut as we were making a start in the small hours of the morning, by starlight, saying: 'Please say it again before you go.' And we left him in the darkness murmuring to himself: 'Jesus.' There were times when we preached and then endeavoured to dismiss the crowd, but they would not go. Often I was very tired and did not feel like preaching again, but as they hung around to hear more, and asked question after question I could not but gladly respond to the appeal.

One of the most fearful features of heathenism is its heartless cruelty, knowing no bounds, and not even hesitating at torture and lingering death. Thus only a few years in the past a regular trade was carried on in little boys. They were taken northward and sold for salt or grass cloth. Their purchasers tightly bound every joint and every limb to make them swell, as the flesh was then considered better for eating. Then after two days, if they were not already dead, scalding water was poured over them preparatory to eating them.

In other villages a milder form of cannibalism is secretly practised to this day. If a man is suspected of being possessed by an evil spirit, they say that, if he is only killed, the spirit will enter another person, and still continue his bad magic in the village. So, to annihilate man and spirit, they all share in eating him. But apart from cannibalism there are poison trials, secret societies, and cruel customs sufficient to fill books. A little Christian boy, converted as the result of the work of our neighbouring white missionary Mr Wilding, recently refused to attend the dance of the secret society Bambudje. So the members of the sect put him upon a platform of matting in a hut, over a slow fire, and smoked him to death. The whole family then disappeared. The people said that disease had carried them off, but of course it was the poison of the Bambudje, and no natural disease. In one village, where we would desire to place a white missionary, the old chief recently died, and shortly afterwards, foul play being suspected, they exhumed his body, and found three of his wives who had been buried alive with him.

The other day, passing along the forest path, we came to a smoky village. Fourteen huts were burned to the ground. There was blood on the ground. A man had been taken by an evil spirit, and had killed four men outright; two more he had slashed fearfully with a knife. Then he hacked down a lot of the village palms and bananas, and set fire to the huts, burning up the greater part of the food on which the people relied to keep them till next harvest. As we went to bind up the poor sufferers, the murderer stood at a distance looking on, leaning upon his loaded gun. But no one dare interfere with him or restrain him, for they reverenced the evil spirit which possessed him.

A little girl, a sweet, little, plump, black girlie sat rocking herself to and fro outside a hut the other day, crying, 'Father's given me away, he has given me away,' while the tears dropped from her grief-stricken face, and made lines down her little bare tummy. It was quite true. Two old women, renowned witch doctors, had commenced their incantations outside the father's hut, and he, fearfully afraid, had offered to appease them with whatever they would – the little girl.

During our journey, my wife noticed in one great village two women sitting in chains. We made enquiries and found that they were two of the chief's 60 wives. Tired of the dull monotony, the slavish ignominy, and the filthy immorality of their lives and surroundings, they had run away. But they were caught five days' journey away, and brought hack in chains to learn submission.

Why do I tell you all this? If I wished to harrow your souls, I could multiply such cases. But on the other hand I fear I have often been too prone to paint the bright side of the picture. No, my purpose is not to pain you. Listen! The chief of 60 wives came to my wife and me, saying, 'I know that we are bad. We're in the forest, and don't know the way out. Come and live with us. We will give you the best of the land. Ask what you will – goats, chickens, sheep. My villagers will build for you. You will not have to walk, for we will carry you in a hammock. Only come and tell us about God and this, what do you call Him, Jesus.'

In that same village, chief, headmen, wives, and 600 villagers stood and sat listening to the Word of Life. Then, before daylight dawned, people were around our tent with the sick to be prayed for. Some burnt their charms and believed in Jesus. Were it not that the eyes of the Catholics are upon us – eager to anticipate and thwart our every move – I could tell you of district after district where chiefs and people send out the same Macedonian cry, 'Come over and help us.' We cannot, even with the missionaries coming, tackle more than one third of all the great area visited by my wife and myself. And even if we could gospel all of it, this is but a wee bit out of this Christless land. We all should have some aim in life. Here in Elisabethville (today's Lubumbashi), one of Africa's most beautiful and opulent towns, a continual round of suicides tells of the heartlessness of mere money-making. Livingstone, the great pathfinder of Central Africa, cried, 'I will open a path into the interior or perish.' He had one purpose as Jesus had, who 'set His face as a flint.' I know that many dear ones who read this desire to be wholly given to the work of the Lord, that time and means are only held in trust for Jesus.

May it not be that this account of Africa's need will lead some to surrender and cry: 'Lord Jesus, You who died for me and live for me, to the last pant of my breath, to the last fibre of my muscle, to the last cent of my wealth, I pray that You would help me to carry the beautiful news of free salvation to these waiting needy souls.'

One aim – one purpose – all absorbing."

10

A trip to the Lomami River

Having heard from England, Holland, and America that new missionaries were preparing to come out to the Belgian Congo (today's DRC), Brother Burton felt it necessary to find the thickest populations, the direction of the main roads of population travel, the areas in which the Kiluba language is understood, and to spot healthy sites, with a view to locating the oncoming workers to the best advantage. Having had several of the Lomami River people with them at Mwanza for about a year, some of whom had been converted through the faithful testimony of one of the Mission's evangelists who visited them, Brother Burton had often been begged to settle along the Lomami River. Hence he chose that route for his journey of survey. They were absent from home exactly six weeks and the details of this wonderfully interesting journey are recorded in his Journal, excerpts from which are freely taken in this chapter.

"On Saturday, September 6th, 1919, by 6:30 a.m., a large crowd of men, eager for the journey, had gathered outside the enclosure of our Mwanza house, to be 'taken on' as carriers of our hammocks, tent, and equipment. As my wife and I sat at breakfast a number of our Christians waited in front of the door to wish us God speed and a safe return. Several wee Kanguba youngsters accompanied us some distance into the forest and seemed quite proud of my remark that before long they too would be able to shoulder their loads and accompany us.

The vast majority of officials and traders in this country know no Kiluba and a mere smattering of Kiswahili. Consequently they would point to a village asking, 'What is that?' The guileless Luba answering: 'Kibundji ' It's a village – the name for a village in their language, is then marked down on the map as 'Kibundji.' Many similar errors occur on existing maps, so that in travelling I carry a prismatic compass and triangulate where possible to keep an accurate record of villages and paths.

There is something infectious about Congo travel, and as we thread our way in 'Indian file' along the little wriggly forest paths, the carriers drop their Kiluba, speaking Kiswahili, the language of the caravan, shouting to each other of other journeys they have been on, and keeping up a continual chatter of advice and encouragement to those who are taking their first trip, while, occasionally, they break into a weird and melodious travel song. We camped at Lubembei, where we have an out-school, and after a day spent in New Testament translation, and a delightful dip in the Lungui river we called an afternoon Gospel service. A devil-possessed lad in this village was recently delivered in Jesus' Name. Also an old man was mightily convicted and wished to become a Christian, but was not prepared to give up his fetishes. He fell ill, had ten fetishes made to guard and heal him, and died soon after. His deserted hut stands near by the ten ugly wooden dolls in which he put his trust – an eloquent testimony to the inefficiency of fetishism. These two facts have mightily impressed the people, though the Catholics have tried to counteract the effects by declaring that we use sorcery.

Sunday, September 7th. We do not, as a rule, like to remain at one village from Saturday till Monday, as the carriers, if inactive, get into mischief with the local inhabitants. We prefer making a short move of four or five miles. Thus, today, we moved camp to Lubinda. The young trees on the hills were extremely beautiful. Every variety of red, scarlet, brown, fawn, lake, etc. in the early leaves. As I sat in my carrying hammock reading, 'The ox knows his owner, and the ass his master's crib, but Israel does not know, my people do not consider,' I could not but apply the passage to these Baluba. The birds and flowers, the trees and hillsides all seemed to be enjoying the bright Sunday morning, and only man, poor Christless rebel man, fails to recognise the tender loving hand of a heavenly Father.

When we arrived at Lubinda, we camped under a magnificent 'Kakunkula' tree. So far as we could discover it must be about 50 years old, but the shady, spreading branches were sufficient to shelter 15 such tents as ours, being 261 feet in the circumference of the tree's shadow.

The village is in two parts, divided by the Lubembei river. On each side are rivals, Mwana Bute Kalume, and Shiku. The former desires to establish an independent chieftainship, while the latter is loyal to the chief Luamba, of the whole Ngoimani valley. We had a blessed afternoon meeting with the former village and a moonlight service among the subjects of the latter. Mwana Bute had a diseased arm, which had pained him for years, and despite big sums in goats, cloth, etc. given to witch doctors, he only grew worse. Then during the first meeting that we held in his village he asked us to pray for his healing, with the result that he was at once healed.

Though his arm has given him no trouble since (four years), yet Mwana Bute is by no means a Christian. The afternoon meeting was opened for testimony, and some of our lads spoke blessedly.

Monday, 8th. We were away by 5 a.m. An early start enables one to travel in the cool of the day, but, alas, on this occasion, it also meant that in the semi-darkness my hammock carriers dipped me in a crossing stream.

We had a splendid reception at Kisanga. We have selected a site for a mission in this village, as several large districts can be worked from it. In the evening between 150 and 200 people listened attentively to the Gospel. My wife was amused to notice eleven women sharing one pipe, passing it round from one to another.

We had intended to help Brother Gatzke build a nice little station here. It is healthy, there is splendid timber, and in every way would make a fine centre from which to radiate the Gospel. But, alas, Brother Gatzke has gone back to South Africa, and, at least for a time, our plan has miscarried. The chief, his counsellors and people were all eager to have a school. May God speedily send His own appointed messenger. In the meantime we are working Kisanga and the villages ahead by fortnightly visits from our itinerating evangelists (Since writing this Brother Hodgson has taken charge of Kisanga Station).

Tuesday, 9th. We reached Mpiana early. There seems to be a fairly big population in the village, but it is very stretched out. Every man lives beside his own gardens in the bush in order to scare off the elephants, which would otherwise work havoc during the rainy season nights. The country round about seems to be very little inhabited. Only a few small scattered hamlets.

We had a delightful swim in the Mbungui. Not far off is a small pool which the inhabitants declare to be inhabited by their gods. They say that when they go to the pool and ask questions, a ripple or movement in the water indicates an affirmative reply, whereas silence and stillness means 'No'.

During the afternoon a big red puff-adder was seen in the trees near our tent. I shot it. But the people afterwards expressed disapproval, as they believed it to be possessed by the guardian spirit of the village. One of our evangelists, who was here some time ago, was given shelter in the house of a man whose little girl had a twisted neck. Charms and superstitions had for a long period been resorted to, but the neck remained crooked. At night, before retiring, our evangelist prayed, laying hands on the girl in Jesus' Name, and on awaking in the morning her neck was straight.

We had a fine afternoon meeting, somewhat disturbed, however, by the pompous behaviour of the Chief, who came late, just as I had well gripped the attention of the people, and refused to be seated, till his own particular mat had been fetched.

Wednesday, 10th. We reached Matabongo early. The Chief was most civil and respectful, but the people were very fearful of us, as unscrupulous recruiters of labour employ all sorts of subterfuges and underhand means to obtain workers.

In the cool of the afternoon I took my rifle and went to get meat for the carriers. I wounded a buck, but owing to the hastiness of the man who accompanied me it struggled off into the bush and was lost. I always tell my men that after I have shot, even if the game falls, they must remain low, lest they frighten off a wounded animal by revealing their presence. But in the excitement of the moment they almost invariably jump up and rush forward, with the result that, if an animal is not absolutely disabled, it frequently makes a last dash for liberty, only perhaps to die in some inaccessible spot.

On return to the village, I found that my wife had already started the meeting, and had a big crowd for such a sparsely inhabited district. There are a number of small hamlets within 25 miles of here, and a couple of evangelists might work them all from Kakongolo and Kijima.

Thursday, 11th. About an hour after we started a thunderstorm broke and we had a severe couple of hours. Fortunately we got up the tent before it struck us, so that neither carriers nor loads got wet. After passing a ridge of ironstone hills, we wound for the last five miles of our journey beside the Kiankodi river – a very thinly populated piece of country. The river is a beautifully clear stream about the same volume (at Ngole where we camped) as the Orange River in the Free State, or the Ribble at Whitewell near Preston. The dense luxuriance of the tropical vegetation surpassed for height and beauty anything we have previously seen. Enormous trees, tangled to their very tops with giant creepers, while the undergrowth impenetrably thick hung over the swiftly running water.

The first Ngole village which we reached numbered about seven huts, and our tired carriers refused at first to go further, though everyone in the village was suffering from a fearful disease of scabs and running sores, known as 'musa.' However, we finally travelled another mile on to a high ridge, and camped near the huts of the petty chief. He was a quiet unassuming man.

The Kiankodi plain is rich in salt, and most of his people were away gathering it. In the afternoon we climbed a hill at the back of his village. My wife found the ascent rather taxing, but we were well rewarded by a magnificent view. We could see hills to the east of the Lovoi River in the south, the Kasongo Nyembo hills about 50 miles west, and the hills shutting us off from the watershed of the Luvidyo River to the north east. Over these hills, about 30 miles from where we stood are the famous cannibal chiefs of Twite Munza and Twite Kabombwe. They are outlaws. Their country is high and healthy and the population is very large. Oh, may we soon see the Gospel preached in their villages. Twite Munza's people are gradually coming under control and some of them now pay the tax, but it is probable that Twite Kabombwe's spirit and the vicious cannibalism (which they practise with the smelling out of sorcerers) will call for a military action.

Away to the west also could be seen in the dim distance the blue plain of Mungu Sungu's country which is reigned over by those devil possessed women. The people appoint their chieftainesses according to a belief in incarnation. After one woman dies, they wait till some woman is taken by the usual paroxysms of demon possession, when she, and they, believe that the spirit of the departed Queen has returned to resume her reign.

In the evening I invited two old men to sit with us by the fire and talk. At first, we allowed them to ramble on in their happy, simple, irresponsible way, about the salt, and the days when they smelted iron, and how a raid of Kabinda's men swept down, carried off their forges and tools, and forbade them to work in iron any more. Tales of hunting, travel, and pages of local history they gave us around the fire. One old man remarked on our great wisdom. He said: 'But of course you're so old!'

I said: 'How old are we?' He said: 'I don't know. I cannot count my own years, and I'm only grey on the temples. How should I tell your years when your face and hands are all white? You must be my grandfather's age.'

Presently we turned the conversation into the topic of God's great salvation through Christ Jesus. Like the householder of Matt. 13, we produced from our treasure 'Things new and old,' telling of the God whose Name and acts they know, and of His Son Christ, of whom to this very night they had never heard – of the creation in all its glories around them, and of the new creation of all those who enter into the Lord Jesus.

As I and the other Congolese unfolded gently, to these two old blacks around the campfire logs, the precious treasures of God's grace and love, they seemed astounded.

One remarked: 'I always knew that those stars were eyes; for I've seen them wink as they looked at me. But well! well! Just to think that all I have to do is to lift my hands up there (suiting the action to the word) and speak to God, in the Name – of what do you call him – Yesu Kidishitu, and He will save, and heal, and keep me!'

After further talk they thanked us and went off into the night. Once in a lifetime they had heard the Word of life. How heart-breaking the thought, and then perhaps out again into heathen night forever. While self-satisfied Christians at home ask, 'Why should we go to the heathen?' and 'Isn't my money my own to do as I like with?'

How I wish that many at home might thus taste that concentrated essence of pure delight in telling of Jesus to eager ears and hungry hearts for the first time. They would need no persuading to come, to give, and to pray for these dark children of night and superstition.

Friday 12th. We followed the Kiankodi along our whole day's march through a country infested with tsetse fly, which made travelling rather unpleasant. My wife was continually and badly bitten. We camped at Kasakai. My wife found one poor old woman so ill that she could only just move out of her hut into the sunshine. She had come with her relatives to the saltpans, and as she was too ill to return at the end of the season they left her alone. How cruel Christless heathenism is! My wife, after praying with her, sent her some boxes of matches with which to buy food, but it was a long time before she could be persuaded to accept the gift, as she could not believe that it was a matter of free grace. She said she thought that we were going to involve her in some obligation, with a view to getting hold of her relatives to work on the mines. How very like many poor sinners who cannot accept the glories of God's free grace in Christ Jesus because they think that it is merely a trap to involve them in all sorts of legal obligations which they are unable to fulfil; whereas in reality it is 'mercy from first to last.'

However heavy their loads, our carriers always contrive to take with them a little musical instrument consisting of eight to ten strips of iron, stuck into a piece of flat wood about as big as one's hand. Holding the instrument ('Kadimba,' or 'Kisandji') in both hands, they snap the strips of iron with their two thumbnails, producing very plaintive, soothing music. Some of our carriers are most dextrous at it, and after a long day's tramp, when the load is laid down, and a shady tree is found, they pass many a quiet, tranquil hour, producing pleasant minor notes and trills on their 'Kadimba.'

In the afternoon two sub-chiefs of Kabongo came to the service, with a considerable crowd of people. Our helpers preached well, and I had great liberty and joy in telling out the Gospel message also.

Next day we camped at Kakolwe. 'We had an evening Gospel meeting, but only a few attended, and these were fidgety and inattentive. One cannot always tell, however, where the Gospel seed will find root. 'Instant in season and out of season' – 'Sow beside all waters,' – 'To every creature,' – these are our orders and so we can leave the results with God.

Sunday 14th. We remained at Kakolwe for Sunday, sending an evangelist on ahead to hold services at Kabwilu. Our afternoon's Gospel meeting was attended by a larger and more respectful crowd than yesterday. We had a bathe in the Lubende stream. It is the last time that we shall touch water flowing eastward to the Lualaba (the upper reaches of the Congo River) for some weeks, as tomorrow we pass over the watershed, and into the basin of the Lomami River.

On strolling along the village in the semi-darkness towards the tent, we were arrested by an animated conversation. Two or three old men were speaking away some 50 yards off, beyond a manioc garden, where they could scarcely be aware of our presence and we were delighted to hear one of them give an accurate and full summary of my Gospel messages of both yesterday and today, while the others occasionally asked questions and expressed approval. I must confess to disappointment at the apparent indifference in yesterday's meeting, and so this was God's tender and loving way of allowing me to see that the Word had not altogether fallen upon deaf ears. We went to sleep with the dismal howl of a hyena in our ears. He had evidently been attracted to the village by the smell of roan antelope flesh, which my workers are smoking over slow fires.

Monday, 15th. The villagers at Kabwila gave us a tremendous reception, cheering vociferously, and running beside us until we had long left their village behind. Presently the beautiful little lake Boya came into sight. Then across the Lubiai stream with its beautiful raphia palms, and up a well made road to the Belgian state poste of Kabongo. We were most kindly and courteously received by the Administrator, an intelligent gentleman, who took us on to his veranda, gave us coffee, and put a fine, big two roomed house at our disposal.

As we sat chatting, the great chief Kabongo came with a whole crowd of sub-chiefs and counsellors, to arrange for some details of tax collecting. He is an old slim man, and conducted himself with a great amount of pomp and ceremony. He was dressed in a long black dress coat with a red blanket round his shoulders, and had on a felt hat, with red feathers in the rim, and a big bunch of white feathers on the top. I had a chat with him about the Munza country, and also about the first chiefs of Kabongo. He says that the man who founded this village on the Lubiai was the notorious Kongolo, who buried his own mother alive because she giggled in his presence.

Mr Miller of the American Methodist Episcopal Mission has commenced work here, and the chief has built him a big school in the village. Just now, however, both Mr Miller and his wife, with their little son, are away (Kabongo later became the responsibility of the CEM under Mr Harold Womersley).

I asked the chief to call a big meeting in the afternoon and, when my wife and I reached the village, the local Christians got together a crowd of about 400. I sent a polite message, asking chief Kabongo to be present. He came with a lot of ceremony. He objected to removing his hat during the service. I gently but firmly insisted, pointing out that though we wished to give him all the respect due to a great chief, yet God is greater than all: 'King of Kings, the Ancient of Days'. For a time he was obdurate and, as there were about 300 looking on, I felt it was a crisis, and we must see that King Jesus and not King Kabongo was given supreme place. When I refused to commence the service until my wish was complied with, at last the chief went off, removed his hat, and various other paraphernalia and, returning in a white suit, he took a keen interest in the whole service, and afterwards took us to see his houses, etc.

Down each side of his enclosure is a row of huts for his wives, while in the centre are two great single room huts, each about 20 feet in diameter. There is nothing European about them. They are simply the old fashioned Luba huts, but the most beautifully built that I have ever seen. Thatching, lattice work, and mud smearing have all been carried out with the most accurate symmetry, and altogether they represent the most perfect pieces of purely Luba architecture that I have ever seen.

In the evening we were invited to dinner with the Administrator, and had a most interesting talk, during which he gave me notes of the best centres in his administrative territory for mission work, and also promised to lend me his map if I care to stay and copy it.

Tuesday, 16th. I spent all day copying the map and, finishing about 4 p.m., went to bid goodbye and have a cup of tea with the Administrator, during the taking of which I was able to have a talk on spiritual lines, which I trust may not be altogether fruitless.

Wednesday, 17th. Arrived at Tombe, a very long village, consisting of a double row of huts with a road down the centre. The inhabitants are exceedingly noisy and impudent. I had a very rowdy meeting attended by 300 or 400. What with the continual chattering of the women about my wife, who is the first white woman that many of them have ever seen, and the fear of many that we had soldiers in hiding, ready to pounce upon them and treat them badly, sending them to the mines, etc., the service was somewhat unsatisfactory, but at least, we had the opportunity of preaching Christ.

We chose a route through the country of the Bene Mpeta and Bene Musengai, who are mildly cannibal. That is if they detect anyone practising witchcraft or casting evil spells, they kill and eat the culprit. The Kabongo administrator told me that on crossing the Lukuvu River we might know we were in cannibal land, but at Tombe, our carriers all huddled together, half frightened, half in fun, declaring that this was their last week, and that within the next few days they would be sauce for sweetening manioc mush.

Thursday, September 18th. After a splendid morning walk we entered the dense forest along the edge of the Luguvu River. It is a deep narrow river, with many tracks of hippopotamus along the banks. After about 2½ hours the carriers reached the little hamlet of Mukola, and were preparing to camp when we arrived. I made them shoulder their loads and go on to Mukomba, another eight miles march. Mukomba is a village of about 50 huts, and we found the people timid and intelligent. They grow castor oil, pineapples, etc. No one would suspect them of the horrid practice of eating human flesh. They gathered respectfully and listened to the Gospel.

Later, three or four lads came to the tent, asking, 'Can we by believing, become God's children in one day?' So I explained how that instantly and eternally we may become God's children. 'Then,' they said, 'now, as we become His, you will go away tomorrow, and no one will remain to teach us about Jesus. Please write us a page of God's words, that, if anyone who can read passes our village, we may ask him to read to us, even if only one of God's words, that we may know more.' So I wrote them out a page of texts, which they very carefully carried off, wrapped in banana leaf. I wonder who will read them that precious page of God's words? I know that 'Blessed are they that hunger and thirst after righteousness, for they shall be filled' so that somehow, God alone knows how He will satisfy the longing hearts.

Friday, September 19th. We had prepared ourselves to receive a somewhat cold or hostile reception from the Musengai population, but we were surprised, on reaching Kulu Kahehula (their first big village), to see neatly built houses, and a beautifully swept street, while the grass cloth which they weave is neater than we have hitherto seen.

The situation is beautiful, on the clear limpid Luhujia stream, and nestling on a little table land, between high grassy hills crowned with patches of forest. After winding for a few miles along the hills, and a stiff climb over a ridge, we dropped into Kinombe, a village of some 120 huts. As Kinombe is in the very heart of the Musengai hills we approached with some misgivings, and I think we should not have been altogether surprised to see skulls on posts, and old men gnawing bones. But we were surprised to see neatly built huts, nestling among the palm trees, and a well hoed path connecting different parts of the village.

My wife – the first white woman to visit the Bene Musengai – received a tremendous ovation of cheering, greeting and hand clapping. We were conducted courteously to the chief, who gave us a kindly reception, and put at our disposal the veranda of his beautifully built little house. Before we had been there many minutes – what a sight for thirsty missionaries after a 19 miles travel far from civilisation – some youngsters came with pineapples and lemons for sale.

In the afternoon we held a meeting. There were about 150 people present, but though there was no actual discourtesy, it was the first meeting they had ever had, and the first time they had ever heard the precious Name of the Lord Jesus, so that at every pause there was a big noise which had to be quelled before we could proceed.

Certainly there were eager faces, and intense listening from some, but though we had prayed earnestly for a time of blessing, yet, when I dismissed the crowd, my wife and I turned to each other, remarking, 'What a strange disturbed, unfinished, unsatisfactory sort of meeting.' The people, however, did not disperse, and the chief after talking eagerly for some time with some old men came back to me, saying, 'Look, Bwana, we've heard what you say, and so far, so good; but we want to get at the root of the matter. How do we get audience with God? How does the Name of Jesus affect the matter? What can a man do to be made good? Show us how to pray. We understand that Salvation is a gift, but how do we receive it? We want properly to understand.'

The people crowded round. A whole bank of eager black faces, intelligently taking in every word. What a joy it was to answer question by question, to show them how prayer is made, and how a sinner can be made clean. Again and again they put clear and straight thinking questions, hanging on every word of my replies. The sun was almost on the horizon when the chief said, 'Now, Bwana, I understand and am satisfied. We shall ask God to send some one to teach us, and we want to do as you say.' Really, I never had a sweeter, straighter response to the Gospel message in my life.

In summarising, let me say that the country is well watered and beautiful in the extreme; the population of the Bene Musengai, I would put at 600 living in three big and three small villages (all within ten miles of Kinombe), while their neighbours, the Bene Mpeta to the north number about twice as many. God grant that these sweet happy, frank people may soon have a regular and faithful gospel ministry in their midst. The fact that in their desire to rid from their midst those who practise secret black art they have killed and eaten them should not make one despise them. Rather it shows the length to which their religion carries them, and I believe that when the grace of God takes hold of them they will be prepared to go to similar lengths in His service for the true religion.

Saturday, September 20th. In the early morning the people came streaming into the village from Mukombo, 19 miles ahead. They said that the white administrator from Kisengwa is to visit their village. We have continually prayed that God will put us in the road of those who can give us information and surely this is His answer, so that today we feel He has blessedly answered prayer. We had a long tramp from the Bene Musengai, passing two deserted villages en route; almost all the inhabitants had decamped into the bush on the approach of the white man.

Some time after midday we reached Mukombo. It is a fine big village. I would estimate the inhabitants at 600 or 700. The whole place is well laid out, neatly built huts being aligned on each side of a wide nicely swept street, with rows of pineapples along the front of each hut.

I had a long talk with the administrator, and he lent me his map of the district which I copied. He is the only white man in this whole district – about 100 miles long by 50 miles wide – and there is not a single missionary, black or white, Roman Catholic or Protestant.

In the north the people speak Kiswahili; in the south Kiluba, and a little Kituba, while among those in the east Kisongye is spoken. With the exception of two districts the population is not big. These districts we hope to see in the next fortnight.

The Administrator tells me that, a few days ago, while attempting to collect tax in the small village of Beikija, which we found deserted en route, he was attacked by poisoned arrows, and muzzle loading guns, and had quite an exciting time. Also he says that, although the district of Kisengwa has been under white administration since 1902, yet only quite recently the ex-administrator surprised some of the Bene Kipete (whose villages we are to pass (D.V.) the day after tomorrow) in a cannibal feast, and they decamped so hurriedly that they left behind a piece of smoked human arm with hand and fingers. He managed to capture 25 of the culprits, and they are now in detention at Kabinda (today in the East Kasai province).

Sunday, September 21st. Altogether last night and this morning my wife and I finished eight chapters of Testament translation. I had a visit from the chief and his elders. We explained that we had come with God's words, and desired that his people should hear. So he promised to call an afternoon meeting. He was very friendly and expressed a desire to have a missionary in his neighbourhood that all his people might be taught. Certainly the district is healthy. We have had no mosquitoes, and slept without nets. Also from here several big villages can be reached. We shall see later whether any better spot exists as a centre from which to reach this people. In the afternoon, despite a shower of rain, some 300 or 400 people attended the Gospel meeting, and on the whole they listened well, though, as it is the first time these people ever heard Jesus' Name, naturally a Gospel service called for many remarks and questions.

In the evening the people held a drum and whistle dance. They all wore white grass matting loincloths and, as they danced in rhythmic motion in a great circle around a fire, the effect was weird and ghostly. Their tune was not unmusical, produced by whistles of reed, resembling panpipes.

Monday, 22nd. We made an early trip through to Kichima, a village of some 400 people, built in a single long street with houses on either side. At the end of the village are a number of ruined huts, evidently just destroyed. There were recently two rival chiefs – each with his own following – appointed upon the death of the old village headman. These proceeded from defiance to insult, then to pillage and affront, and finally to open war. After several deaths the one part of the villagers either fled or yielded, leaving the other part in possession.

When offered food I explained that we did not need it, being well provided, but they begged us to accept it. One poor chap brought an egg, saying, 'I have no more, but if you don't accept this as a token of goodwill, then I will imagine that you consider me as the dirt beneath your feet.' It is not often that we have seen so kindly a spirit.

In the afternoon a crowd of about 250 gathered to hear the Gospel. We blessedly felt God's power. A rain storm broke over us while the meeting was in progress, and the people fled to shelter, but as soon as it was over, they were back again in added numbers. The interest was intense, and every few minutes I had to stop, while there was a burst of surprise, or to give them a chance to turn excitedly to each other, and tell over again some point which had specially gripped them.

When all was over the crowd would not disperse. They stood as if rooted. One old man shouted: 'Here's a wonderful thing! We've lived here a lifetime, and seen wicked white men come, who stole our goods, and abused our wives and our sisters. But at last a man has come in peace and with a real white woman. And, we have heard words of our creation and salvation. What answer shall we give to the white man?'

I explained that it was not I – the messenger – who needed a reply. But God Himself and Christ His Son who awaited a reply.

The village head stepped forward and, sitting at our feet, said: 'Bwana, we have never heard those words before, and tomorrow morning you are leaving us. May we not ask a few questions?'

I gladly assented and for a long time they eagerly asked and listened, some 270 or 280 people solemnly drinking in every word. I think I never met a more whole-hearted, guileless response to the Gospel message in my whole life. I have spoken with men in South Africa, who told me how exultant they were when, after three or four years of hard toil for insignificant gains, at last they found diamonds which rewarded all their toil; I have heard tales of following for days on the spoor (tracks) of a herd, and of the final shot which brought down the longed for trophy, and of the triumph as the hunter stood over the dying body of some great beast, that amply rewarded all his toils, but I am sure that no thrill of joy and pure delight can surpass that which a Gospel preacher experiences when he sees Congolese pass that precious Name from lip to lip for the first time, and realises that his hearers are giving a glad and immediate response to the claims of the Lord of Lords and King of Kings – Jesus Christ, the most lasting of all joys, the worthiest of all themes, the most miraculous of all results.

Tuesday, 23rd. We left the village with many wishes for a good journey, the people assuring us that they will continue to pray to God in Jesus' Name until He sends them a teacher of their own. The village head said : 'I will show you a short cut across the open country where you may be able to shoot a roan antelope.' But after a tramp of four or five miles he led us into a little hamlet where some of his relatives and his mother live. There he asked me to sit down while he called the people together that I might tell them 'words to be amazed at.' Then I saw that it was not a roan antelope that he had led us by this circuitous route to find, but he had brought us there that his people might hear of Jesus and, after I had finished, he himself stood up and volubly, earnestly, and accurately told them practically all that I had preached on the previous afternoon, especially urging them 'not to forget that holy Name of power and authority – Jesus Christ.'

After a couple of hours' tramp we reached a swamp of most magnificent raphia palms. The beautiful ferns, the palm fronds of some 30 feet average length, and the wonderfully soft, brightly coloured mosses, lichens, and flowers which carpeted and festooned this marsh, fully repaid us for half an hour's struggle through mud, quake bog, and water – along slippery logs and on half submerged stumps, with a growth so dense overhead that one had to move carefully in the gloom. Then we went on for two or three hours over undulating country past the Kitania lake and the village of Koni.

About 70 years ago Kitania Lake was the site of a flourishing village, in a low lying valley, with the lakes of Mwebo and Dijiba only three or four miles away. A woman noticed, one day, while digging up sweet potatoes that water oozed through, so instead of going to distant streams, she and her fellow villagers drew water close at hand. But the spring became stronger and stronger till one day some hidden barrier burst and the whole village was swamped, only two individuals (whose children at present inhabit Koni) escaping, and the neighbouring lakes dropped several feet in depth. Then both the new and the two original lakes rose till the former level was reached. Clearly the whole phenomenon was due to a subterranean connection between the lakes, but the population attribute it to an insult to some local deity who had been offended because the people did not give him enough beer. By all accounts the inhabitants of Koni are cannibals. Even their nearest neighbours acknowledge it. As we passed their pretty little hill-side village they shouted, 'White man we greet and welcome you, but had you been the Administrator from Kisengwa, we would not want you here, for we refuse to pay the tax.'

Finally we arrived at Kabulo Kisanga, a village of some 550 people. They met us at least a mile from the village. Several sturdy fellows, shouting welcomes, pushed our hammock carriers aside and seized us, running us into the village in fine style. There the women came trotting round like bats round a candle, clapping their hands in welcome to the first white woman, and uttering shrill yells, patting their mouths the while, to give the effect of a strange intermittent trill. The chief was an ignorant, impudent young fellow, and I had to call him to order severely, after which he behaved tolerably well, and brought us some pineapples as a peace offering.

One of the most trying experiences of a tramp preacher in Central Africa is the continual gaze. Some white men drive the inquisitive gazers off with a hippo hide sjambok (whip), but we gladly welcome them. Nevertheless, it is a very real trial, after a long march to sit and be a gazing stock for 300 or 400 pairs of keenly scrutinising eyes. Paul said: 'God hath set forth us apostles last, as it were appointed unto death, for we are made a spectacle unto the world and to angels and to men' (1 Cor. 4, 9). Old and young, men and women, stand round in a solid wall, hemming one in, and as one sits on the first load to be set down in the village, and mops the dust and perspiration from one's face, remarks pass freely among them, for they have not yet found out that we understand all that they are talking about.

No action of ours, or article we produce is too small for scrutiny and comment. The fact that I eat with my wife, walk beside her, and even get up to allow her to sit down, is a never ending source of wonder, and the poor, down-trodden, despised, beaten, degraded local women – the meaning of whose name in their language is a synonym for weakness and shame, and who are bought and sold as sheep or goats – are the first to raise their voice in criticism.

Lady missionaries who come to the Congo to bring their message of liberty to Africa's dusky daughters, must be under no misapprehension. The Hebrew slaves as well as their Egyptian overlords resented the attempt at their emancipation (Ex. 2, 14: 5, 2; 6, 9; 14, 12; 16, 13) and Africa's women are the first to raise objections when we bring them news of their freedom. They cling to their superstitions more tenaciously than the men, and they resent monogamy on the ground that if a man has several wives, there is less work for each one to do.

Thursday, 25th. After about ten miles of open country we reached the Lomami River. It is a very different river from the Lualaba (the upper reaches of the Congo). The latter is skirted with broad plains and marshes, but the Lomami has hills down to the water's edge, very little marsh land, and is beautifully wooded along the banks. It has an even depth of about six feet, and runs over a gravely bottom, so that the people propel their boats with poles rather than paddles. Every few hundred yards one comes upon rapids and waterfalls, some of which are of enchanting beauty. There are numbers of hippopotami and crocodiles. Also the sleeping sickness fly, palpalis, is very plentiful.

We camped at the village of Kijiba – eight miles from Mwana Tshofwe. The people on this side of the Lomami, between the boundaries of the rivers Lukashi, Ekekei and Idimbi, are Bekalebwe, a most interesting and intelligent people. They build their villages on the hill tops – unlike the Baluba, who build as a rule scattered villages down in the valleys and beside the water courses. Their houses are large and well built, in beautiful streets, each house enclosed by its own fence of living trees, and in its own neat garden.

Their skill in ironwork and basket making is considerable. Also their gardens are very creditable. Though only dug with the hoe, yet they are absolutely straight, dug in regular parallel rows from top to bottom of the hills.

Their language is very similar to Kiluba, so that I can understand much that they say. Like the Baluba, between Kabongo and here, they make grass cloth clothing from Makulo and Makombo palms.

In the evening we had a blessed little meeting, though I had to speak through an interpreter. I suppose 150 were present. Some time after our arrival the chief at Mwana Tshofwe, having heard of our coming, sent his head man through to welcome us.

Friday, 26th. This morning the old sub-chief of Kishiba sent for us to pray for him as he had a sore chest and back. It is really blessed to see how, during this trip, God has honoured prayer with the laying on of hands in Jesus' Name. Again and again when our carriers have been taken ill they have come for prayer, and have been restored. Hence, though many of them are unconverted, they help to spread the fame of Jesus' Name, and recommend others to come for prayer.

Our reputation has gone before us. My wife, being the first white lady in all this region (at Kabinda there are three ladies, but these people of Mwana Tshofwe have never had a visit, as Kabinda is five days' journey distant), came in for the lion's share of the attention. Round upon round of cheers, scores of little children running ahead to stand in line and salute, then dashing on to line up and salute again. Dear old African mothers rushing from their gardens to clap their hands in joyful greeting, and then back to work again.

Some six miles before we reached Mwana Tshofwe our hammock carriers were pushed aside, and a crowd of sturdy perspiring men took turns in carrying us. Considering the fact that practically the whole road from the Lomami River up to Mwana Tshofwe is a continual climb, this help was most timely. Arriving in the village, with a population of about 800 or 1,000, the chief met us in the main street and, greeting us with a clumsy courtesy, took us to the shade of his veranda. Here we found a white man, the agent of the 'Bourse de Travail du Katanga,' (Katanga Labour Exchange) at Kabinda. He was most kind, gave us tea and, though he was on the point of leaving, he gave me a full hour's conversation, telling me the position of the biggest towns, and of the tribal boundaries, as well as a lot more useful information.

How wonderfully God has provided us with friends and information at every step of this journey. We have completed 250 miles of our journey, have located with rough accuracy some 300 towns and villages, and have covered half our trip. Ebenezer! God has wonderfully, blessedly sent along tax collectors, chiefs, travellers, and Government Agents to enable me to find out heavy centres of population, the language, distribution, etc. 'Shall the axe boast itself against the one that swings it, or the saw against the one who uses it to cut?' We have had nothing to do but move along in His will, and gather the information which our Father has laid ready to our hand.

During the three days' stay at Mwana Tshofwe both we and the men were showered with presents, and had again and again to refuse gifts, real bona-fide gifts, expecting nothing again. These gifts included sheep, goats, fowl, eggs, etc. Each morning we were given a tin can of goat's milk, and again and again presents of monkey nuts, bananas, sugar cane, etc.

On Friday evening the biggest crowd gathered that I have ever preached to, headed by the chief and his elders. I should judge there were 550 or 600 present.

Saturday, 27th. In the morning I visited Kiungu, the biggest village of this district – estimated population, 3,000. The distance from Mwana Tshofwe is eight miles. The chief and his elders, despite gathering rain clouds, gave me a most respectable hearing. Two Roman Catholic lads from Kabinda, on a visit to their relatives, did their best to be impudent and upset the meeting, but the chief had them turned out of the village for their rudeness, and apologised to my evangelist, Shalumbo, saying that they were strangers.

On the journey home I took refuge from the rain in a small village. The people vied with each other to show me kindness. I was given a raphia palm bed and mat on one of their verandas for my midday siesta (nap). They brought me sugar cane, monkey nuts (peanuts), and bananas, killed a goat for my carriers, and in every possible way showed their love and appreciation. Again in the afternoon we had a big meeting at Mwana Tshofwe.

Sunday, 28th. Before we got up this morning there were sick people outside the tent waiting for prayer, and two men desiring to accept salvation in Christ Jesus. One of these had a big packet of gourds, nutshells, horns, and grass cloth packets, filled with charms and magic which he had brought to burn.

The chief's eldest son – the heir apparent, a nice intelligent fellow, visited us, and later took us to see the home that he is building, with nice big airy rooms with high ceilings. He said that all the people were so glad to welcome the white man and had done all in their power to manifest their appreciation at our visit; but why, oh why, were we not staying with them? They wanted someone to stay always and teach all their villages of the book that God had sent to man.

He was so absolutely frank and genuine that it is very hard to think of leaving tomorrow. This district is one of the most promising – perhaps the most promising – for reaching large masses of eager, hungry people within a comparatively small area that I have seen. The people are kindly; the country is open, with superb views on every hand. The villages being built on hilltops, however, visitation would be tiring, and especially to anyone with a weak heart.

In the evening after the last service (during which we blessedly re-alised God's power), the chief and his counsellors asked me if I wouldn't make their country my home. They declared that they would withhold nothing from me. Such appeals are most pathetic. An old man present, with practically all his village, has burned his fetishes. At another vil-lage (Kabwe) they have had regular evening prayer since the visit of our evangelist Shalumbo, a little over a year ago.

Monday, 29th. We were ready for the march by 3:30 a.m., but several were waiting for a final word, and some sick were waiting to be prayed with. Also some old fellows wanted to know: 'You have God's words. What are you going to do for us?' I said, 'I can make no promise at present, but I have asked God to send a missionary here, and am writ-ing to England to tell them about you all, and I am sure that He will answer in Jesus' Name, and send you a missionary.'

As we left the village the early morning sun broke over the green highlands and mist shrouded valleys of the Bekalebwe country, and as I sat in my carrying hammock I opened 'Lesser's Translation of the Old Testament' at Isa. 9: 'The people that walk in darkness have seen a great light: they that dwell in the land of the shadow of death – a light shines brightly over them. You have multiplied the nation and made great their joy; they rejoice before You as with the joy in har-vest, as men are glad when they divide the spoil. For the yoke of their burden, and the staff on their shoulder, You have broken the rod of their oppressor – For a child is born unto us, and a son has been given unto us, and the government is upon His shoulders.'

Truly, after 19 centuries of darkness, at last the blessed light of Jesus is breaking in upon the subjects of Mwana Tshofwe.

We camped at the little ironworkers' village of Nkoto on the Ekekei River, and I had a lovely swim in its waters. Most of the people seemed too busy at their forges to attend the Gospel meetings, but a few lis-tened earnestly to Shalumbo, and the others who could preach to them in their own KiKalebwe (Kisongye). As several of the carriers are suf-fering from tick fever (contracted at Kabongo, where the intermittent fever tick is bad), I determined to stay over a day at Nkoto to write letters and give them further rest.

Tuesday, 30th September. The iron smelters were at work this morning by 4 a.m. shouting to hoes and axes to come out of the red iron ore. Their charcoal furnaces are simple clay receptacles about four feet high behind, where the bellows go and an additional depth of three feet at the front, where the iron metal is run out.

It takes about 14 hours to get the iron from the ore, and they put in six big wicker baskets (each with about 50 pounds weight) of ore, to get enough iron for 10 to 20 hoes, while the same amount of charcoal is burned up in the operation.

Wednesday, 1st October. We were misled in the early morning and, having gone some distance before we discovered our error, had to retrace our steps. Hence we halted for breakfast at the very big village of Lusala, near the big flat-topped Neumba hill, which has been in sight, off and on, ever since we left Kibanza, and has been a great help to me in correctly mapping this country, making such a conspicuous landmark for triangulations.

The old chief of Lusala – who boasts about 500 villagers and rich iron deposits – came very respectfully and humbly, saying that, since he understood that we were explaining the words of God, and he much desired to hear them but had never had the opportunity, would we please let someone stay and explain these 'matters of eternity' to his people. So Shalumbo stayed for a service. He states that an enormous crowd gathered, and listened earnestly. Moreover they begged him to persuade the white man to send someone to live at Lusala and always teach them.

Arriving at Kabashilange, our stopping place, a village of about 250 people, we found ourselves in the centre of a considerable crowd doing honour to their far-famed 'Nkishi' or idol, named Tambwe, which was made by four powerful magicians at a price of 200 francs and a woman. The woman, frightened to become the wife of a magician, ran away, but was brought back and forced into submission, though screaming and almost incoherent in her terror.

The 'nkishi' is about two feet six inches high – a wooden figure covered with charms, etc. It is carried about by two women, who may not touch its sacred person, but hold it by two long poles attached to its arms. Moreover, as it is carried, a drum and rattle band is in attendance, while little girls sweep the ground before it, as it is stood upright, with grass cloth bundles filled with magic charms. The father of a certain man – Somwe – was lost, and the idol was paid a big sum to find him. The poor tired women attendants dragged it uphill and down dale, through stream and forest, now and again professing to get on the scent, but in vain.

So Somwe and many of his family, hearing of the Gospel from our Christians, threw up fetish worship, burnt their charms and professed faith in Christ.

Just across the Ekekei River about two miles distant is the village Lualaba Iwa Nsangwa, a village of some 500 people; but the tree across the river, which served as a bridge, has been swept off by flood, so I contented myself by preaching at Kabashilange, leaving our Christians to cross the Ekekei and preach in Lualaba. They found the river neck deep and very swift, but they were repaid for their journey by a splendid service. We also had a big crowd listening while we urged the people of Kabashilange to turn from idols, and trust in the Lord Jesus. In fact all night they did not sleep, as the people pressed into the hut which had been allotted to our preachers, and begged them to tell more.

Next day we camped at Midumbu, welcomed by chief Mulenda to a well kept white man's rest house. This is a fair-sized village, built along a single wide street, and containing 120 houses and 240 people.

The Kisengwa Administrative District which we have now re-entered is a difficult one to encompass with the Gospel, as one only finds the villages at very long intervals. There are but four large villages outside the Bene Kipete, namely Mukombo, Dipesa (Kitanza), Kimoto (Mukunu) and Bidikwibwe (Kasendu). As, however, all these and also the Bena Kipete are within three days' march of Mukombo, which is a healthy populous village, this would seem the best spot for a mission site in Kisengwa District. They are all Kiluba speaking villages.

The people of Midumbu speak a mixture of Kiswahili, Kikalebwe, and Kisongye, but understood me well enough when I spoke Kiluba to them.

Friday, October 3rd. We had a varied country today. Leaving Midumbu we soon left the light scrub lands, and came out into open country. As we neared the Lomami, we entered most beautiful dense forestland. Presently we came to an abrupt slope, which led down amid tangles of pineapple to the Administrator's garden. Mr Phillips, the Administrator, gave us a kind reception, put the travellers' rest house at our disposal, invited us to dinner and a most interesting chat, and finally gave us a basket of fruit and vegetables to help us along the road.

Saturday, October 4th. After a lovely march through dense bush, across the Lukashi River on a strange bridge of poles, and another march in open country, we reached Muninga, the village chief Mpeko, just as the people were preparing to go to battle with Engo of Kabongo (some ten miles further on).

However, on hearing that a white man was coming, they desisted, and stayed to hear the Gospel.

Monday, October 6th, 1919. We plunged into the bush, emerging in the lovely mango and lemon avenue of the Katompe where there are coffee plantations. Here we met our evangelists Kadimi and Gideon with their wives. They had a very successful rice harvest and, having sold well, they have freely given their time all this dry season to evangelising all along the Luvidyo River, which, it will be remembered, we approached near its source at Ngole.

This place was started 17 years ago by the Comité Spécial du Katanga (a Government-backed Company that owned the rights to the land) as a rubber plantation, and then abandoned by them. The coffee is a later development. There are now 56 hectares under cultivation, producing 30 tons of coffee which is sold at the absurdly low figure of 1.75 francs (14d or 8c.) per kilo, or about 7d. or 4c. per pound, and all who taste it declare its flavour superb.

In the evening we had a very blessed service in Katompe village. About 250 were present and the power of God came down blessedly upon us. There is salvation for asking, 'Whosoever shall call upon the Name of the Lord shall be saved' (Rom. 10, 13). Who knows how many from among the villages that we have passed have reached out in faith in Jesus' Name and found that great salvation which comes to 'whosoever shall call.' And seeing that the Name and Authority of the Lord Jesus Christ has now reached these people, what a tremendous responsibility devolves upon us, His ministers, to baptise, to teach, to form assemblies, and to carry out all in accordance with God's Word! (In 1921 a Congolese evangelist was placed in this village).

Tuesday, 7th October. Today we leave the beaten track of the Kongolo-Kabinda route, and turn into the long, dripping grass of the tsetse fly-infested bush. Before long, my poor wife's limbs and face were so fearfully stung and poisoned as to be swollen into knobs and eruptions, while for a time the irritation was so severe that she could no longer rest in her carrying hammock. But the poison had evidently affected her head as well for, on getting out, her brain reeled and she fell to the ground. Moreover, her feet were in such a state that she positively could not walk without assistance. So we had to put her into the carrying hammock, hasten to a near village, get up the tent with all despatch, and as the tsetse flies were bad even in the village we had the mosquito nets put up, and got her to bed as soon as possible. A hot bath was the only thing that seemed to allay irritation. However, the Christians gathered and prayed with me, and God graciously answered, so that by evening my wife was comparatively easy once more.

The rain set in mercilessly soon after we reached camp – in the miserable little village of Kilume – so that we could not hold a service. Almost all the people, however, must have heard the Gospel, for all day long our men were visiting one and another in their huts, and telling them of God's love in sending His Son to be the Saviour of the world.

Wednesday, 8th October. On the journey again, but this time with my wife's feet in my cycling hose and her body swathed in a blanket.

Moreover, with a cow's tail switch to clear off the flies which would attack hands or face so that, while I was bitten, she escaped lightly. Personally, tsetse fly bites don't seem to affect me beyond the initial prick of their sting.

We camped at Kihombo, a little village. This district is very poorly inhabited. One of my carriers took my rifle, and managed to kill a wart hog, which the carriers eagerly divided. It has the reputation of being the sweetest meat in the bush, though its face is enough to put a white man against it. Surely no more ugly animal (not even a hippo) walks on this continent than a wart hog!

Thursday, 9th. A long journey through open forest. The carriers spotted three hartebeest in the distance and, as I stalked them with my rifle, two great buffalo suddenly rose from the bush and rushed right across my path at less than 100 yards range. So, leaving the hartebeest, I shot one buffalo, breaking a leg. A long chase followed, and finally Mr Buffalo kicked his last, and became 1,000 pounds of prime beef, to the huge delight of the carriers. We always make a point of kneeling around the fallen game, and ascribing the success, not to the gun or huntsman, but to our Heavenly Father. In this way our carriers learn to realise their dependence upon Him.

We passed the village of Lubidje, and some smaller hamlets, finally camping beside the marshes of the Luvidyo River at Twite Ntenga, where heavy winds and threatened rain prevented our holding a big service.

We have now reached the fringe of the heavy population around Hanga Nkolwa (Ankoro) though the main village is 30 miles distant.

Friday, 10th. From Twite we passed a succession of villages ranging in population from two or three families to some 200 to 400 in the biggest centres. The Catholic priests have four catechists in these villages and, humanly speaking, in another couple of years, the people will be almost impossible to reach. Throughout this dry season some of our Christians have been evangelising here and find a ready response.

We ferried across the Luvidyo River within a few hundred yards of the spot where it falls into the Lualaba. The stream is about 25 yards wide and navigable for about six miles from its mouth, making the big villages of Shimbi and Kanombe accessible from Lualaba by boat. From here to Ankoro, 20 miles southward, and to Kabalo, 35 miles northward is one long succession of villages without Christ and without hope. We camped at Kikasu.

Saturday, 11th. From early morning till after midday we passed along a well hoed path with some 13 villages, some of them small, and the largest (Hanga Nkolwa, or Ankoro) having a population of about 500, a Belgian Government Poste, and a Greek trader's store at which we were glad to replenish our stock of sugar, flour, etc.

We camped at Bale, a small village about five miles south of Ankoro – six days' journey along the Lualaba river bank from Kabumbulu. Just north of this spot the River Luvuwa, running out of Lake Moero, flows into the Lualaba. It is navigable as far as Kiambi but, so far as I can discover from local people, the villages on its banks are few and small, excepting Kiambi itself.

At Bale our helpers could purchase practically no food. The village is new, the manioc gardens are not yet giving crops, the bush buck and wild pigs are making serious inroads into the cultivation, and the people (a weakly diseased, scrofulous little crowd) seemed to be subsisting on roots, lizards, and the like. Hence the carriers begged us not to remain there over Sunday for another day of hunger.

Monday, 13th October. After a halt in the bush to lop down a tree and get a splendid feast of wild honey, and a long tramp into the hill country, we reached Kahia, a village of about 150 people, at the foot of a fine wooded mountain. The chief seemed a respectful, intelligent, young fellow, and my heart was much drawn to him. We halted to preach. It was a most blessed and impressive service. The first time that they have heard of Jesus' Name. How eagerly they listened!

We felt sorry to leave them with so small a testimony to this great Gospel. But perhaps they have heard enough to make them hungry for more. 'Blessed are they that hunger and thirst after righteousness, for they shall be filled.'

Leaving Kahia, we tramped along a most beautiful forest path, with mountains looming up above us through the treetops to our left, for another six miles to Mpianambayo, the village of Chief Taha. My interest in this village – though I had never before set foot in it – extends back for three years, to a time when I was nursing a sick trader through black water fever in his camp at Kabumbulu. During an interval of his convalescence, as the sick man slumbered, I slipped out into his veranda to get a breath of fresh air. A man was sweeping the yard and, as my heart was full of the message of Calvary, I spoke to this man of his soul, of God's love gift, and of eternal salvation. He eagerly listened, and later in the day told me of great villages two days' journey over the hills where his family live, and where God's words have not been heard. He evidently returned to his village and told them, for more than a year later a deputation came to Brother Salter at Mwanza, asking us to send them a missionary at Mpianambayo. Months and years have slipped past, but though we have prayed constantly, yet this is the first time I have been able to preach there.

The village is beautifully situated in the head of four valleys, with great hills all around, densely afforested, and with such a wealth of tangled creepers festooning the tree tops as one doesn't often see. We camped beneath a mighty teak tree. The chief had had too much palm wine, and his constant interruptions during service somewhat hindered the preaching of the Gospel, though there were some who manifested real earnestness. Within a few miles radius of his village there are several other large towns.

After some 18 miles we reached Kilulwe, renowned far and near for its ironwork. The ore is much richer than that which we saw at Nkoto. One big basketful will produce iron for from ten to 16 hoes.

The old chief Kilulwe came to meet us in the most extraordinary get up. He had a sort of halo round his head made of blue, black, and white beads, a similar bead-covered insignia across his breast, a very keen, well-made authentic local knife stuck into his belt, a beautiful little leopard skin around his loins, and most extraordinary of all, an elaborately carved staff in his hand, on the head of which were artistically carved two Baluba women arm in arm.

From here, I got a fine set of triangulations. There is a fine population around Kilulwe, and being upon the hillside it is a healthy position. In my opinion (though further surveys would be necessary to substantiate the matter finally) it would be better to supervise the district from a European station at Kilulwe than at Mpianambayo, which latter is surrounded by hills, and is therefore hot and enervating.

By the afternoon, the Chief, who had become offended, had recovered from his sulks and attended the Gospel with a big following, though his whole attitude was that of graciously condescending to patronise our meeting with his august presence and I fear that he will have to bend his bead-crowned head considerably lower before he can enter the strait gate of Salvation through repentance toward God and faith in the Lord Jesus Christ.

Friday, 17th October. Home! Oh what a welcome home the Mwanza population gave us! Christians and heathen alike. Far into the night they came to say how glad they were of our safe return. We praise God that under the care of Sisters Toerien and Rickow the work has gone on well in our absence, and fresh manifestations of His grace have been seen in precious souls added to the Lord."

11

A Luba Pentecost

Mwanza, January 20th, 1920:

"My heart is so full of praise to God that I scarcely know where to commence in telling you of the great blessings of the last fortnight. I have repeatedly asked your prayers that God's Holy Spirit might be poured out upon Lubaland. Let me tell you how wonderfully our Father has answered.

We are in the habit of assembling our believers every three to six months for fellowship, teaching, and conference. Those who at the last conference started out to teach, returned to this conference with a blessed harvest of believers: seven from one village, twelve from another, 15 from a third, and so on. What a joy it was to welcome these young Christians, and to feed them from God's Word. They seemed never to be tired of listening. I started the first meetings at 6 a.m. for our leaders, teachers, and evangelists, and from thence onward we didn't have a moment to ourselves until late in the evening. Our last regular meeting was a gathering at night on our veranda to teach them new hymns. In a week or so those eight to a dozen fresh hymns will be ringing out into villages nearly 100 miles apart.

Even that was not the end of proceedings, for a number of little lads would gather at Sister Toerien's house to pray for the baptism of the Spirit, or, having been filled with the Spirit themselves, to pray others into blessing. This would proceed until nearly midnight, but so eager were some youngsters that, though they had to start work at 6:30 a.m., we could hear voices of earnest prayer coming from one hut long after midnight.

Some of you know soon after our arrival at Mwanza, we were joined by some freed slaves. These had been carried away from Lubaland many years ago, and sold to the Portuguese in Angola.

There they heard and received the Gospel of Christ through the faithful ministry of British and American missionaries. Then on their emancipation they started back to their own land with the good news of the Saviour, Whom they had found. While loyal and faithful to the light that they had, these dear fellow-workers steadfastly resisted the truth of the baptism in the Spirit, and some of them had no time for Divine healing, the laying on of hands in Jesus' Name, and so on. Anything outside of their own particular line of truth and conduct, they firmly refused, saying 'Oh, they didn't do it in that manner in Angola.' We have always endeavoured to foster and encourage the affection between these freed slaves and their spiritual fathers in Angola, but their stubborn opposition to the truth, and the fact that it influenced our growing local Christian church against these blessed and vital truths of God's Word, led us to see that we must raise a strong clear-cut issue between what God's Word says, and what the missionary tradition and precedent from Angola says.

So with earnest crying to God, and with hearts brimful of love to all parties, we raised a definite note from the commencement of the convention upon the supreme necessity of God's children being endued with power from on high. Moreover, we determined to cast the matter on the Lord, that we would willingly work with one person entirely surrendered to God, and filled with the Holy Spirit, rather than with a thousand who powerlessly blindly follow the Scriptureless traditions of men, and ignore the simple instructions of the Word of God. Thus, then, for the first four days of the Conference, we ceaselessly hammered upon the one dominant note of submission to God's Word.

On the fourth day of the Convention, Thursday, in our morning meeting there were about 160 present, to whom we spoke on Mark 16, 15 to 18: 'These signs shall follow those who believe.' There was a solemn, heart-searching time, and God's power was wonderfully felt as those present frankly acknowledged that they did not bear the hall-mark of Scripture, in that these signs did not accompany their ministry. Then at the invitation to come forward to pray for, and to receive the Holy Spirit, almost the whole of the congregation came forward. Even the most stubborn opposers were ashamed to hold back. At once the whole of the front of the chapel was a tightly wedged mass of earnest believers with their heads down and their shiny backs heaving with the emotion of prayer.

When an angel came down and troubled the pool at Bethesda, the first to enter the troubled water was healed, but at Mwanza, God Himself was troubling the waters, and all who entered were blessed. Some strong men, with earnestness of purpose, took a clean header; little youngsters, who have only known Jesus within the last few weeks, nevertheless scrambled in as best they knew how; while some more dignified and aged elders of the community, with still possibly some lingering hankerings after the fast disappearing traditions of the past, had first to try the water, and finding it not too cold to the toes, managed ankle deep, then knee deep, waist deep, and finally – Oh, Hallelujah! – the same result as with those who took the first clean header. Waters to swim in, a river that couldn't be passed over, bringing life and healing to everything within its reach.

To return from analogy to fact, it was not many minutes after we started praying that the first few were filled with the Spirit. And then they helped us by laying hands upon, and praying with others. It was only those on the outskirts of the crowd that were within reach. The whole of those in the centre of the crush were out of our reach, but not out of God's. Oh, how they cried, and groaned, and grovelled in the dust, as they wrestled their way to victory. The noise of this great visitation was heard in a village one and a half miles away. Truly the mountains of pride and self esteem were broken down, and the valleys of fear and mistrust were filled up, the crooked places of schisms, quarrels, suspicions, and party spirit were made straight, and the result is the same as in John the Baptist's time, that all flesh is seeing God's salvation (Luke 3, 5-6).

There sat one middle-aged woman apart on her little stool (in all our assemblies the women and men prefer to sit apart) and, as she nursed her baby, the look of her face was one of pharisaic disdain, as much as to say, 'Fancy disturbing yourselves like that! I'm sure I'm far too dignified for anything so grotesque.' But as the power of God came down, and dozens of little lads were crying and beating their breasts, or rolling their perspiring little faces in the dust in the agony of their appeal, or magnifying Jesus in Kiluba, or in the new and heavenly language of the Spirit, there were very few in the room who were untouched, and it was utterly impossible to tell how many received the Holy Spirit. Presently the portly woman, mentioned above, began to feel the movings of the Spirit, and stool and baby went anywhere, as she abandoned herself to God. This was not the only baby that Sister Toerien rescued during the service. Oh, what a different woman was this once haughty lady next day, when she received the Holy Spirit, and walked up and down with hands uplifted, praising God in new tongues.

We have grieved much over the haughtiness of one or two older Christians but, what a change the Spirit has wrought. One old man always took a front seat and lost no opportunity for impressing upon everyone in truly local fashion, the greatness of his own importance and piety, but from the time that the Spirit fell upon him, he has taken his place at the very back of our chapel, to keep the door and to keep the noisy children quiet, while, when later in the services I asked for some volunteers among the youngsters, to clear the pool which we used for baptism from mud and slime which had silted into it, he was the first to offer for this undignified and dirty job.

That first wonderful meeting lasted from 10 a.m. to 3 p.m. For three hours the whole place was swayed by God's Spirit. Many fell as though dead and those who had no room to fall on the floor fell on each other.

At least two cases occurred of those who praised God in beautiful English, and I also heard snatches of French, and Dutch or German. And almost all who spoke in tongues had languages with beautiful clear R sounds, which is significant, since in the natural a Luba cannot properly pronounce this sound. Then when all was quiet, of course, I had to explain it all from Acts. 2, that 'this is that,' and that Christ Jesus 'being by the right hand of God exalted has shed forth this which you now see and hear.' Since then it is hard to say which has been the most wonderful meeting. Congolese have been coming and going all the time, so that one cannot give an accurate number of our visitors, for some would stay for two or three days and go away, others would go and come back again. But it was manifestly unwise to let all the believers go back home after a week's meetings as originally intended, since some remained cold, hungry, and unblessed, while others in the full flood tide of a new-found power and blessing were in danger of being carried into excitement and folly, unless taught from Scripture more of God's purpose and desire in pouring out His Spirit. But an average of considerably over 100 visitors must have been here for the fortnight's meetings. Moreover, since this is the busiest part of the gardening season, when every day's labour will give big returns at the end of the rainy season, almost half of the believers were unable to attend, and those who did come only did so at a big personal sacrifice – which, however, God wonderfully rewarded.

My work was chiefly among the men, my wife helped the women, and Sister Toerien the boys and girls. Over 150 children were at the Sunday School in the middle Sunday of the Conference, and more than half of them were under the power of God, while a number were filled with the Spirit exactly as in Acts 2, 4; 10, 46; 19, 6. The hours between the meetings were fully occupied in answering questions, giving advice and encouragement, and in listening to confessions of sin. This last is all the more wonderful since hitherto horses could not drag confessions from a Luba. All their lives long they have lived in such deception and hypocrisy that, to confess a sin, when they had not been caught redhanded, would appear to them the height of absurdity. 'But when He (the Spirit of Truth) is come, He shall convince the world of sin' (Jn. 16, 8), and during this convention the burdened ones have forced themselves upon me whether I would or no.

And, oh, what fearful pages of crime were unfolded. But against

the hideous background of disgrace and shame, the Cross of the Lord
Jesus is all the more resplendent. How precious it was to kneel with
these stricken, guilty lads, pour out our heart's burden to God, and
see them go away humbly, gratefully rejoicing, yet still amazed at the
stupendous fact that 'The blood of Jesus Christ, God's Son, cleanses
us from all sin.'

All our out-station teachers have gone back home today, excepting
one; and they are all baptised in the Spirit, as are also my chief carpenter, the three pupil teachers who help my wife in the school, etc.
Several of the strangers who came back with us from the recent long
trip in the Bekalebwe country have also received the Holy Spirit. Last
Thursday we baptised 57 believers in water; men and women, boys
and girls, Baluba and Bekalebwe. In the case of several of these, I had
hesitated previously, but now 'Can anyone forbid water that these
should not be baptised, who have received the Holy Spirit just as we
did?' (Acts. 10, 46).

There must be now nearly as many more believers awaiting baptism in our various out-stations. Though many had already left for their
homes, yet on the last Sunday 87 believers gathered around the Lord's
Table, to show forth His death in the emblems of His broken body and
poured out blood – 'Until He comes.' When my readers remember how
less than four and a half years ago I was stranded on this mission hill,
with my only companion and chum, Brother Salter, slowly coming back
from the very jaws of death, with fever; how we stood in the midst of
the desolation of rocks and long grass, and forest, and looked across to
the villages nestled among the trees; how having scarcely a word of the
language we could only pray, pray, pray for those thousands who had
never even heard the Name of Jesus. When you remember this, you
can understand how our hearts nearly burst, and how often the well-
springs of our being overflowed in boundless thankfulness to God, and
how again and again when we sought words to praise Him, for this
band of rejoicing Christians, all that we could pour out at His feet was
tears of gratitude.

We have often grieved at the hidden bickerings and smouldering
jealousies among our young Christians, Bekalebwe against Baluba and
both against the Angola freed slaves, while these last again were divided
into two camps, representing the two denominations working in Angola, and each party considering itself better than the other. The two
chief causes of strife we will call S. and W. They live near each other, and
though outwardly friendly, the grudges of their hearts were plainly seen.
S. had a mighty humbling, and was filled with the Spirit early in the
meetings, whereupon W. gave up praying for this great blessing, and
made no bones about proclaiming the other Christians to be humbugs

and their blessing a hoax, since he himself had felt nothing and received nothing. I called W. aside to try to help him, for while so many others were receiving blessings, he was left stranded high and dry. But my ministries were fruitless, and so my wife and I could only pray. In the middle of one night, God awoke S. and told him, go and call W., and lay hands upon him, and pray that he might receive the Spirit. So accordingly S. and W. – erstwhile at loggerheads – were soon praying together under the stars. Before long the power came down; W. was mightily filled with the Spirit, and so great was the noise that the other Christians came running out of their huts, lighting their resin torches, to join in the thanksgiving as they saw these two old antagonists, with hearts aglow, alternately hugging each other for joy, and praising and magnifying God in new tongues.

Now the rumour soon spread abroad among the villages that 'Bwana Burton preaches till he has his hearers under his spell, and he then touches them, whereupon they tremble, fall down, turn to God, and speak foreign languages.' But, praise God, this illusion was soon banished for, on the third day after the Holy Spirit was outpoured, a man entered who had heard of Christ at Mr Wilding's Mission, but had never heard any teaching concerning the baptism in the Spirit. We had scarcely started the meeting – in fact we were just having a few preliminary hymns – when the power of the Spirit fell upon him as he sat in his seat, and immediately he commenced volubly and fluently to praise God in an unknown tongue.

Now that you have heard what our blessed Lord is doing, compare notes, and I'm sure that some of you will remember that Thursday, January 8th (when the experience of Pentecost in Jerusalem became actually the experience of Lubaland) was a day when you yielded to the Spirit's promptings and gave yourselves very specially to prayer for our work.

Now, beloved, pray for our Congolese teachers, and for the bands of young believers, that they may be used as clean and faithful vessels for the carrying of blessing in Christ Jesus to thousands. Pray for us. Our health is none too good and duties are many and pressing. Pray for the band of men and women at present preparing to come out and join us in the work. Pray for the speedy completion of the Scripture translation, and for blessing upon the books, tracts, etc., now in the course of preparation."

12
What about the heathen:
are they lost?

"People often ask 'Are those poor heathen, who have never had the opportunity of hearing the Gospel, to be eternally damned for not believing in Jesus Christ?'

Now, as this is a subject which gets to the very root of all missionary endeavour, it is necessary to put aside all preconceived notions on the matter, and refer to what God says about it in His Word. And the question and answer are plainly put in Rom. 10, 14-18: 'How shall they hear without a preacher?'

'But, I say, have they not heard? Yes, it is true that their sound went into all the earth, and their words unto the ends of the world.'

In other words, a revelation has come from God to every man. They have heard. For God says: ' That was a true light, which lights up every man that comes into the world' (John 1, 9). 'The grace of God that brings salvation has appeared to all men', (Titus 2, 11.) 'My eyes have seen Your salvation, which You have prepared in the sight of all people' (Luke 2, 31).

Some will ask: 'How has that revelation come to all mankind?' And – 'How much do they know of God?' To answer this we must refer to Psalm 19, 1-4, from which the quotation in Rom. 10, 18 is made. Here we see that God is made known through his creation. 'The heavens declare the glory of God and the skies clearly show His handiwork. Day after day they pour out speech; night after night they clearly show knowledge. There is no speech or language where their voice is not heard. Their voice is gone out into all the earth, and their words to the end of the world. In the heavens He has pitched a tent for the sun.' Thus we see that day and night, heaven and earth, are constantly telling out God's glory in every clime and nation. They were established with this purpose in view. 'Let them be for signs and for seasons', said God, in Gen. 1, 14. The hills spoke to David of their Maker, and His steadfastness. 'I will lift up my eyes toward the hills from where my help comes. My help comes from the Lord Who made heaven and earth' (Ps. 121, 1-2). 'In the same way He did not leave Himself without a witness, in that He did good, and gave us rain from heaven and fruitful seasons, filling our hearts with food and gladness' (Acts. 14, 17). These fruitful seasons are telling us of God's faithfulness and goodness even where no missionary society is at work. In fact, all over the world pioneer missionary societies find that those to whom they go already know of a great creator God, Who orders all, Who maintains all, and Who rules over all. So, as Romans, 1, 19-21 so aptly puts it, 'Since what may be known about God is plain to them, because God has made it plain to them. For since the creation of the world God's invisible qualities – his eternal power and divine nature – have been clearly seen being understood from what has been made, so that men are without excuse. For although they knew God, they neither glorified him as God nor gave thanks to him.'

Now man says that they are excusable because they do not know; but God says that they are without excuse because they know. And God calls 'Look to Me and you will be saved, all the ends of the earth' (Isa. 45, 22). That is to say that to the ends of the earth, whosoever will but even look to God for salvation may find it, for God will send the messenger, God will reveal Jesus, God will Himself do all that is necessary for the one who will simply look.

This knowledge of God through creation is not, however, the only thing which the heathen know. Rom. 1, 28-32 shows that they have a knowledge of sin and its consequences. In verses 29 to 32 is a list of twenty-three sins, with the conclusion that mankind: 'Who, although they know what the righteous legal demand of God requires when it points out that those who do these things deserve death, not only continue to do them but affirm those who do them too.' Our experience in Lubaland absolutely confirms this testimony. The Baluba know of God. They have at least 16 different names for Him, and recognise His sovereignty and power in many ways. Moreover, although adultery, lying, necromancy, murder, etc., are rife, yet the people know that these things are wrong. Their own proverbs prove that they, being without the law, yet 'have the work of the law written in their hearts' (Rom. 2, 14-15). Another startling fact now comes to light: During the dispensation of the Holy Spirit every land and nation has had the gospel message. Those lands which are darkest, and most Christless today, once had the Gospel, for Paul writes in Colossians 1, 6, 23 that the 'gospel . . . is come unto . . . all the world', and 'which was preached to every creature which is under heaven.'

It is true that all people once had the Gospel. But 'men loved darkness rather than light because their deeds were evil.' (John 3,19). The whole attitude of these people has been aptly described by Job 21, 13-15, 'They spend their days in wealth, and in a moment go down to Hell. Therefore they say to God, depart from us; for we do not desire to know about Your ways. What is the Almighty that we should serve Him? And what profit is there for us if we pray to Him?' Therefore God has left them to walk in their own ways, and 'Because they did not like to retain God in their knowledge, God gave them over...' to their own passions and unnatural behaviour (Rom. 1, 28).

Now the whole position becomes clear. No one can bring a charge against God for not sending a further revelation to people who are rejecting the revelation which they already have. And, moreover, no one can bring an indictment against God for condemning to eternal separation from Himself (with all that that involves) those who do not wish to retain Him in their thoughts, and who, when they knew God, did not glorify Him as God, and were continually unthankful toward Him.

But 'whoever has will be given more, and will end up with great abundance' (Matt. 13, 12). And so when God sees a company of those who want Him, then He sends the missionary to preach Jesus, Who is the way to God. 'No man comes to the Father but by Me.' Jesus said (Jn. 14, 6). This is a fact of the greatest importance. No one will ever be saved apart from Jesus Christ. 'He that has the Son has life, and he that does not have the Son of God does not have life' (1 Jn. 5, 12).

Those millions of heathen who have gone down to a Christless eternity are not to be regarded with pity and sympathy, as having been the victims of God's negligence. Truly the Church has been negligent, and will receive justice meet for her negligence. But God has not been neglectful. He has revealed Himself through nature, and wherever there has been a heart to recognise and acknowledge that revelation, He has also given a revelation of His Son, the Lord Jesus, in grace. Jesus said: 'Blessed are they that hunger and thirst after righteousness, for they shall be filled' (Matt. 5, 6). God will always find means to fill the hungry or thirsty one. Never, in the annals of eternity will anyone be able to rise before God, with the charge: 'I was hungry and thirsty after righteousness but You did not fill me.'

Therefore, we regard those heathen who died without salvation as millions of rebels against all that God could do to lavish upon them His kindness, show them His faithfulness and power, and attract them to Himself. They have neglected and forgotten God, and we read, 'The wicked shall be turned into Hell, and all the nations that forget God' (Ps. 9, 17). Those nations have in the past known Christ, but have forgotten Him. And now, though they know God through His handiwork, these forget Him also. So God will righteously turn them into Hell.

Hell, a place of no hope!

In these days many are openly teaching, and others are secretly teaching, that there is hope of salvation after death. Some indeed are saying that God would not be just if this were not so. But God Himself says, 'When a wicked man dies his expectation perishes and the hope of unjust men perishes too' (Prov. 11, 7). When? When he dies! His hope perishes!

'The grave cannot praise You. Death cannot celebrate You. They that go down into the pit cannot hope for Your truth' (Isa. 38, 18). These false teachers belittle God's word, paralyse missionary enterprise, and leave the heathen to eternal doom, by saying that they that go down into the pit can hope. God's word says they cannot hope for His truth.

God says, 'The person who is often reproved but blatantly refuses to listen will suddenly be destroyed and there is no changing the outcome' (Prov. 29, 1). Even though these false teachers say that there is a remedy, God says that there is none. Even were there annihilation after a period of punishment in Hell, that would be a hope. It would at least be a hope of release. But no! God says, 'The smoke of their torment ascends up for ever and ever' (Rev. 14, 11); and again, 'These shall go away into everlasting punishment' (Matt. 25, 46).

Before closing this matter we must guard against those who would make the revelation of God through nature, an excuse for refusing to go and preach the salvation of Christ through grace.

If we had no other inducement than Christ's command 'Go into all the world, and preach the gospel to every creature' (Mk. 16, 15), we are responsible for obedience to that command.

But also 'faith comes by hearing and hearing by means of the word of God' (Rom. 10, 17).

And if it may be said that through us, as through Peter, 'God has also granted repentance resulting in life to the Gentiles' (Acts 11, 18). What a joy and what a reward is ours in thus snatching brands from the burning!

Seven busy months followed the outpouring of the Spirit at Mwanza. The three white missionaries were working at a pressure far beyond their strength. Again and again they went down with fever. New Congolese preachers were sent out, and new schools were built, all of which called for Brother Burton's constant supervision, while Mrs Burton's work among the women was richly blessed, and Miss Toerien, with the children, experienced similar times of refreshing and power from on high.

Numbers were converted to Christ, and baptised, both at Mwanza and in the rapidly increasing out-stations, while under the fresh impetus of revival the whole work was going forward in leaps and bounds.

At last the joyful news came that Brother Salter was returning from his furlough with a band of six workers. What a welcome they received! As soon as possible they took over the work of the mission, while Brother and Sister Burton, and Sister Toerien at once started out for their well-earned furlough.

And none too soon, for Sister Burton's strength and health, formerly so good, gave way, so that at Elisabethville (today's Lubumbashi), Bulawayo, and Johannesburg she was in such weakness and suffering that it was only with difficulty she reached the homeland. Here, however, with congenial atmosphere, loving friends and wholesome food, she rapidly recuperated.

While the workers on the field, now increased to ten in number, have been spreading the gospel message far and near with glorious results, the missionaries on furlough have been recruiting more new workers. Thus, by the month of August 1922, there should be fifteen white workers, and between 30 and 40 Congolese evangelists, actively working together for the furtherance of God's kingdom in the Congo Evangelistic Mission.

This brings to a conclusion what transpired during the first five years of the mission planted by Burton and his fellow workers in the Congo. God can be praised for what He did then and for what He has been doing ever since. This work continues not only in the Congo but in other countries of the African continent.

More can be learned by subscribing to the Central African Missions' monthly magazine – CONTACT – available from the CAM office:

355 Blackpool Road, Preston, Lancashire PR2 3AB, England
Tel: 01772 717830   Email: admin@camafrica.fsnet.co.uk